THE COMPLETE GUIDE TO
BATHROOMS

Ideas & Projects for Building & Remodeling

CREATIVE PUBLISHING international

CHANHASSEN, MINNESOTA

www.creativepub.com

Contents

Copyright © 2003
Creative Publishing international, Inc.
18705 Lake Drive East
Chanhassen, Minnesota 55317
1-800-328-3895
www.creativepub.com
All rights reserved

Printed in U.S.A. by R. R. Donnelley
10 9 8 7 6 5 4 3 2 1

President/CEO: Michael Eleftheriou
Vice President/Publisher: Linda Ball
Vice President/Retail Sales & Marketing: Kevin Haas

Executive Editor: Bryan Trandem
Creative Director: Tim Himsel
Editorial Director: Jerri Farris
Managing Editor: Michelle Skudlarek

Editor: Thomas G. Lemmer
Art Director: Kari Johnston
Project Manager: Julie Caruso
Technical Photo Editor: Paul Gorton
Copy Editors: Karen Ruth, Dane Smith
Mac Designers: Andrew Karre, Jon Simpson
Illustrators: Jon Simpson, Earl Slack
Studio Services Manager: Jeanette Moss McCurdy
Photographers: Tate Carlson, Andrea Rugg
Scene Shop Carpenter: Randy Austin
Manager, Production Services & Photography: Kim Gerber
Production Manager: Stasia Dorn

THE COMPLETE GUIDE TO BATHROOMS
Created by: The Editors of Creative Publishing international, Inc.,
in cooperation with Black & Decker. Black & Decker® is a trademark
of The Black & Decker Corporation and is used under license.

Library of Congress Cataloging-in-Publication Data

The complete guide to bathrooms : ideas and projects for building and remodeling
    p. cm.
At head of title: Black & Decker.
Includes index.
  ISBN 1-58923-062-0 (soft cover)
  1. Bathrooms--Remodeling--Amateurs' manuals. I. Creative Publishing International.
  TH4816.3.B37 C66 2002
  643'.52--dc21

2002034962

ISBN 1-58923-062-0 (softcover)

Portions of *The Complete Guide to Bathrooms* are taken from *Bathroom Remodeling, Customizing Your Home, Finishing Basements & Attics, Home Plumbing Projects & Repairs, Advanced Home Plumbing; Basic Wiring & Electrical Repairs; Advanced Home Wiring, The Complete Photo Guide to Home Improvement.* Other titles from Creative Publishing international include:

New Everyday Home Repairs; Carpentry: Tools • Shelves • Walls • Doors; Building Decks; Workshop Tips & Techniques; Carpentry: Remodeling; Landscape Design & Construction; Built-In Projects for the Home; Refinishing & Finishing Wood; Exterior Home Repairs & Improvements; Home Masonry Repairs & Projects; Building Porches & Patios; Flooring Projects & Techniques; Home Plumbing Projects & Repairs; Basic Wiring & Electrical Repairs; Advanced Deck Building; Great Decks & Furnishings; Remodeling Kitchens; Stonework & Masonry Projects; Sheds, Gazebos & Outbuildings; Building & Finishing Walls & Ceilings; The Complete Guide to Building Decks; The Complete Guide to Painting & Decorating; The Complete Guide to Creative Landscapes; The Complete Guide to Home Masonry; The Complete Guide to Home Carpentry; The Complete Guide to Home Storage; The Complete Guide to Windows & Doors; The Complete Photo Guide to Home Repair.

Introduction

Few rooms in the home serve as great a role in our daily routine, relaxation, and health as the bathroom. In the bathroom we brush our teeth, shave, put on makeup, soak in the tub, and retreat from the world. It's a place that must work with sanitary efficiency and, ideally, satisfy our cravings for privacy and luxury.

Remodeling an outdated or poorly designed bathroom, or even adding a brand-new one, can create a space that better suits your needs. New hardware and a fresh coat of paint can transform a dingy half bath into a more attractive space. Changing the layout of fixtures could make a bathroom more usable for a growing family. Annexing the closet space of an adjacent room can provide the necessary space to add a sauna to a master bathroom. And thanks to the safer and more accessible fixtures available, an updated bathroom can be designed to be more hospitable for the physically challenged or the very young.

The Complete Guide to Bathrooms is a comprehensive guide to all aspects of remodeling bathrooms. With clear definitions, step-by-step instructions, and full color photos and illustrations, this book gives you the knowledge to plan and successfully complete any bathroom remodeling or addition project.

The book is divided into three convenient sections to ease you through each phase of the bathroom remodeling process.

Designing & Planning Bathrooms: Dreaming up all the possible style, design, and layout options is probably the most fun aspect of remodeling a bathroom. But as fun as this is, at some point you must determine which of those great ideas will meet your particular needs while also fitting within your actual space and budget. The first section of the book guides you through each step of the planning stage, from initial concept to contacting building inspectors. No matter how simple or extravagant your new bathroom design may be, you will be able to create a working plan and budget that is right for you.

Roughing-in Bathrooms: Because most bathroom remodeling projects require a basic knowledge of carpentry, plumbing, and wiring techniques, the second section of this book is devoted to what is referred to as the "rough-in." Here you will learn the basic skills and proper techniques for demolition and installation of the house systems. Projects include: building partition walls, installing water-supply and drain-waste-vent pipes, and wiring electrical circuits.

Bathroom Remodeling Projects: With the bathroom rough-in complete, the third section of the book will show you how to install all the standard bathroom fixtures, wall and floor surfaces, cabinets, lighting and more. You will also find easy-to-follow directions for large-scale custom building projects, such as ceramic tile countertops, tiled shower bases, and glass block showers, as well as installation instructions for luxury amenities, including whirlpools and saunas.

In addition, the book also provides a "Portfolio of Bathroom Ideas" to help you generate practical and creative ideas for redesigning your bathroom. Dozens of inspiring photos display different bathroom types, styles, and layouts.

Even if you choose to hire professionals to do the rough-in work or install the fixtures, *The Complete Guide to Bathrooms* remains a useful tool. This book will give you an increased understanding of the work involved in remodeling a bathroom, to help you work with contractors and make the best use of your money.

Portfolio of Bathroom Ideas

Whether you are showering or shaving, a great bathroom enables you to take care of your needs in a comfortable, attractive, and convenient setting. It is a place you can retreat to in privacy, spending uninterrupted time tending to your needs in a relaxed and pleasant fashion.

When designing a new bathroom or renovating an existing one, style should be as big a consideration as function. From the choice of materials to the layout of fixtures, the space should reflect your individual sense of style through the use of particular colors, textures, and patterns.

To help you generate practical and creative ideas for your bathroom remodeling or addition project, the following pages contain a number of color photographs displaying different bathroom types, styles, and layouts. Use these photos to inspire your plans for the perfect bathroom.

© Jessie Walker

Every element of this bathroom (above) is influenced by its Egyptian theme. The decorative bird faucet handles, basket-weave textured sink, and painted mural of the pyramids are used to shape a distinctive and highly personal bathroom.

© Robert Perron

A feeling of privacy is critical to a good bathroom design, especially in large family baths designed to be used by more than one person at a time (above). This bathroom layout provides many separate and distinct task areas to meet everyone's needs.

The custom-built vanity (below) and corner-mount toilet (left) in this half bath not only make good use of the limited space, but also add character to an otherwise plain, cramped bathroom.

Visual appeal is as important as function in a luxury bathroom (bottom). This room uses custom stone tile, designer plumbing fixtures, and a hand-painted emblem on the wall to create a showcase bathroom. The whirlpool is suitable for relaxed bathing by one or two people, and the glass-enclosed toilet stall and fireplace add a luxurious touch.

A double-sink countertop and vanity help make this bathroom suitable for a large family (right). The separate shower and tub, extra towel rods, ample cabinet space, and plenty of open floor space create a bathroom that can be used by several people at the same time.

This large family bathroom (middle) has plenty of space between fixtures and provides many separate task areas to create a comfortable environment for multiple users. Soft colors, decorative molding, and recessed shelves add to this bathroom's inviting and soothing tone.

This cozy family bathroom (far right) was created for little money, primarily through the use of color and pattern. The yellow tile with black border on the walls complements the checkerboard floor, while the classic style fixtures help accentuate the retro look of the room.

A private bathing area has been created in this room (left), although bedroom and bath occupy the same space. Set off from the rest of the room and placed along one wall, the whirlpool tub and stand-alone shower seem like a separate room. A private stall containing a toilet is located to the left of the shower.

This luxury bathroom (below) provides the ultimate escape from a stressful day. The whirlpool and glass-enclosed steam shower offer the therapeutic benefits of a trip to the spa, while the strategic placement of the fixtures, cabinets, and large casement windows helps create an open and relaxing atmosphere.

© Karen Melvin

© Jessie Walker

© Jessie Walker

Repetition of textures, colors, and themes throughout a room can lead to a successful mix of styles, such as in this bathroom (above). For example, both the mirror frame and the shelf opposite the mirror have bowed sides to match the legs of the vanity. Each of these elements is also painted black, which is used as an accent color in the tile and checkered shower curtain.

A combination tub-shower, equally useful for a quick morning shower or a relaxing evening soak, helps create a versatile family bath in a modest space (above). A soothing atmosphere is established through the use of color and the matching tile of the shower and floor.

Through the use of designer fixtures and a variety of finish materials, this stylish bathroom (above) exists within an otherwise typical bathroom layout. The bottom half of each wall is bumped out and tiled to match the floor, and capped with a stainless steel shelf that circles the room.

A deep bathtub unit is a great way to create more room in—and lend a distinctive look to—a small bathroom (left). The use of bold colors in the molding and accent tiles helps brighten an otherwise dark space.

This stylish bath (above) proves that a universal bathroom doesn't have to look or feel like a hospital room. The design mixes many accessibility features (barrier-free shower, grab bars, movable cabinets) with vibrant colors, interesting textures, and distinctive materials to create a comfortable space for users of all abilities.

White and pink are the primary colors used in this half bath as the base colors for the walls and in the floral patterns of the drapes and rug. Groupings of fresh flowers accent the room, helping to create a light garden feeling.

This country bathroom contains antique furniture and fixtures that were customized to meet current code requirements. The cast-iron tub was refinished and re-plumbed, antique light fixtures were cleaned and rewired, and an old dresser was modified to adequately support the sink and countertop.

© Karen Melvin

Photo courtesy of Kohler, Co.

With a little creativity, an attic space that otherwise would have been used for storage is transformed into this cozy guest bathroom (far left). White walls and fixtures matched with full-size windows at the gable-end allow plenty of light to consume the space.

This bathroom, designed for accessibility, incorporates a tilt mirror, wheelchair-accessible sink and counter, and attractive tub/shower combination with grab bars.

The tall cabinets and a pedestal sink in this bathroom introduce vertical lines into the design, which help keep the high ceilings from dwarfing the small room. To remedy the lack of counter space, each cabinet has a fold-down door that is used as a work-surface.

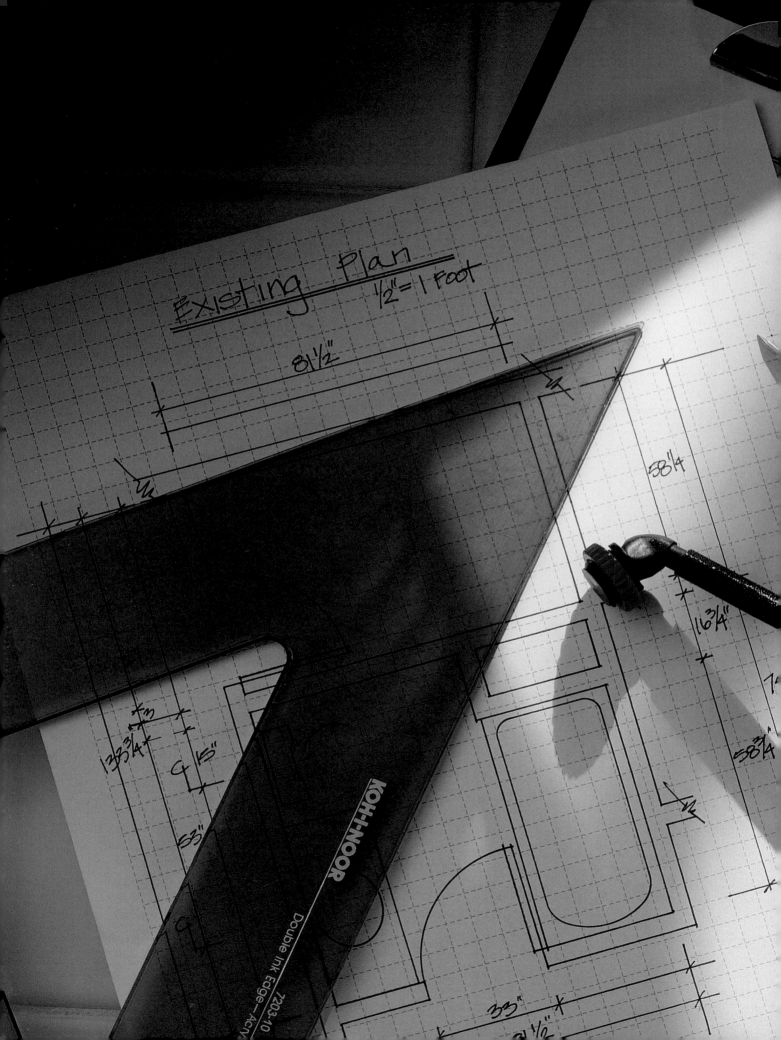

xisting Space

e measurements

81 ¾

75½

PICKETT   P-232 A·ES

**Designing&
Planning**

Designing & Planning Your New Bathroom

© Karen Melvin

Bathroom remodeling projects are high on many homeowners' wish lists. Whether you repair a leaky faucet, redesign the layout of fixtures, or tear out and start over, a bathroom remodeling project should make your bathroom more efficient and comfortable. Before you rush out to buy new fixtures or flooring, however, consider three elements of your new bath: type, style, and color.

What type of bathroom are you remodeling or building? The three basic types are family baths (both large and small), master (or luxury) baths, and half (or guest) baths. Each has its own requirements for space, fixtures, and layout. To help you determine what type of bath you want, consider who uses the bathroom and how often, where the bathroom will be located, what features you want most, and whether the bathroom must be accessible to someone with physical limitations.

Next, think about your bathroom's style. Since the bathroom is one of your home's most-used spaces, it should blend in with the overall style of your home. Look through magazines, attend home shows, or visit open houses for ideas. You will find design ideas that range from American, English, and French Country to Contemporary, Southwest, and Colonial.

Then, think about color. Your choices of bathroom type and style often will influence your choice of color. Consider the overall style of your home when choosing colors for fixtures, flooring, and lighting. Remember that children grow up, and that you can grow tired of trends. Try to think about how the bathroom will function in years to come. The best option may be to choose neutral-colored fixtures and tile, then add color accents with wallpaper, paint, or towels.

A bathroom remodeling project involves lots of planning; thinking about what you want is the first big step. However, you must also consider your needs, budget, and space. This first section of the book discusses:

- Determining Your Needs (page 17)
- Three Levels of Bathroom Remodeling (pages 18 to 19)
- Choosing Bathroom Fixtures & Materials (pages 20 to 41)
- Designing for Accessibility (pages 42 to 47)
- Building Codes & Design Guidelines (pages 48 to 49)
- Drawing Plans (pages 50 to 51)
- Creating a Budget (page 52)
- Working with Professionals (page 53)

Determining Your Needs

A bathroom is divided into three activity areas: the toilet, the sink, and the shower/tub. Successful bath design considers the relationship of these areas, allowing for accessibility and safety.

Half Baths

Also called powder rooms or guest baths, half baths are small rooms designed for visitors to use. They can be as small as 20 sq. ft. and often are located near entrances or entertainment areas of a home. It's often best to have their doorways open into hallways, rather than dining rooms, living rooms, or other public areas.

Half baths typically feature only a toilet and vanity or pedestal sink finished with smaller fixtures and finer materials. When designed as a guest bath that includes a shower, these rooms require more space and are called three-quarter baths.

Family Bath

The family bath is often located near the sleeping areas in a home. It is used by more than one family member, and it often must provide storage for toiletries, towels, and cleaning supplies. It features at least one sink, one toilet, and a shower and tub.

The typical family bath can fit in a 5 × 7-ft. area. A larger bath may allow room for extra features, such as a double-bowl sink or separate shower and tub area. A small family bath may conserve space by combining the tub and shower, incorporating recessed shelving, and featuring space-efficient fixtures and storage cabinets. Fixtures and finishes should be low-maintenance, highly durable items, such as ceramic tile and enameled fixtures.

© Christian Korab

NOTE: Bathrooms for children must be safe for them to use unsupervised and should be easy to adapt as the children grow. Features that make daily hygiene easier and safer for children include single-handle faucets with anti-scald guards, adjustable showerheads, safety plugs, grab bars, smaller toilets, lowered sinks, and vanities with built-in step stools.

Master Bath

A master bath is a sanctuary for the owners of the house, usually connected to the master bedroom. It is typically quite large, and may have separate activity centers containing features such as a whirlpool tub, shower, partitioned toilet, and multiple sinks and vanities. It may even feature a sauna or steam room. The fixtures and finishing materials generally feature ceramic tiles, custom cabinets, and upscale accessories.

© Karen Melvin

Three Levels of Bathroom Remodeling

Will it be enough to simply install a new faucet, recaulk the tub, and paint the walls? Or is this the time to make some real changes—add that second sink, install the whirlpool you've dreamed about, or even annex that hallway linen closet and make the bathroom bigger? These options actually represent the three distinct levels of bathroom remodeling: makeover, layout change, and expansion.

A *makeover* involves cosmetic changes and replacement of fixtures or accessories. Generally speaking, it is less expensive to make cosmetic changes than to make structural changes.

You can accomplish a lot with a makeover. You can bring a room to life with new colors, patterns, and textures; silence leaky, dripping fixtures forever; or improve safety with grab bars and nonskid appliqués. You can also increase storage space with efficient vanities, medicine cabinets, or linen closets, and you can sweep away condensation and odors with a new vent.

Keep in mind, however, that cosmetic changes do not solve structural problems. You may be able to make a space feel larger through decorating techniques, but it won't be any easier for two people to actually use the room at the same time.

A *layout change* represents the next step in remodeling complexity—rearranging some or all of the fixtures within the existing space.

You can often make significant improvements in the way a bathroom can be used by changing the layout. Adding a second sink or enclosing the toilet in its own private niche, for example, might make it possible for two people to comfortably use a bathroom previously suited only for one.

A layout change is a substantial undertaking, usually involving extensive mechanical work, as well as general demolition, reconstruction, and finishing of surfaces. Because of this, costs are higher than with a simple makeover.

If you need an overall bigger bathroom, *expansion* may be the best option.

Small, narrow bathrooms such as this one are found in hundreds of thousands of homes. The illustrations on these pages show three ways this bath might be remodeled.

Each house has its own opportunities for finding extra space, but possibilities include closets that adjoin baths, small bedrooms no longer needed for their original purpose, or any adjoining room that could sacrifice some of its space.

Adding space to your bathroom increases the cost by more than just the additional square footage of the room itself. When you annex other spaces, the construction process is no longer contained within one room. For example, if you patch over a hallway closet door in order to incorporate the closet space into the new bathroom, you'll also have to paint the hallway and repair the flooring and trim.

Each level of remodeling—from modest makeover to extravagant expansion—can be applied to any size or type of bathroom, which makes it difficult to accurately set average costs. However, you can figure an initial estimate of the costs for the new bathroom you envision by using the information provided on page 52.

Level 1, Makeover: In the makeover, we've replaced the toilet so it matches the tub, changed the window treatment from curtains to shutters, painted the walls, and added a sliding shower door. We've also installed a new vanity cabinet, countertop, faucet, and mirror. With the addition of wainscoting, we've made the room appear slightly wider.

Level 2, Layout Change: A room this size offers limited ways to change the layout. One possibility, assuming this is not the primary bathroom, is to convert it into a more "interesting" half bath for guests. In this drawing, the room dimensions haven't changed, but we've removed the tub, relocated the sink and redecorated in a contemporary style.

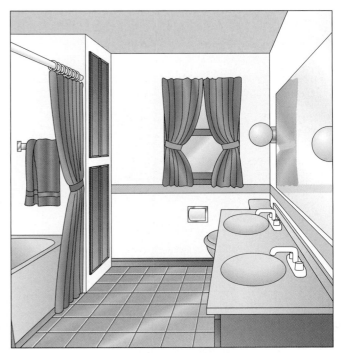

Level 3, Expansion: In this example we've added about 30 inches to the width of the room by annexing an adjacent closet. By doing this, it's now possible to make this room workable as a shared bath with a double vanity. Additional storage space has also been gained.

There is a wide variety of bathroom fixtures and materials available on the market. Compare the function, style, and price of similar products to help find the items that will work best in your new bathroom.

Choosing Bathroom Fixtures & Materials

Bathroom fixtures and materials have changed dramatically in recent years. Tubs can rival health-club spas, toilets and shower heads are more water efficient, and the options for sinks run the gamut from stainless steel and hand-painted china to wood basins and glass bowls.

The products you choose will determine how well your new bathroom works, how it looks, and how long it will last. Your choices also play a large part in determining how much your remodeling job will cost. Before you begin creating plans, develop a shopping list of products to be installed in your new bathroom. For instance, a shower that's separate from the tub requires a different floor plan than a one-piece shower-and-tub combination. Then as you complete your plans, make final fixture and material decisions.

Pages 21 to 41 discuss the most common bathroom fixtures and materials available, but there are several other good resources for bathroom product information:

• Consumer home magazines, as well as interior and architectural design magazines, often feature bathroom design ideas. Many have reader reply cards so you can send away for manufacturers' brochures. Also, consumer advocacy magazines, such as *Consumer Reports*, periodically rate bathroom fixtures according to performance and price.

• Many manufacturers and distributors maintain Web advertising sites on the Internet, often containing photo galleries, reference materials, and online catalogs.

• Home centers or kitchen and bath showrooms allow you to browse through actual displays to see how various products look and how much they will cost.

• Contractors are good sources of informed advice and can often steer you to stores where you will get straight answers as well as fair deals.

• Organizations such as the National Kitchen & Bath Association (NKBA) publish information on industry trends, products, and services and can help locate certified professionals in your area.

• Professional bathroom designers may be able to help you choose and combine different fixtures, materials, and colors to create an attractive and functional bathroom that suits your home and the needs of your family.

Tips for Water Conservation

Because nearly 75% of water used in a home is used in the bathroom, your water conservation efforts should start here:

• Don't let water run while shaving, washing your face, or brushing your teeth.
• Take short showers. Turn off water when lathering with soap or shampoo, then turn it on to rinse.
• Install a water-efficient showerhead (2.5 gal or less per minute; required by code in many areas).
• Install a toilet dam or plastic bottle filled with water in the tank of older toilets. Make sure the item doesn't interfere with the toilet's operation.
• Install a low-flow toilet (1.6 gal or less per flush; required by code in many areas).
• Avoid unnecessarily flushing the toilet. Replace or adjust toilet handles that stick in the flush position, allowing water to run.
• Check for leaks by adding food coloring to the toilet tank. Color will appear in the toilet bowl within 30 minutes if there is a leak. Replace any corroded, worn out, or bent parts.

Bathtubs & Whirlpools

Because a bathtub or whirlpool is often the largest component of the bathroom, its placement anchors the room. There are a wide variety of shapes, sizes, and materials available to accommodate just about any situation. The three basic types of tubs are: attached-apron, deck-mounted, and freestanding.

Attached-apron tubs are the most common. They are enclosed on three sides by alcove walls. Whirlpools (page 23) and one-piece tub-and-shower combinations (page 24) are also available to fit standard-size alcoves. See pages 160 to 163 for installing attached-apron bathtubs.

Deck-mounted tubs and whirlpools rest on the subfloor and are surrounded by custom-built decks or platforms. Typically, these tubs have a larger capacity than attached-apron tubs. Although the cost of the tub itself may be comparable to that of attached-apron models, the final cost of installation will be higher due to the construction of the deck.

Freestanding tubs are available in both modern and traditional claw-foot styles. They're usually made from cast iron, which retains heat well and is virtually indestructible. Though they can be heavy and difficult to move, they are typically easy to install. Because the plumbing is exposed, pipes need to have an attractive finish.

When selecting a tub, consider not only the style of the tub or how much space you have available, but also that it is comfortable for the primary users. Many modern designs feature gentle curves, sloping backs, and armrests for more comfortable bathing.

Rectangular tubs are the most common and are often combined with showers. They come in a wide range of lengths, widths, depths, and colors in addition to the traditional 30" × 60" × 14" white version.

Space-saving square and triangular tubs fit into corners to help open up small bathrooms. Like rectangular tubs, these also can be combined easily with a shower.

Oval, round, and hourglass shapes are usually larger and work well in master or luxury bathrooms. Extra-deep tubs (as much as 22" to 24" in depth) are great for soaking, but can be difficult to stand up in as well as get out of. For safety, a deep tub should be set into a deck so you can sit down to enter.

Attached-apron tubs are an efficient use of space and are often combined with a shower to create a tub-and-shower combination.

Freestanding tubs are available in the traditional claw-foot design as well as up-to-date modern models.

(continued next page)

A deck-mounted tub often is the focal point of the bathroom, providing both visual appeal and a luxurious bathing experience.

Space-saving corner tubs are available for small bathrooms. Often these smaller tubs are deeper than standard tubs, which allows for more comfortable bathing.

Tub shapes and sizes vary dramatically to accommodate the space available and the look you desire.

Bathtubs & Whirlpools (continued)

Tubs are manufactured from many different materials, each with its own advantages and disadvantages:

Fiberglass is an inexpensive, lightweight material that comes in many different colors. It is easily molded, so tub units can include seats, grab bars, soap dishes, and shampoo shelves molded into the sides. Though fiberglass has many benefits, its surface can scratch easily and its color will fade over time.

Acrylic, like fiberglass, can be molded into just about any size and shape required. Unlike fiberglass, however, the color runs through the entire substance rather than just the surface coat, making it less likely to scratch or fade.

Enameled steel tubs are shaped from sheets of steel and coated with a baked-on enamel similar to that of cast-iron tubs. However, the enamel layer is usually thin and susceptible to chipping. In addition, enameled steel doesn't retain heat and tends to be noisy. When buying an enameled steel tub, check for a good undercoating that helps muffle sound and retain heat.

Cast iron is the toughest material available for tubs. Iron is cast into a tub shape, then coated with a baked-on enamel that is relatively thick ($\frac{1}{16}$"), resulting in a richly colored finish. The enamel is strong, durable, and very resistant to chips, scratches, and stains. The cast iron itself is almost impervious to dents and cracks. Cast iron is just about indestructible, but it's also heavy—a standard tub weighs between 300 and 400 lbs. Often, the floor framing must be reinforced to support the additional weight. Cast iron is used most commonly for claw-foot and other stand-alone bathtubs.

The enamel finish of old, scratched, or marred cast-iron tubs can be reglazed; however, the finish doesn't last as long as the original and is more susceptible to chips and scratches. Reglazing a cast-iron tub is not a do-it-yourself project, so hire a contractor who is familiar with the process, look for a two-year guarantee and ask to see examples of previous work.

Ceramic and *stone tiles* are used to build custom tubs in unusual shapes and sizes. The floor of a custom-made tub is built with floor mortar (or "deck mud"), and must slope toward the drain a minimum of $\frac{1}{4}$" for every 12".

Whirlpools for home use were developed by Roy Jacuzzi in 1968. A novelty at first, they've become increasingly popular as prices have decreased, systems have become more reliable, and the practical benefits of whirlpools have been realized.

Whirlpools circulate water mixed with air through jets mounted in the body of the tub. The pumps move as much as 50 gallons of water per minute to create a massaging effect that relieves stress and muscle pain. Some jets also can be adjusted to alter both the stream's direction and the proportion of air and water (more air means a more vigorous massage).

Since whirlpools are almost always made from acrylic, sizes and shapes vary tremendously. Prices also vary—whirlpools can range from $700 to $6,000 before installation. Price is determined by the number of jets (from four to ten or more), size of the water pump, and options such as a heater and emergency shut-off switch.

There are a variety of accessories available for whirlpools. A multi-speed motor allows you to choose from various settings, from a gentle, relaxing soak to a vigorous massage. An in-line heater maintains the water temperature. There are also grab bars, mood lights, pillows, timers, mirrors, and touch-pad controls available for convenience and comfort.

Before investing in a new whirlpool, review the maintenance requirements of the tub. Some whirlpools require elaborate maintenance for the pumps, timers, and controls, and many roomy models require an extra-large water heater to fill them.

Whirlpools can generally be installed by a skilled homeowner familiar with the basic techniques of carpentry, plumbing, and tile setting. Some whirlpools are small enough to fit in the alcove size used for standard bathtubs, though most models require the construction of a surrounding deck or platform. See pages 166 to 171 for installing a deck-mounted whirlpool.

Photos this page courtesy of Kohler, Co.

Deck-mounted whirlpools are the most widely available and come in many shapes to fit different needs.

Standard-size recessed tubs with whirlpool jets are available to fit into standard-size tub alcoves.

One-piece alcove showers made of fiberglass or acrylic fit between finished walls.

Neo-angle showers offer a unique look, and also save space.

Showers

Showers can be split into two broad categories: those that are combined with tubs, and those that stand alone. Within those categories, there are a number of styles and materials available. Most materials used in showers are also used in tubs (see page 22).

Tub-shower combinations are the most common shower design. They use space efficiently and are generally cheaper to install than separate tub and shower units. A shower can easily be added to an alcove tub by extending the tub faucet to include a showerhead, then waterproofing the walls using fiberglass, acrylic, or solid-surface surround panels (pages 164 to 165), or ceramic tile (pages 184 to 191). One-piece molded fiberglass and acrylic tub-and-shower units are also available.

Stand-alone showers are ideal for bathrooms that don't have enough space for a full-sized tub, or as a supplement in master or luxury bathrooms. They can be purchased prefabricated or can be custom-built using a design of your own choosing:

• One-piece alcove showers are the most common option for do-it-yourself installation. The stall is molded from a single piece of fiberglass or acrylic, with no seams, making it easy to clean and maintain. There is a wide range of shower stall sizes and styles available, some complete with seats and steam bath capacity.

• One-piece neo-angle showers are designed to fit into a corner, taking up slightly less space. They are generally made from acrylic or fiberglass, and have doors that open at an angle.

• Shower surround panels are used to construct simple, inexpensive shower stalls. Individual panels are usually joined together into a three-sided unit, then bonded to the walls of a framed alcove above a preformed shower base made of PVC plastic, fiberglass, acrylic, or solid-surface material (pages 146 to 147).

• Freestanding showers are complete units that are not attached to walls on any of the sides. They range from inexpensive sheet metal or fiberglass units to elaborate glass block showers.

• Custom shower stalls can be designed to fit into odd spaces. The floor is built using mortar and a waterproof membrane (pages 148 to 153). The walls can be finished with ceramic tile, glass block, or a solid-surface material. Specialized options, such as seats, steam bath units, and soap dishes are incorporated into the design.

• Barrier-free showers are designed for elderly or physically challenged users. The shower entrance has a low base curb or is without a curb altogether, providing easy access to the shower. One-piece molded units are available, or barrier-free showers can be custom-built. Most have built-in shower seats and grab bars. See pages 42 to 47 for more information on barrier-free showers.

There are a variety of shower accessories available that can make a shower more convenient and comfortable:

• Shower doors and curtains are usually purchased separately from the shower itself. Options range from simple plastic curtains costing a few dollars to custom-made tempered glass doors costing a thousand dollars or more.

• An overhead light ensures safety in the shower. Make sure that any light installed in a shower area is moistureproof.

• Multiple showerheads, shower towers, and steam showers (pages 40 to 41) can create a more luxurious shower. Steam showers require extra plumbing, wiring, and a shower stall with doors that seal tightly.

Photo courtesy of Swanstone

Solid-surface shower stalls are easy to install, clean, and maintain.

©Jessie Walker

Custom-tiled showers can be built to accommodate unique spaces and desired options.

Photo courtesy of Seattle Glass Block/Pittsburg Corning Corporation

A glass block shower adds a distinctive and luxurious look that can brighten any bathroom.

Sinks

From highly decorative to purely functional, sinks are available to match almost any space, budget, and taste. The most significant difference between sink types is in the method of mounting them. The three primary types available are wall-mounted, countertop, and pedestal.

Wall-mounted sinks are bolted to the wall, taking up little space. Because there is no vanity, wall-mounted sinks offer easy access to the plumbing hookups. They are a good option for utility bathrooms or half baths where exposed plumbing and lack of storage space are not serious drawbacks.

Pedestal sinks are wall-mounted sinks that rest on decorative pedestals that partially hide the plumbing. Pedestal sink styles range from old-fashioned to ultra-modern. A pedestal sink is an attractive choice for small guest bathrooms where space is at a premium.

Countertop sinks include sinks that fit into a countertop cutout or that are formed as an integral part of the countertop. They are often combined with vanity cabinets, which provide extra storage space and hide the plumbing. There are several different installation options:

• Self-rimming sinks drop into a cutout in the countertop; the rim of the sink overlaps the edges of the cutout. They are the most common and least expensive style of countertop sink.

• Integral sinks, usually made of solid-surface or cultured marble, are molded into countertops (page 35). Integral sink-countertop units are easy to install and maintain. Integral sinks range in price from very economical to quite expensive, depending upon the material used.

• Undermounted sinks are attached with clips beneath a cutout in the countertop. Since the edge of the cutout remains exposed, undermounted sinks are often used with solid-surface or stone countertops. They are usually more expensive to install than self-rimming sinks.

A pedestal sink is attractive and takes up less space than other sink designs.

Wall-mounted sinks are perfect for bathrooms with limited space.

• Flush-mounted sinks are installed so the top of the sink aligns with the top of a tiled countertop, creating the effect of an integral sink. Flush-mounted sinks vary in cost, depending upon the tile you use for your countertop.

Like bathtubs, sinks are made from a variety of materials:

Cultured marble, also known as cast polymer, is an inexpensive material often used to create integral sink-countertop combinations to fit standard vanity sizes.

Porcelain (vitreous china) is often used for self-rimming sinks. It has a durable, glossy surface that is nonporous and easy to clean. Porcelain sinks are readily available in white and almond; other colors and designs can be special ordered.

Solid-surface material is long-lasting and easy to clean; scratches and most stains can be buffed or sanded out. It is one of the more expensive choices for bathroom sinks, but its durability and ease of care help justify the price. Solid-surface sinks are available in self-rimming, under-mounted, and integral models, with a variety of colors and patterns to choose from.

Stainless steel brings a high-tech look and durability to bathroom sinks. It is available in either a satin or mirror finish. Price varies according to thickness or "gauge"—the lower the gauge number, the thicker the steel. Look for 18-gauge material with a noise-reducing undercoating.

Enameled cast iron is an extremely durable material. Made of thick, heavy iron with an enamel coating, these sinks are available in only a few shapes and sizes, and are rather expensive. A low-cost alternative is *enameled steel*. However, it is lightweight and not very durable—the enamel coat tends to chip easily.

Tempered glass is used to create stylish bowl sinks for bathrooms. Undermounted styles can be lit from underneath to create a moody glow.

Other materials, such as concrete or wood, can be used to create sinks for exotically styled bathrooms. Before selecting a sink made from an unusual material, consider the shipping time, installation procedures, and day-to-day maintenance.

Self-rimming sinks mount on to any type of countertop and are the most common style of bathroom sink.

An undermounted sink can be made of a contrasting color and material to achieve a specific look, or it can be chosen to match the countertop.

A bowl sink creates a distinct visual effect in a bathroom.

Faucets & Showerheads

Faucet style has a significant impact on how your bathroom will look and how your fixtures will function. The two factors that affect the style most dramatically are the number of handles and the shape and length of the spout.

Faucets are available in both single- and double-handled models. Most traditional faucets have two handles, while more contemporary-looking faucets often have one. Most spout styles are available in both models.

Spouts vary in length, height, and size. When selecting a spout for your sink, tub, or shower, coordinate it with the fixture. For example, a tall spout, which drops water from a greater distance, needs a deep sink basin to contain the additional splash.

There are three basic types of faucets: sink faucets, bathtub faucets, and showerheads. Within each type there are a number of styles.

Sink faucets are used frequently every day in bathrooms, so they should be selected to complement how the sink will be used most often.

• The standard sink faucet is classic, cost-effective, and suitable for almost any style of sink. Standard faucets have short spouts that extend just over a sink basin.

• Crescent, or gooseneck, faucets have tall, curved necks that can add an elegant look to a deep sink.

Two-handled faucets come in a variety of designs, from classic old-fashioned to ultramodern.

Bathtub faucets mount on the wall above the tub, on the tub itself, or on the deck of the tub.

• Standard bathtub faucets are the most common selection for tubs. They can accommodate extensions to create bath-shower combinations.

• Crescent faucets are usually mounted on the tub or tub deck to create a sleek, elegant look.

• Waterfall faucets provide a wide, flat stream of water. They are perfect for filling large tubs and whirlpools quickly.

Showerheads are available in many different configurations. By law, showerheads can deliver no more than 2.5 gallons of water per minute. The configuration of the showerhead is determined by the way it is mounted.

• Fixed showerheads are usually mounted on shower walls, although there are varieties that can be mounted on the ceiling.

• Handheld showerheads can be moved around relatively freely or placed in a stationary holder mounted either on the

wall or above the faucet. Hand-held showerheads make it easier to clean children, pets, and the shower or tub itself.

• Multiple showerheads can be mounted in a variety of different ways. Two or more showerheads may be mounted together on a wall, or, in larger showers, they may be mounted across from each other to spray from opposite sides.

• Body sprays are adjustable sprayers that are mounted on the shower walls, usually in a series of three or four.

Once you have chosen a style, examine the construction and finish of the brands and models you're considering. Generally, a well-made faucet will feel heavy and solid in your hands. Stay away from lightweight faucets with plastic inner components, as well as from models that have washers or O-rings. The best overall choice for durability is a solid-brass, corrosion-resistant faucet with a ceramic disc valve. These faucets are expensive, but virtually indestructible.

Single-handled faucets are the most common type of bathroom faucet, with many different designs to choose from.

Faucets with widespread handles can be mounted in a variety of positions, providing greater accessibility to users.

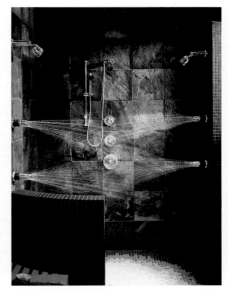

Showerheads are available in many styles, from wall-mounted heads to handheld sprayers with adjustable spray settings.

The finish on a faucet affects its appearance, price, and maintenance. The most popular choice is chrome, which is durable and easy to maintain. Polished brass is vulnerable to tarnishing and requires more maintenance than chrome, while colored epoxy on brass is long-lasting, easy to clean, and available in a variety of colors. Pewter, nickel, and gold finishes are also available, though somewhat expensive.

No matter which type of finish you select, examine each faucet for scratches and other imperfections before you purchase it.

SAFETY NOTE: Anti-scald valves (page 142) protect you and your family from scalding hot water by preventing sudden changes in water temperature frcm a faucet or showerhead when water is run in another part of the house. They are required by code for new construction. High temperature stops can also be installed on existing faucets to prevent the water temperature from rising above a preset level.

Waterfall faucets deliver a large volume of water to bathtubs and whirlpools.

Wall-mounted faucets are stylish fixtures for use with undermount and bowl sinks.

Toilets

As with most other bathroom fixtures, toilets have significantly changed in recent years. New designs are efficient, durable, and less susceptible to clogs.

Federal law mandates that new toilets consume no more than 1.6 gallons per flush, less than half the volume used by older styles. New, low-volume toilets save as much as 20,000 gallons of water per year in a typical home.

A number of options in the construction of toilets affect the style of the toilet:

• Two-piece toilets have separate water tanks and bowls. Two-piece toilets are less expensive and more common than one-piece toilets.

• One-piece toilets have a tank and bowl made of one seamless unit. One-piece toilets sit lower and have fewer crevices so are easier to clean than their two-piece counterparts.

• Elongated bowls are roughly 2" longer than regular bowls. They can be more comfortable for large or tall people. Elongated bowls take up slightly more floor space.

• Elevated toilets have higher seats, generally 18" rather than the standard 15". This style is more convenient for very tall people or for someone who has difficulty sitting down or rising from a seated position.

The basic types of flush mechanisms available are gravity- and pressure-assisted.

Gravity-assisted toilets take advantage of the principles of physics. The original design is simple—water is allowed to rush down from an elevated tank into the toilet bowl. The pressure of the cascading water flushes waste away and rinses the bowl clean. A variety of hardware and floats are available to regulate the water level in the tank and maintain a watertight seal between flushes. The power of the flush is determined by the force and quantity of water entering the bowl.

Photo courtesy of Kohler, Co.

Toilets are available in a variety of styles and colors to suit almost any decor. Two-piece toilets are the most widely available.

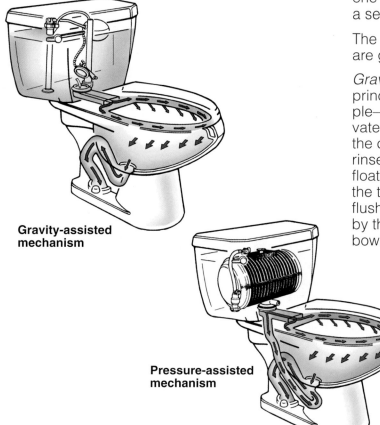

Gravity-assisted mechanism

Pressure-assisted mechanism

Gravity-assisted toilets are now designed with taller tanks and steeper bowl walls to increase the effects of gravity.

Pressure-assisted toilets are more expensive than standard toilets, but they can reduce your water usage significantly.

The flush mechanism of a pressure-assisted toilet boosts the flushing power by using either compressed air or water pumps.

Requirements for decreased water usage have prompted design changes in gravity-assisted toilets. Newer gravity-assisted toilets have taller, thinner tanks and steeper bowls to increase the effects of gravity.

Pressure-assisted toilets rely on either compressed air or water pumps to boost flushing power. Increased flushing velocity results in fewer backups and greater cleansing power.

Pressure-assisted toilets carry a higher initial price tag, and their additional moving parts can make them more susceptible to failure than standard toilets. These toilets aren't as simple to adjust or repair as gravity-assisted toilets, and some models can be noisy.

There are now toilets available that have dual-flush systems, which offer a combination of flushing options to suit your specific needs. Developed in Australia, where water conservation is a necessity, these toilets have two buttons on the top of the tank, allowing you to select either an 8-ounce flush for liquids or a 1.6-gallon flush for solids.

Bidets & Urinals

A *bidet* (bee-DAY), is a type of washbasin that allows for personal cleansing. It is usually installed next to the toilet. A bidet needs its own water supply and drain. There should be storage space for towels and soap nearby.

Any institutional men's room is almost certain to have a *urinal*, and for good reason: they are sanitary and easy to use. Some manufacturers are now producing urinals for home use. If there are a lot of men in your family, a urinal may be something to consider.

©Jessie Walker

©Robert Perron

Vanities can be combined with wall cabinets and medicine cabinets to get the look and storage space you desire.

A simple vanity provides convenient storage in a bathroom with limited space.

Cabinets

Bathroom storage space is typically in short supply. In fact, creating better storage is one of the most common reasons people remodel their bathrooms. As you analyze the space you have, keep in mind three basic categories: cabinetry, open shelving, and traditional linen closets.

If your bathroom is large enough for cabinets, first decide what types and sizes you want. Next, consider construction details, materials, and finishes. Finally, decide whether stock cabinets suit your needs, or if you will have your cabinets custom-made. There are a few types of cabinets commonly used in bathrooms:

• Vanities hide plumbing, provide storage, and hold up the countertop and sink. They can be as simple as a box with a door or considerably more elaborate. In addition, a vanity is often a bathroom's visual focal point and sets the decorative tone for the whole room.

Most stock vanities are 31¼" tall, and range in width from 18" to 48", generally in 3" increments. Smaller cabinet units can be joined together to make larger vanities of virtually any length. Custom-built vanities are often 33¼" tall, but are available in whatever width you specify.

When shopping for a vanity, investigate storage amenities such as divided and undivided drawers, adjustable and fixed internal shelving, built-in hampers, roll-out shelves, and tip-out sink fronts.

• Medicine cabinets offer storage space beyond the reach of young children, as well as quick access to everyday toiletries. Most are designed with a mirror on the door and are installed above a sink. Medicine cabinets can be either surface-mounted or recessed into walls between studs to exploit otherwise unused space (pages 226 to 227).

• Linen cabinets are tall and narrow, taking advantage of floor-to-ceiling space. If you don't have a linen closet or are eliminating an existing linen closet to create more space, a substantial linen cabinet may be a good idea.

• Wall cabinets, because they are shallow, are versatile storage units for small spaces like bathrooms. They can be installed on any available wall space—the most popular spot is over the toilet. Cabinets designed for this area, called toilet toppers, are typically 6" to 8" deep, 24" wide, and 30" tall. Wall cabinets can even be mounted low and topped with a counter.

Wall-mounted cabinets are a good way to make use of space, such as above a toilet.

©Robert Perron

Medicine cabinets offer convenient storage.

Photo courtesy of Wellborn Cabinet, Inc.

Open shelves can display decorative items and keep toiletries within easy reach.

Photo courtesy of Wellborn Cabinet, Inc.

Whatever type of cabinet you're considering, you'll have the choice of stock or custom-made.

Stock cabinets are mass-produced and warehoused for quick delivery. Usually less expensive than custom cabinets, they are sold by building centers, lumberyards, and some bath design showrooms.

Custom cabinets are built to order by a cabinetmaker or cabinet shop, so you get exactly the combination of size, style, material, and finish that you want. Another option is to adapt cabinets built for other uses—such as antique bureaus, desks, or kitchen cabinets—for use in your bathroom.

Though stock cabinets typically are less expensive than custom-made, there is a wide range of prices within each category. If your budget is especially tight, spend your time choosing among options in stock cabinetry. Even if price is not a primary factor, you may find that stock cabinets fit your needs perfectly.

On the other hand, if you want cabinets that are unusual in size, materials, finish, or features, custom cabinets may be the answer. Start shopping for custom cabinets early; contact a

cabinetmaker, a designer, or a kitchen and bath showroom to get the ball rolling, and plan on at least six to eight weeks from design to delivery.

Other storage options for bathrooms include shelves and closets.

Shelves are a useful addition to bathrooms that don't have room for elaborate cabinetry. Large, open shelves can provide a place to keep towels and linens handy, while a shelf mounted under the mirror can allows space to store a few toiletry items in a guest bath.

Shelving can be recessed or surface-mounted. *Recessed shelves* take advantage of the space inside the walls, between the studs, offering the look of custom cabinetry without the cost. *Surface-mounted shelves* are easier to build and often less expensive than recessed shelves because they are not enclosed.

Linen closets generally extend from floor to ceiling, providing efficient storage space for linens and other bathroom items. Adding or relocating a closet requires significant construction—walls almost always have to be moved or built. If you plan to create a new closet in your bathroom, consult a contractor.

©Karen Melvin

Stone countertops offer durability in addition to the look and feel of luxury.

Countertops

When choosing countertops for your bathroom, it's important to consider cost, installation requirements, and maintenance of the countertop materials. Each countertop material offers its own distinctive look, along with a set of advantages and disadvantages.

Cultured marble is composed of a gel coat over a substrate of ground natural stone blended with polyester resin. Designed to resemble stone, it is frequently formed into seamless sink and countertop combinations that are inexpensive, easy to install, and available in standard sizes to fit stock cabinets. The primary disadvantage of cultured marble countertops is that the gel coat can stain, craze, and scratch over time, and once damaged, it is difficult to repair. Clean cultured marble with non-abrasive products only.

Laminate countertops are composed of a thin layer of plastic laminate bonded to a substrate of particleboard. They can be purchased in custom-built or post-form styles. Post-formed countertops have no seam along the backsplash or front edge, and can be cut to any length for easy installation. Custom laminate countertops are fabricated to fit spaces of any shape or size.

Plastic laminate is a relatively inexpensive material and is available in a wide variety of colors and patterns. When choosing a pattern or a color, look at samples that are large enough to give you a good idea of how a whole countertop will look. Often, especially with patterns, a small chip does not accurately represent the way an entire counter will look.

Although they are relatively tough, laminates aren't indestructible—they can be damaged by hair dyes and caustic bathroom cleaners.

Solid-surface material is a homogeneous blend of manufactured polyester or acrylic resins. It is molded into ¾"-thick countertops with solid color running throughout. There are many colors and patterns to choose from, including styles that mimic the look of granite or marble.

Prefabricated solid-surface countertops with integral sinks are available in stock sizes and are easy to install. However, because solid-surface is machinable, it is often custom-fabricated. Fabrication is a difficult process that is almost always done by professionals.

Solid-surface material is virtually impervious to stains and mildew. If the joints are done correctly, there are no seams or cracks in the surface to attract dirt or encourage mold. Also, most scratches and discolorations can easily be sanded out of solid-surface material. Routine cleaning is easy, but check the manufacturer's recommendations regarding abrasive cleaners.

Stone offers beauty and durability that's hard to duplicate. Stone countertops are usually made from ¾"-thick slabs that are installed by professional fabricators. Because stone is so heavy, vanities and cabinets may need to be reinforced so they can support the extra weight.

Granite and marble are most frequently used materials for countertops, while slate and limestone are occasionally used. Granite is more durable and stain-resistant, while marble offers a wider range of colors. Stone is also available in tile form. Though more expensive than ceramic tile, it is far easier to work with than stone slabs.

Make sure to get recommended cleaning procedures from the dealer when you purchase a stone countertop. Procedures can vary depending upon the sealant used on the stone surface.

Ceramic tile countertops are composed of glazed ceramic tile applied to a cementboard and plywood substrate (pages 234 to 239). There are many colors, styles, and textures of tile available, allowing you to choose anything from the bold style statement of a colorful mosaic to the elegance of classic white tiles with textural accents.

Ceramic tile will withstand normal sink-side splashing, but standing water should be wiped up so it doesn't soak into the grout. Grout lines can be susceptible to deterioration and should be sealed to prevent stains, mildew, and water damage. Most manufacturers recommend that you clean ceramic tile with a damp cloth and simple household cleaner.

Glass, concrete, wood, and other materials can also be incorporated into your countertop design to create a unique look. Make sure to get all the facts before deciding to use materials not commonly found in bathrooms. Inquire about installation procedures, maintenance, durability, delivery times, shipping costs, and hidden costs of any extras that may be necessary.

©Karen Melvin

Polished limestone is a durable, warm-toned surface that must be professionally shaped and installed.

Photo courtesy of Dura Supreme Cabinetry

Countertops made of solid-surface material can be molded with integral sinks, and are available in stock sizes that can be inserted into countertops that are custom-ordered to unique sizes and shapes.

Photo courtesy of Kohler, Co.

Ceramic tile can be incorporated into the countertop. It is moisture-resistant and easy to care for and clean.

Recessed light fixtures help create non-directional lighting. (above photo)

A combination of general lighting, task lighting, and accent lighting sets a luxurious tone for soaking in this whirlpool tub.

Lighting

Once you've created a basic bathroom layout, plan how you will light the space. If you need help with your lighting plan, electricians and sales people at lighting stores can provide guidance on style, brands, and lighting effects. You might even want to have a lighting designer draft a complete lighting plan for your new bathroom.

Combine different types of lighting to ensure personal safety, provide ambience, and permit various uses of your space. There are three basic types of lighting:

• General lighting usually involves overhead fixtures that efficiently illuminate the entire room. These lights provide a base that can be improved with specific task and accent lighting. Standard ceiling-mounted fixtures are common, often in combination with a vent or fan.

• Task lighting provides brighter, functional light for specific activities. The mirror area is a common place to find task lighting in bathrooms; wall-mounted light fixtures known as sconces are popular choices because they illuminate without casting shadows. Dedicated task lighting for the shower, tub, and toilet also may be appropriate, especially if those fixtures are separated by privacy partitions. Lights in these areas must be moisture-resistant.

• Accent lighting can be used to highlight points of decorative interest, such as architectural details or a piece of artwork. Soft, diffused tones are created by bouncing the light off of surfaces rather than glaring directly onto them. This indirect lighting can make a small room appear larger, especially if walls are light-colored and reflective.

There are types and styles of lighting fixtures to suit any decor and almost any space requirements. Surface-mounted fixtures are attached directly to the walls or ceiling. They are easy to install and available in a wide variety of styles.

Recessed fixtures are mounted so that the light is flush with the surface of the ceiling or wall. They are unobtrusive choices for overall lighting, casting light without drawing attention to themselves.

Track fixtures are literally tracks that supply power to several small lights that can be positioned as you wish. Track lighting is appropriate for accent lighting as well as for general lighting.

Portable fixtures such as floor and table lamps should be used only in bathrooms with plenty of counter or floor space. CAUTION: Avoid using extension cords in bathrooms, and never place electrical cords near water.

Heating & Ventilation

When making decisions about your bathroom heating system, consider room size, the number of windows, and the type of heat in the rest of the house. Consult a plumber, mechanical contractor, or electrician before making final decisions. There are four basic choices for auxiliary heat in bathrooms:

• Electric heaters can be mounted on the ceiling or walls either by themselves or as part of light/vent/heating units. Toe-space heaters are frequently tucked into spaces below vanities.

• Heat lamps use infrared light bulbs to provide radiant heat. Both surface-mounted and recessed fixtures are available for installation on the ceiling or walls.

• Radiant floor-heating systems installed beneath the flooring material warm the floor by circulating either hot water or electricity. *Hot-water systems* are designed to be the main heat source for a room, and are typically tied to a full house system. *Electric floor systems* (pages 198 to 201) are designed to make a single room more comfortable, not to be its sole source of heat. This type of system is especially popular underneath ceramic or stone tile floors.

• Towel warmers keep towels toasty and can keep a small area of the room warm. Dozens of varieties, both hot-water and electric, are available in wall-mounted and floor models.

Good ventilation protects surfaces from moisture damage, deters the growth of mold and mildew, and keeps the bathrooms air fresh. Vents with electric fans (pages 252 to 255) are required by Code in any bathroom without natural ventilation. The best plan is to install a vent with an exhaust system that carries stale or moist air outdoors.

Vent fans are rated by the number of cubic feet per minute (cfm) they can handle. Purchase a unit with a rating at least 5 cfm higher than the cubic footage of your bathroom. Avoid models that merely recirculate the air—they're cheaper and less complicated to install, but they aren't adequate for this important task.

Most vent fans are installed in the center of the bathroom ceiling or over the toilet area. Units installed over tub or shower areas must be GFCI-protected and rated for use in wet areas. Local building codes may have specific requirements, so check with your building inspector or HVAC contractor before selecting a ventilation unit.

Photos courtesy of SunTouch Floor Warming

Radiant heat floor systems keep hard surfaces warm to the touch and heat the room.

Photo courtesy of Broan-NuTone, LLC

Vent and light combinations serve the dual purpose of lighting the room and reducing moisture and odors.

Photo courtesy of Ceramic Tiles of Italy

©Karen Melvin

Photo courtesy of Pittsburg Corning Corporation

Natural stone and ceramic tiles can be combined to create custom-designed wall surfaces.

Design statements can be made with different paint techniques.

Glass block walls allow light to penetrate the wall, while serving as a partition.

Walls & Ceilings

In a layout change or expansion remodeling project, you may need to add, move, or replace walls. Listed below are the most commonly used wall materials for bathrooms:

• Drywall is the most commonly used material and works well for most bathrooms, except for the area around tubs and showers.

• Greenboard is a water-resistant drywall, good for tub surrounds or areas exposed to moisture.

• Cementboard is undamaged by water and is used under tile in tub and shower surrounds.

• Glass block is a popular choice for interior bathroom walls and shower stalls. The translucent blocks let light in while still offering privacy.

Wall and ceiling finishes should coordinate with the other design elements of the bathroom, withstand moisture, and be easy to maintain. For tub and shower surrounds, wall finishes should be waterproof. Also consider waterproof surfaces behind sinks and toilets.

• Paint finishes range from flat to glossy (sometimes called enamel). Glossy finishes are best for areas that will be cleaned often. While latex (water-based) paints are suitable for nearly every application, alkyd-base paints are sometimes restricted by local regulations because

they are a petroleum-based product.

• Wallpaper does not hold up well in bathroom environments unless it has been specially treated to withstand moisture. Choose smooth-textured vinyl or vinyl-coated wallpaper.

• Ceramic wall tiles are thinner and less expensive than floor tiles. They are durable, easy to clean, and available in hundreds of colors and textures.

• Stone wall tiles are one of the most expensive wall coverings. Consider using stone as an accent, or for one wall behind a pedestal sink.

• Solid-surface material manufacturers offer their products in ¼" sheets for use as wall panels. Solid-surface materials work well for backsplashes, but are more commonly used in tub or shower surrounds (pages 164 to 165).

• Tongue-and-groove wood planks and sheet panels can be used for wainscoting in bathrooms. Finish all wood in bathrooms with a durable urethane or a gloss enamel paint.

Like walls, bathroom ceilings need moisture-proof finishes that resist the effects of high humidity. A smooth, scrubbable surface is best. Avoid textured ceilings which will peel in humid conditions, and are difficult to repair or repaint.

Flooring

Bathroom floors need to be durable; they should stand up to daily use, frequent cleaning, and moisture. Choose textured materials to provide better traction on floors that often will be wet.

• Resilient vinyl flooring is the least expensive flooring material. It is simple to install, easy to clean, and available in a huge variety of colors, patterns, and styles.

Vinyl flooring comes in two types: tile and sheet. Vinyl tiles are easy to install and many styles come with peel-off adhesive backing. However, tile is not the best choice for bathroom floors because the many seams allow moisture to soak between the tiles and ruin the adhesive bond. Though sheet vinyl is more difficult to install than vinyl tiles, it has few or no seams. It comes in 6-ft. and 12-ft. widths and is cut to fit the floor (pages 192 to 197).

• Ceramic tile is a versatile material available in an almost endless variety of sizes, patterns, and colors. There are three main types of ceramic tile: *glazed ceramic tile* is fired, coated with a colored glaze, then fired again to produce a hard surface layer; *quarry tile* is an unglazed porous tile that is softer and thicker than glazed tiles; and *porcelain tile* is extremely dense, hard, and naturally water-resistant (pages 202 to 209).

• Natural stone tile is a premium—and expensive—flooring material. Granite, marble, and slate tiles are the most common stone products for floors. Installation also can be costly as natural stone requires a subfloor of poured mortar or cementboard.

• Hardwood floors are difficult to totally waterproof, even with a thick polyurethane coating. Humidity causes the wood to expand and contract, compromising the integrity of the protective coating and eventually warping the wood. Hardwood floors are appropriate for half baths where moisture and steam levels are low.

• Carpeting typically doesn't have the water resistance required for bathroom floors. If you choose carpeting, be sure to select one that's designed especially for bathrooms.

The condition of your existing floor may affect the cost of installing new flooring. If the subfloor must be replaced or repaired, more time and money will be required. Consult a professional to assess the state of your subfloor and recommend repairs.

Photo courtesy of Armstrong World Industries, Inc.

Vinyl flooring is a popular choice for bathrooms because it is relatively inexpensive, durable, and easy to clean.

Photo courtesy of Kolbe & Kolbe Millwork Co., Inc.

Ceramic floor tile, a popular choice for bathrooms, is durable and water-resistant.

©Karen Melvin

Stone floor tile creates an inviting atmosphere with natural appeal.

Custom saunas can be built to fit the look of your bathroom and can include any features you desire.

Some prefabricated saunas can rival custom-built saunas in style and quality, and are often less expensive.

Home Spa & Luxury Bathroom Amenities

More and more homeowners are installing luxury amenities to bring the therapeutic benefits of a trip to the spa right into their own homes. Master baths and luxury bathrooms are becoming larger in size to create a space that offers total relaxation and an escape from the rest of the world.

Whirlpools have become a standard fixture in master baths. A whirlpool circulates water mixed with air through jets mounted in the body of the tub to deliver a soothing hydromassage. See pages 23 and 166 to 171 for more information on whirlpools and their installation.

Saunas allow you to sweat out the day's tension in the privacy of your home. They are often prescribed by health professionals as a way to relieve everyday aches and pains, and joint problems.

Saunas are most commonly built of soft aromatic woods, such as cedar, redwood, or white spruce. The temperature in a well-made sauna averages 170° to 180°F. Saunas require no water other than the small amounts that are sometimes splashed on the heated stone to increase humidity, so extra plumbing, waterproof floors, and moistureproof surrounds are not necessary.

Little space is required to accommodate a sauna; a 4-ft. × 4-ft. minimum size is recommended for comfort. A sauna can sometimes be fit into a space little bigger than a closet. Saunas can be custom-built in any size and shape to fit your bathroom design, or you can purchase a prefabricated kit that includes the heater and all precut parts. See pages 172 to 177 for installing a sauna from a prefabricated kit.

Steam showers and steam rooms are one of the latest luxury additions to the home bathroom. Steam heat speeds up all of the chemical processes in the body, helping to rid the body of toxins. Some acrylic shower units are available with preinstalled steam capacity; separate steam generators are used in custom-built steam rooms. Steam rooms and steam showers require extra plumbing and wiring, as well as doors that seal tightly.

Shower towers are units that combine valves, multiple showerheads, handheld sprays, body sprayers and water jets using only one water line connection. A shower tower is designed to provide therapeutic hydromassage for aching muscles. Most units require a minimum ¾" dedicated supply line.

A variation of the shower tower, the body spa system incorporates the tower design into a unit that forces a large volume of water quickly through jets for hydromassage therapy. The water collects in the basin and is recirculated back through the system. NOTE: Due to the amount of hot water required to run these systems, you may need to upgrade your hot water heater before installing a shower tower or body spa system.

In addition to the above amenities, many homeowners design their luxury bathrooms with plenty of additional space to house exercise equipment or electronics to contribute entertainment, ambience, and convenience.

Use common sense and follow your local electrical codes when installing electronics in bathrooms. Devise an electrical plan that provides plenty of outlets for the appliances you will be using—overburdened outlets are particularly inappropriate in bathrooms. Make sure to locate all cords and electrical items well away from tubs, showers, and sinks.

Photo courtesy of Kohler Co.

Steam rooms and steam showers must be fully enclosed units with doors that seal tightly to trap the steam produced by the generator. Steam therapy provides many health benefits.

Photo courtesy of Kohler Co.

Shower towers are equipped with multiple shower heads and body sprayers to provide a therapeutic hydromassage for aching muscles.

A bathroom designed for accessibility creates an environment that helps everyone feel more comfortable.

Designing for Accessibility

You've decided on a bathroom makeover, or opted for an new, expanded luxury bathroom to pamper yourself. As you choose your bathroom fixtures and materials, consider improving the safety and accessibility of your bathroom as part of your project. Many products that enhance safety and accessibility can be easily installed in less than an hour. During a major bathroom renovation, integrating these features is even easier. While considering safety and ease of use, you'll need to include nearly all aspects of the bathroom: flooring, fixtures, cabinets, showers and tubs, electrical systems, and doors. Also included are considerations specific to walker and wheelchair users.

Flooring surfaces in combination with moisture from showers, baths, and sinks can create hazardous surfaces. One easy way to improve a slippery floor is to add a slip-resistant glaze to new or existing ceramic tile. For shower floors, add non-slip adhesive strips or decals.

If you are replacing your floor, look for mosaic tiles, vinyl, and cork materials. All are good

flooring choices for the bathroom. Opt for matte finishes because they tend to be less slippery than polished surfaces and they reduce glare—an important consideration for people with vision problems. The vertical offset of the threshold between the bathroom floor and hallway or room flooring should be no greater than ¼". Install transition wedges if needed.

No matter what's on your floor, make sure all bathroom floors are level. Area rugs should have rubber backing to prevent slips and falls. Remove area rugs when a bathroom is used by wheelchair or walker users.

Fixture selection is very important in making a bathroom easier to use. Inflexibility and loss of strength due to illness, injury, or aging can make reaching, bending, and twisting difficult. Toilets, faucets, sinks, cabinets, tubs, and showers can all be adapted or changed for increased useability.

Toilet height is important for people with limited leg or joint strength and back injuries. An easy way to make the toilet height more comfortable is to purchase and install a height adapter that raises a standard toilet seat 2" to 5". These simple products snap onto a standard toilet in less than 5 minutes.

On the other hand, toilets that are 19" or higher are cumbersome for short people and wheelchair users. Because a wheelchair seat usually is 18" high, a toilet seat is most comfortable when it is 17" to 18" high. Choosing an elongated or oval seat style will add surface area for ease of transfer on and off the toilet. If transfer to or from the toilet is particularly difficult, consider an adjustable-height toilet, or a model with a power-lift seat.

If you are replacing your toilet, consider a wall-hung style that can be installed at any height. Wall-hung styles also provide additional clear space for maneuvering a wheelchair or walker. (See page 44 for more information on clear approach spaces for the bathroom.)

A bidet or an integral personal hygiene system costs a little more, but is a nice feature to consider with a new toilet because they help people with physical disabilities maintain independent personal hygiene. (See box on page 31.)

Install grab bars on walls around the toilet so a wheelchair user can safely transfer to and from the toilet. (See pages 262 to 265 for installing grab bars.)

Photo courtesy of Toto USA

An integral personal hygiene system can be installed to help people with physical disabilities maintain independence.

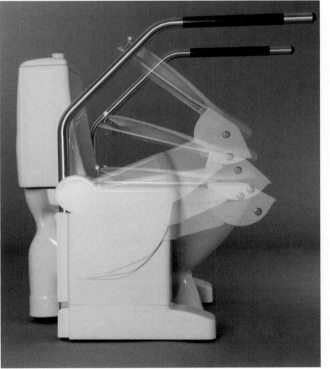

Power-lifts make toilet use easier for people with limited leg or joint strength.

Faucets and showerheads can be made more safe with anti-scald guard and volume-control devices. These simple devices help prevent burns from sudden surges in water temperature, and they are easy to install. Most can be inserted in a standard faucet in minutes.

Replacing double-handled faucets with single-lever styles will make them easier to use. A single lever gives the quickest water control with the least amount of effort. Pull-out sprayers on sink faucets allow for washing hair without using the tub or shower. A luxury option is a faucet with motion-sensor operation for hands-free use. Make sure the sink's drain control is accessible and easy to use. A rubber plug and chain is a simple solution to this problem.

Changing a standard showerhead to an adjustable showerhead mounted on a vertical slide-bar allows people of all sizes to set the water spray at a comfortable height. Adjustable showerheads are especially helpful for seated users. Look for models that can be hand held for best control. When mounting a showerhead, make sure the bottom end of the bar is no higher than 48" from the floor. (See pages 244 to 245 for installing an adjustable showerhead.)

(continued next page)

Approach Spaces & Clearance
Room for Wheelchairs & Walkers

A bathroom should be planned with enough approach space and clearance room to allow a wheelchair or walker user to enter and turn around easily. The guidelines for approach spaces (patterned areas) and clearances shown here include some ADA guidelines and recommendations from universal design specialists.

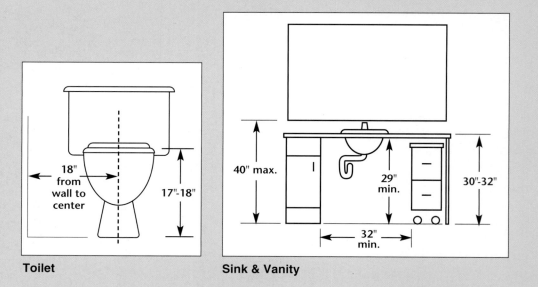

Toilet

Sink & Vanity

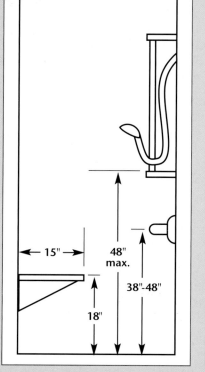

Shower

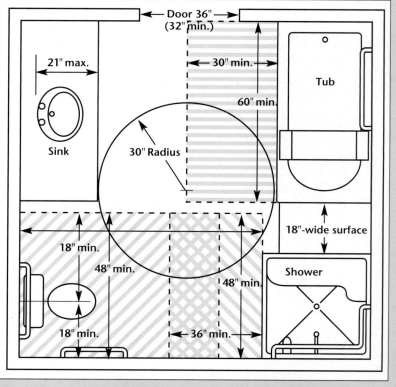

Floor Plan

Designing for Accessibility (continued)

Vanities and cabinets are easier to use if handles are C-shaped pulls, or magnetic touch latches that require a simple push to operate. Many styles are available at building supply centers, or you can order custom styles from cabinet distributors.

Wall-mounted cabinets and medicine cabinets often have shelves that are difficult to reach. Adding pull-down hardware will bring items within reach for seated people or those with limited mobility. Another simple solution is to add a fold-down step stool under base cabinets. Or, simply remount the medicine cabinet to the side of the sink, rather than behind it, to minimize reaching.

Comfortable countertop height depends on the user. For seated people most countertops are too high for comfortable use. A tall person or someone with a back injury might find most countertops too low. Equipping a bathroom with countertops installed at varied heights serves both seated and standing users. Mount sections of countertop at 34" to 36" for standing users, and 30" to 32" for seated users. Position a vanity sink toward the front of a cabinet to minimize reaching. Sinks installed within 21" of the front edge are best. When that's not possible, consider mounting the faucet controls at the side of the sink, rather than the back.

If you are replacing your sink, choose a style that is shallower at the front and deeper at the drain for seated users. Or install a wall-mounted sink, positioned at 30" to 32". Providing a clear space that is 29" high by 32" to 36" wide under sinks and lowered sections of countertop allows seated users to comfortably reach the vanity. Use fold-away doors, remove face frames on base cabinets, or install roll-out base cabinets to gain clear space. For a finished look and for level wheelchair access, always finish the floor under fold-away or roll-out cabinets. Then insulate pipes or install a protective panel to prevent burns to seated users.

Electrical systems in the bathroom can be easily changed to improve safety and make the bathroom more comfortable. There are several changes you can make without ever lifting so much as a screwdriver. Change the light bulbs above your vanity to glare-free full-spectrum bulbs, which will enhance visibility for people with vision problems. Plug in motion-sensor or light-sensor night-lights to make nighttime bathroom visits safer.

Photo courtesy of Kohler, Co.

Roll-out base cabinets provide the option of seating space at the countertop.

Photo courtesy of Elkay

Side-mounted faucet and drain pulls in combination with a wall-mounted sink are easily accessible.

Photo courtesy of Ginger®

A tilted mirror allows seated or short users to easily see themselves.

(continued next page)

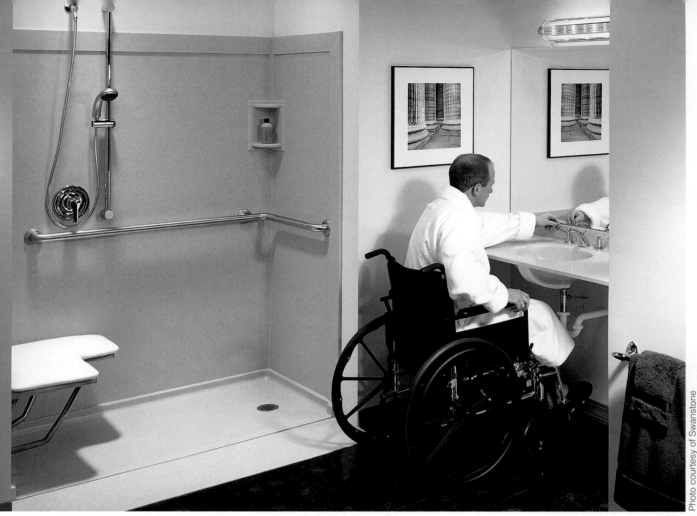

Roll-in shower designs, roll-under sinks, grab bars, adjustable slide-bar showers and open floor space make bathing easier for people with disabilities.

Designing for Accessibility (continued)

Replace all standard receptacles in the bathroom with GFCIs. These devices are required by code and protect your family from electrical shock. (See page 135 for installing a GFCI receptacle.) Install outlets at a minimum height of 18", so wheelchair users can reach them without bending, and install countertop receptacles no more than 21" from the front edge of the countertop. Or consider adding a fold-down electrical strip on the sink cabinet so wheelchair users can have outlets at their fingertips.

Heat lamps, in-floor heating systems, and efficient vent fans in the bathroom make it safer by keeping surfaces drier and less slippery. (See pages 198 to 201 for in-floor heating and pages 252 to 255 for vent fan installation.) Extra warmth in the bathroom makes it more comfortable for the elderly, who are especially prone to chilling. People with limited or impaired movement may take longer to bathe and dress, so they will also appreciate the warm environment.

If your bathroom has a stand-alone or tub shower, install a waterproof light over the area to eliminate shadows and provide added assurance in a slippery environment.

Add a phone jack and telephone to your bathroom so elderly or disabled family members can call for help if they fall or are injured.

Showers and tubs are slippery, have high edges, and often have controls in inaccessible places. Some innovative products can make bathing easier and safer.

First and foremost, install grab bars in and around the shower and tub. Grab bars provide stability on slippery surfaces. They are so important that every bathroom should be equipped with them. (See pages 262 to 265 for installing grab bars.) Adding a shower seat or installing a pull-down or permanent seat in the shower allows elderly or disabled family members to sit while bathing. Ready-to-use tub and shower seats can be purchased from hospital supply stores. Models include transfer seats, seats with backs, and simple stools. These units can be

Photo courtesy of Kohler, Co.

New tub designs include doors, seats, and more comfortable soft materials.

Photo courtesy of Craftmaster Manufacturing, Inc.

Consider installing a pocket door in your bathroom to gain more clearance room for wheelchairs and walkers.

moved out of the way when not in use. If you decide to permanently mount a shower seat in your bathroom, install it at 18" high, and be sure the seat is at least 15" deep.

On tubs, reposition water controls and faucets toward the outside edge of the tub, at a height of 38" to 48", so the water can be turned on and adjusted before getting in to bathe. If you're going to replace your tub or remodel your bathroom, consider a bathtub with a side-access door to eliminate climbing over the side. Look for newer tub styles made from soft materials that are non-slip and comfortable.

Wheelchair users can have great difficulty with standard tub and shower designs. Consider replacing a combination tub and shower with a stand-alone shower. The best designs include a base that slopes gently toward the drain, rather than a curb to contain water. When fitted with a pull-down seat and adjustable, handheld showerhead, roll-in showers can accommodate people with a wide range of abilities.

Many roll-in showers are designed without doors or curtains. Innovative designs include block

walls that separate wet areas from the rest of the room. When a curtain is used, install it on a rod mounted securely into wall backing, so it can support a person who may grab it during a fall.

Doors and doorways can be changed to improve safety and accessibility. The most important thing you can do to bathroom doors—including those on showers—is to reverse the hinges so doors open out. That way, family members can be helped if they fall because they won't be blocking the door swing. Having bathroom doors open out also allows for more open floor space. You might also want to consider replacing the door's hinges with swing-clear hinges that will give you more door clearance.

Some bathrooms have smaller entrances that can make bathroom access difficult. Consider widening doorways to 32" to 36" so wheelchair and walker users can enter the bathroom easily. Or replace a standard door with a pocket door to gain clear space. (See pages 220 to 223 for installing a pocket door.)

Building Codes & Design Guidelines

Because so many activities occur in such a relatively small space, remodeling a bathroom requires careful planning and design. The National Kitchen and Bath Association (NKBA) publishes a list of bathroom design standards to help people plan rooms that are safe and accessible to all users. Some of the basic standards are listed in the chart at the right. Standards specific to universal design can be found on pages 42 to 47.

Your bathroom probably won't conform to all of the recommended standards, but they can help guide your overall plan. What your plan must include is everything prescribed by the local building codes. Page 49 lists many of the common code issues for bathrooms.

The following steps outline the next phase of your project—drawing plans and obtaining permits.

Sketch a plan. Draw your bathroom's floor plan and wall dimensions to scale (pages 50 to 51). Buy or make your own templates for existing and new fixtures, and experiment with different layouts. Remember to plan for both fixtures and plumbing lines, locating any new plumbing near existing waste-vent lines—moving existing fixture drains can add significantly to the cost and difficulty of the project.

Check the building codes. Consult local building codes regarding all aspects of your project, particularly the minimum clearances required around fixtures. The floor space needed for the room will largely depend on the types and number of fixtures included. Consider compact fixtures and built-ins if you are short on space.

Create a scale drawing and materials list. Detail your initial plans, adding all dimensions and fixtures for your new bathroom. Include all plumbing, wiring, and HVAC connections. After completing your drawing, make a materials list, set a timetable, and decide what work you will do yourself and what work you will hire out.

Have your plans reviewed. Take your completed plans to the local building department for review. Getting input early in the process will save you time and expense later. The building inspector will check your drawings and materials list and recommended changes. You also will need to obtain one or more building permits, which include scheduled inspections. Typically, the building inspector will review your work after the framing and rough-in plumbing and wiring are completed and again when the job is done.

Bathroom Design Standards

For more information regarding bathroom design, contact the NKBA (page 266).

- Plan doorways with a clear floor space equal to the door's width on the push side and greater than the door's width on the pull side. NOTE: Clear floor spaces within the bathroom can overlap.

- Design toilet enclosures with at least 36" × 66" of space; include a pocket door or a door that swings out toward the rest of the bathroom.

- Install toilet-paper holders approximately 26" above the floor, toward the front of the toilet bowl.

- Place fixtures so faucets are accessible from outside the tub or shower. Add anti-scald devices to tub and sink faucets (they are required for shower faucets).

- Avoid steps around showers and tubs, if possible.

- Fit showers and tubs with safety rails and grab bars.

- Install shower doors so they swing open into the bathroom, not the shower.

- Use tempered glass or another type of safety glass for all glass doors and partitions.

- Include storage for soap, towels, and other items near the shower, located within 15" to 48" above the floor. These should be accessible to a person in the shower or tub.

- Provide natural light equal to at least 10% of the floor area in the room.

- Illuminate all activity centers in the bathroom with task and ambient lighting.

- Provide a minimum clearance of 15" from the centerline of sinks to any sidewalls. Double-bowl sinks should have 30" clearance between bowls, from centerline to centerline.

- Provide access panels for all electrical, plumbing, and HVAC systems connections.

- Include a ventilation fan that exchanges air at a rate of 8 air changes per hour.

- Choose countertops and other surfaces with edges that are smoothed, clipped, or radiused.

Building Codes

The following are some of the most common building codes for bathrooms. Contact your local building department for a list of all codes enforced in your area.

- The minimum ceiling height in bathrooms is 7 ft. (Minimum floor area is determined by clearances around fixtures.)

- Sinks must be at least 4" from side walls and have 21" of clearance in front.

- Sinks must be spaced 4" away from neighboring sinks and toilets, and 2" away from bathtubs.

- Toilets must be centered 15" from side walls and tubs, with 21" clearance in front.

- New and replacement toilets must be low-flow models (1.6 gal./flush).

- Shower stalls must be at least 30" × 30", with 24" of clearance in front of shower openings.

- Steps must be at least 10" deep and no higher than 7¼".

- Faucets for showers and combination tub-showers must be equipped with anti-scald devices.

- Supply lines that are ½" in diameter can supply a single fixture, or one sink and one toilet. A ¾"-diameter supply line must be used to supply two or more fixtures.

- Waste and drain lines must slope ¼" per foot toward the main DWV stack to aid flow and prevent blockage.

- Each bathroom must be wired with at least one 20-amp circuit for GFCI-protected receptacles, and one 15-amp (minimum) circuit for light fixtures and vent fans without heating elements.

- All receptacles must be GFCI-protected.

- There must be at least one permanent light fixture controlled by a wall switch.

- Wall switches must be at least 60" away from bathtubs and showers.

- Toilet, shower, vanity, or other bathroom compartments must have adequate lighting.

- Light fixtures over bathtubs and showers must be vaporproof, with a UL rating for wet areas.

- Vanity light fixtures with built-in electrical receptacles are prohibited.

- Whirlpool motors must be powered by dedicated GFCI-protected circuits.

- Bathroom vent ducts must terminate no less than 10 ft. horizontally or 3 ft. vertically above skylights.

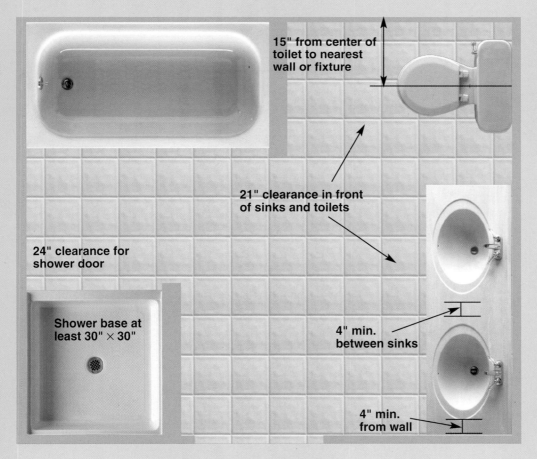

15" from center of toilet to nearest wall or fixture

21" clearance in front of sinks and toilets

24" clearance for shower door

Shower base at least 30" × 30"

4" min. between sinks

4" min. from wall

Follow minimum clearance and size guidelines when planning locations of bathroom fixtures. Easy access to fixtures is fundamental to creating a bathroom that is comfortable, safe, and easy to use.

Drawing Plans

If your new bathroom involves a layout change or expansion, create floor plans and elevation drawings. A floor plan is an overhead view of the floor and the fixtures, while an elevation is a face-on view of a wall and the fixtures. Your drawings will be the basis for contracts with tradespeople and vendors.

To begin, sketch a rough outline of the existing floor plan. Include wall thicknesses and any adjoining space that could be used for expansion. Also note any quirks or jogs in the walls—they may hide pipes or other essentials. Measure and record the size and location of all existing fixtures and mechanicals (heat ducts, wiring, etc.). Make measurements from a fixed point, such as a corner, and record dimensions in inches. Finally, sketch an elevation of each wall. Include the height of ceilings, doors, windows, fixtures, and other features (mirrors, shelving, etc.).

Use the rough sketches to draft a precise scale drawing of your existing floor plan—this draft will be used to trace layout options. Add dimension lines (with measurements) in the margins, then add the existing fixtures, mechanicals, and other architectural features (also with dimensions) in their current positions.

Using the scale drawing of the floor plan as a guide, sketch variations of your new bathroom. On tracing paper, trace the walls with any modifications you want to explore (relocating the doorway, expanding into an adjoining closet, etc.), then draw all the necessary fixtures in their correct proportions, in new locations.

Trace as many versions as you can think of to find the plan that best fulfills your vision and makes good use of your space, while conforming to building codes and accepted design principles (pages 48 to 49).

Use the overall dimensions of your new floor plan to sketch elevation options on tracing paper, just as you did for the floor plans. When you are satisfied with these, draft new elevations to show the precise locations of elements on the walls. In the end, the elevations and floor plans must agree.

Your drawing plans may well be revised again before they are truly final. Revise your drawings as you get more information or better ideas.

A scale drawing shows everything in accurate proportion. After measuring the dimensions of your existing bathroom, draft a floor plan, including any adjoining space that could be used for expansion of the layout (such as the storage closet shown below). The accepted scale for bathroom plans is ½" = 1 ft.

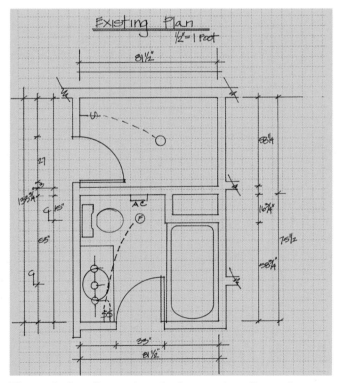

The existing floor plan draft contains dimension lines noting the accurate measurements of the space, including the location of all existing fixtures. This draft also shows the location of electrical circuits.

Bathroom Floor Plan Options

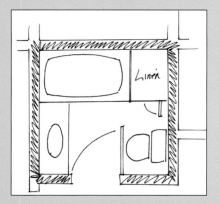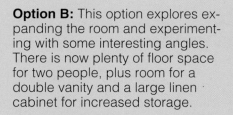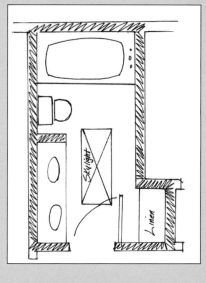

Option A: This floor plan option of the draft on the opposite page shows a layout change within the existing space. The sink and vanity stay in the same place, but the tub and toilet have been switched. There is room to add a linen cabinet, but the space still is very cramped.

Option B: This option explores expanding the room and experimenting with some interesting angles. There is now plenty of floor space for two people, plus room for a double vanity and a large linen cabinet for increased storage.

Option C: The existing room is expanded by annexing the adjacent closet. There's plenty of floor space, a double vanity, and a built-in linen cabinet. This plan has the practical benefits of Option B, but is less expensive to build.

Bathroom Elevation Options

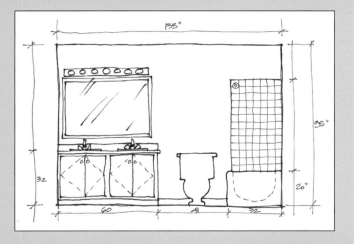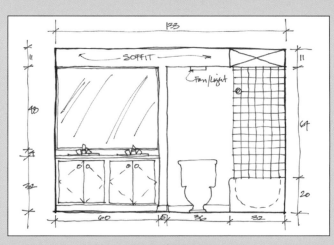

Option A: This elevation shows a simple arrangement with a standard mirror and light fixture. It also shows ceramic tile in the shower area, ending just above the shower curtain.

Option B: This variation shows a custom mirror framed in by a partition wall, and a soffit that runs above the vanity, toilet, and tub. Lights are recessed in the soffit.

Creating a Budget

Creating a detailed budget helps you plan a new bathroom that fits your pocketbook as well as it fits your home and the needs of your family.

Types of Baths	**Range of Cost**		
	Levels of Remodeling		
	$ Makeover	$ Layout Change	$ Expansion
Half Baths	$250 to $5,000	$2,500 to $7,500	$4,000 to $12,500
Full Baths	$600 to $15,000	$4,400 to $19,000	$4,400 to $23,000
Shared Baths	$600 to $19,000	$5,000 to $22,500	$7,500 to $25,000
Luxury Baths	$1,900 to $25,000	$11,000 to $32,000	$19,000 to $44,000

The typical range of cost for a bathroom remodel depends on which level of remodeling and which type of bathroom you are planning.

One of the most important steps in planning a bathroom remodel is to create a budget. A budget is a statement of how much you're willing to spend. It helps you control costs and prevent the project from spiraling out of control.

First, establish an initial budget based on both the amount of money available to you and how much you want to spend. Determine how much of your personal savings you can afford to use, and whether or not you will borrow from a financial institution. Contact several different banks, credit unions, and mortgage companies to compare interest rates for identically structured loans. Loan officers can give you detailed information about different loans and options.

Next, make a list of all the fixtures, materials, and services you are considering using in your project. Estimate the cost of each item listed, then calculate the total project cost estimate. Compare this total with your initial budget. If it is more than the funds you've allocated, decide if you are willing to spend more to get what you want. If the cost is still too high, modify your initial budget based on the estimated costs. There are several options for reducing remodeling costs:

• Consider options other than building additions or expansions into other rooms, such as a layout change or cosmetic makeover.

• Reevaluate which elements are truly important and which you can do without. Prioritize your list, deleting the least important items until the estimated costs match what you're willing to spend.

• Comparison-shop for fixtures and materials. Look for end-of-year closeout sales, or choose good quality materials over luxury products. Also consider used or salvaged items.

• Do some of the work yourself to save on expensive labor costs, but tackle only those tasks with which you feel comfortable.

Balancing what you want to spend with a realistic estimate of costs gives you a working budget that should be quite accurate. You can later devise a final budget based on your detailed drawing plans and the actual quotes from contractors and vendors.

Working with Professionals

Many homeowners hire professionals to plan or complete the more complex or specialized aspects of their bathroom remodeling project. These professionals generally fall into two main categories: design professionals and building professionals.

Design professionals help you plan your project. They are experts at taking ideas and turning them into project plans and blueprints. Their services are expensive, so it's wise to do some planning of your own before contracting with them.

Bathroom designers provide detailed help with the layout and design or your bathroom, and can also act as general contractors. Look for certification by the National Kitchen and Bath Association (NKBA), and the initials CBD (certified bath designer).

Interior designers deal with the functional and aesthetic aspects in bathrooms to help create a specific style. Look for designers certified by the American Society of Interior Designers (ASID).

Architects are licensed professionals who design and prepare detailed construction plans for homes and buildings. Their services are expensive but warranted, and sometimes required for major remodeling projects.

Building designers are similar to architects. They usually have extensive experience in construction and design but less background in engineering.

Design/build firms offer the services of both designers and general contractors to see a project through from start to finish.

Building professionals are the tradespeople who coordinate and complete the construction phase of the project. They all fall under two main categories: general contractors and subcontractors.

General contractors manage all aspects of a remodeling project. They hire, schedule, coordinate, and supervise the activities of all the professionals working on a job. Many will only take major construction projects.

Subcontractors actually complete the work.

Hire design and construction professionals to help with the elements of your project that you are uncomfortable with or incapable of completing yourself.

Subcontractors include all the professionals in the various building trades, such as carpenters, plumbers, electricians, and HVAC (heating, ventilation, and air conditioning) specialists. They can be hired for specific aspects of a project or to help with planning and problem solving.

Before hiring a contractor, check references—including a project currently underway, if possible. Never hire a contractor simply because he or she is the low bidder. Once you've made a selection, meet with the contractor again to make final arrangements and agree on a contract.

Call Your Building Inspector

Building inspectors review your project at various stages to ensure it meets local building code requirements. And although inspectors aren't paid as consultants, they are experts in their respective fields and can be excellent resources for specific questions about building, electrical, or plumbing applications. Inspectors are busy, so keep your questions short. Also request pamphlets or local code summaries, when available.

Roughing-in Bathrooms

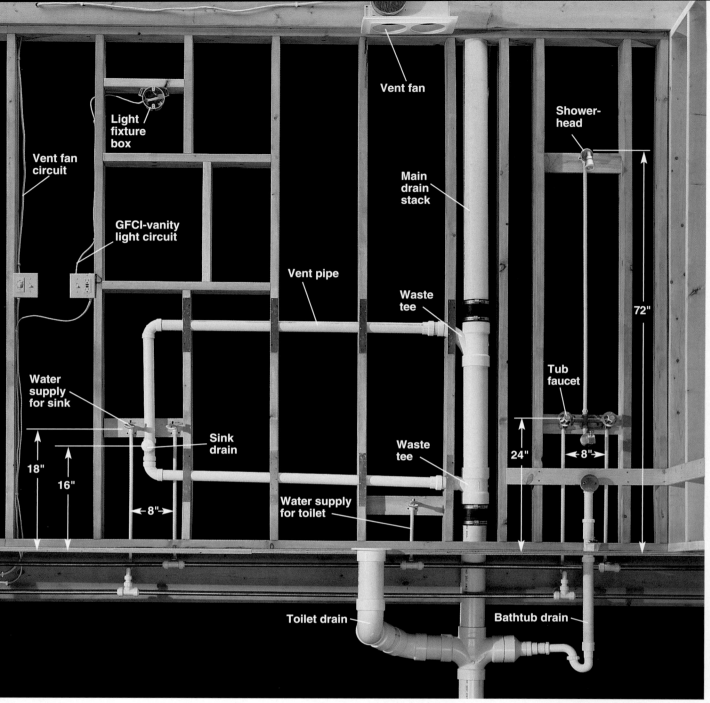

Vent fan

Shower-
head

Light
fixture
box

Vent fan
circuit

GFCI-vanity
light circuit

Main
drain
stack

Vent pipe

Waste
tee

72"

Water
supply
for sink

Sink
drain

Tub
faucet

Waste
tee

Waste
tee

24"

8"

18"

16"

8"

Water supply
for toilet

Toilet drain

Bathtub drain

A basic rough-in for framing, wiring, and plumbing in an average bathroom is shown above. Your actual rough-in will vary, depending on the layout of your bathroom.

Roughing-in the Bathroom

The process of installing new framing, plumbing, and electrical lines is called the "rough-in." This work is completed while the wall cavities are uncovered. Doing your own rough-in work requires some experience. Many remodelers with limited wiring and plumbing experience hire professionals to install new pipes and electrical cable, then connect the fixtures themselves.

Most rough-in projects require a building permit

(page 48). Make sure a building inspector approves the rough-in work before you finish the walls.

This chapter includes:

Preparing the Work Area

Whether they include carpentry, plumbing, or electrical work, most projects share the same basic preparation techniques and follow a similar sequence. Start by checking for hidden mechanicals in the work area and shutting off electrical wiring, plumbing pipes, and other utility lines. Reroute the mechanicals where necessary. If you are not comfortable performing these tasks, hire a professional.

Test all electrical outlets before beginning any demolition of walls, ceilings, or floors. Shovel all demolition debris away from the work area. Clear away the debris whenever materials begin to pile up during the construction of a project. For larger jobs, consider renting a construction waste container.

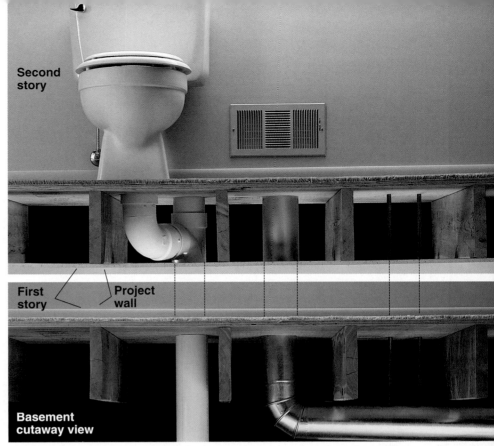

Check for hidden plumbing lines, ductwork, and gas pipes before you cut into a wall. To determine the location of the pipes and ducts, examine the areas directly below and above the project wall. In most cases, pipes, utility lines, and ductwork run through the wall vertically between floors. Original blueprints for your house, if available, usually show the location of the utility lines.

Preparation Tips

Disconnect electrical wiring before you cut into walls. Trace the wiring back to a fixture outside the cutout area, then shut off the power and disconnect the wires leading into the cutout area. Turn the power back on and test for current with a circuit tester before cutting into the walls.

Shovel debris through a convenient window into a wheelbarrow to speed up demolition work. Use sheets of plywood to cover shrubs and flower gardens next to open windows and doors. Cover adjoining lawn areas with sheets of plastic or canvas to simplify cleanup.

Do removal work quickly and easily by using the right tools for the job. A reciprocating saw with a combination blade cuts through old mortar and tile grout, turning a time-consuming chore into a simple job. Always wear eye protection, a dust mask, and heavy gloves.

Removing Bathroom Fixtures & Surfaces

Begin the removal phase of your project by removing fixtures located near the door. Even if you plan to keep these items, get them out of the way so they are not damaged, and to clear the way for removing other fixtures. Also remove cabinets, vanities, electrical fixtures, and accessories.

Remove old bathtubs and shower stalls only after you have created a clear path to get them out. Trim and wall and floor surfaces may need to be removed first. Label all items you plan to reuse, then store them where they won't be in the way. Get help when removing heavy fixtures, like a bathtub.

Turn off water supply and electrical power to the bathroom before removing electrical and plumbing fixtures, or cutting into walls or ceilings.

Work safely: wear eye protection, dust masks and heavy gloves during any demolition and removal process.

This section shows:

- Removing Toilets (pages 60 to 61)
- Removing Sinks, Cabinets & Countertops (pages 62 to 65)
- Removing Bathtubs & Showers (pages 66 to 69)
- Removing Electrical Fixtures & Bathroom Accessories (pages 70 to 71)
- Removing Wall & Floor Surfaces (pages 72 to 75)

Tips for Removing Bathroom Fixtures

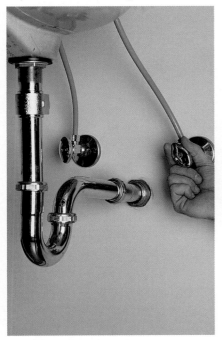

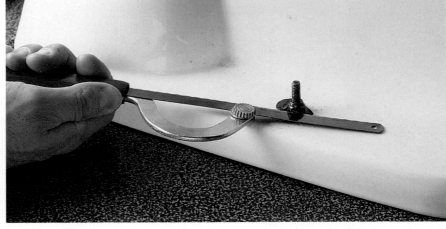

Cut corroded bolts with a hacksaw if you cannot loosen the nut with a wrench and you wish to remove the old fixture intact. Often, floor bolts on toilet bowls must be sawed off.

Turn off shutoff valves, mounted rear fixtures on the water supply lines, before disconnecting water pipes. Sinks and toilets usually are equipped with easily accessible shutoff valves, but many bathtubs and showers are not.

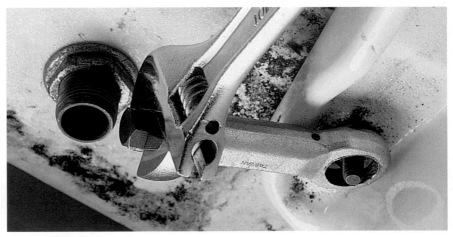

Crack corroded nuts with a nut splitter if you cannot reach the bolt with a hacksaw or wrench. Bolts that connect toilet tanks and bowls (above) and coupling nuts that connect faucets to supply lines can be difficult to reach. Nut splitters are sold at most automobile parts stores.

Turn off the main shutoff valve when there are no individual shut-off valves at the fixture being re-moved. Main shutoff valves usually are located in your basement, near the water meter.

Plug drain pipes with a rag or pipe cap if they will be open for more than a few minutes. Uncovered waste pipes allow dangerous sewer gases to escape into your home.

Most toilets are fragile and should be removed during full remodeling projects, even if you do not plan to replace them. Always use care when handling any fixture made of china or porcelain.

Removing Toilets

The toilet is the first fixture to be removed in most remodeling projects. Loosening corroded or rusted nuts and bolts is the most difficult part of the process. See page 59 for tips on removing problem nuts.

Old toilets that will not be reinstalled may be broken up into small, easily managed pieces, using a sledgehammer. Disconnect the toilet and cover it with a heavy blanket before breaking it. Wear eye protection, long sleeves, and heavy gloves during the demolition.

Everything You Need

Tools: adjustable wrench, ratchet wrench and sockets, screwdriver, putty knife, basin wrench.

Materials: sponge, rag, bucket, drop cloth.

Tips for Removing Toilets

Protect your floor with a drop cloth when removing the toilet, if you plan to keep the original floor covering. Residue from the wax ring seal between the bottom of the toilet and the toilet flange is very difficult to remove from floor coverings.

Disconnect any pipes between a wall-mounted toilet tank and the bowl, after turning off the water supply and emptying the tank. Older toilets often have a metal elbow that connects the tank to the bowl. Set 2 × 4 braces below the tank before detaching it from the wall.

How to Remove a Toilet & Wax Ring

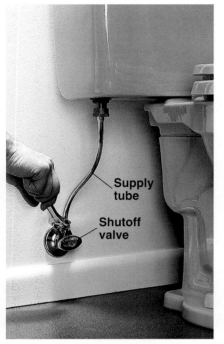

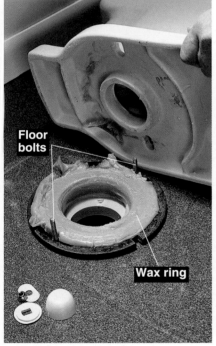

1 Turn off the water, then flush the toilet to empty the tank. Use a sponge to remove the remaining water in the tank and bowl. Disconnect the supply tube with an adjustable wrench.

2 Remove the nuts from the tank bolts with a ratchet wrench. Carefully remove the tank and set it aside.

3 Pry off the floor bolt trim caps at the base of the toilet, then remove the floor nuts with an adjustable wrench. See page 59 for tips on removing corroded or rusted nuts.

(image: additional photo)

4 Straddle the toilet and rock the bowl from side to side until the seal breaks. Carefully lift the toilet off the floor bolts and set it on its side. A small amount of water may spill from the toilet trap.

5 Remove the old wax from the toilet flange in the floor. Plug the drain opening with a damp rag to prevent sewer gases from rising into the house.

6 If the old toilet will be reused, clean the old wax and putty from the horn and the base of the toilet.

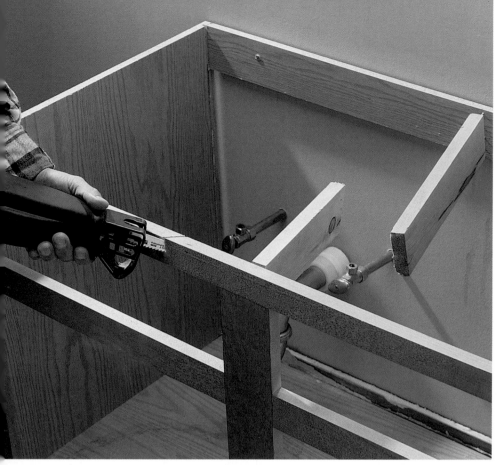

Cut apart cabinets and vanities to simplify their removal and disposal. A reciprocating saw or jig saw works well for this job. Wear eye protection.

Removing Sinks, Cabinets & Countertops

Replacing bathroom sinks, countertops, and cabinets is a quick and relatively inexpensive way to give your bathroom a fresh, new look.

First, disconnect the plumbing, then remove the sink basin or integral sink-countertop unit. Next, take out any remaining countertops. Finally, remove the cabinets and vanities.

Everything You Need

Tools: bucket, channel-type pliers, adjustable wrench, basin wrench, reciprocating saw, hacksaw or pipecutter, screwdriver, utility knife, flat pry bar.

How to Disconnect a Sink

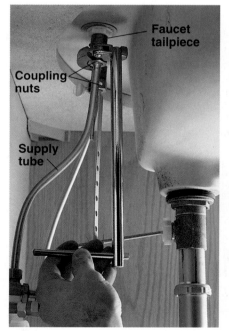

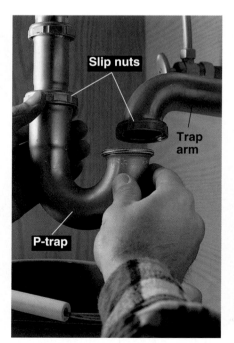

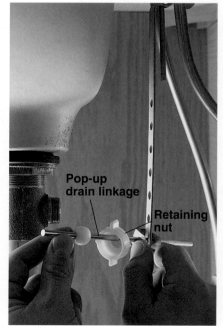

1 Turn off the shutoff valves, then remove the coupling nuts that connect the supply tube to the faucet tailpieces, using a basin wrench. If the supply tubes are soldered, cut them above the shutoff valves.

2 With a bucket beneath, remove the P-trap by loosening the slip nuts at both ends. If the nuts will not turn, cut out the drain trap with a hacksaw. When prying or cutting, take care to avoid damaging the trap arm that runs into the wall.

3 Disconnect the pop-up drain linkage from the tailpiece of the sink drain by unscrewing the retaining nut.

How to Remove a Sink

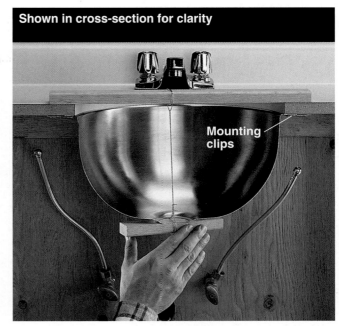

Shown in cross-section for clarity

Mounting clips

Self-rimming sink: Disconnect the plumbing, then slice through any caulking or sealant between the sink rim and the countertop, using a utility knife. Lift the sink off the countertop.

Rimless sink: Disconnect the plumbing, including the drain tailpiece. To support the sink, tie wire around a piece of scrap wood and set the wood across the sink opening. Thread the wire down through the drain hole and attach it to another scrap of wood. Twist the wire until taut, then detach the mounting clips. Slice through any caulking, slowly loosen the wire, then remove the sink.

Wall-mounted sink: Disconnect the plumbing, slice through any caulk or sealant, then lift the sink off the wall brackets. For models attached with lag screws, wedge 2 × 4s between the sink and floor to support it while the screws are removed.

Pedestal sink: Disconnect the plumbing. If the sink and pedestal are bolted together, disconnect them. Remove the pedestal first, supporting the sink from below with 2 × 4s. Lift the sink off the wall brackets (photo, left).

Integral sink-countertop: Disconnect the plumbing, then detach the mounting hardware underneath the countertop. Slice through any caulk or sealant between the countertop and wall, and between the countertop and vanity. Lift the sink-countertop unit off the vanity.

How to Remove a Wall Cabinet

1 Remove the cabinet doors and mirrors, if possible. If the cabinet has electrical features, see the variation shown below.

2 Remove screws or any other anchors that hold the sides of the cabinet to the wall studs.

3 Pull the cabinet out of the wall cavity. Pry the cabinet loose with a pry bar, or grip the face frame of the cabinet with pliers to pull it out.

Variations for Wall-mounted Cabinets

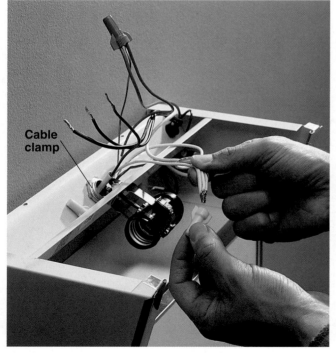

Cabinets with built-in electrical features: Shut off the power, then disconnect the built-in lights or receptacles (see pages 70 to 71). Unscrew the cable clamp on the back of the connection box so the cable is loose when the cabinet is removed.

Surface-mounted cabinets: Support the cabinet body from below with 2 x 4 braces, then remove the mounting screws to free the cabinet from the wall. When removing a large cabinet, have a helper hold the cabinet while you work.

How to Remove a Countertop & Vanity

1 Disconnect the plumbing (page 62), then cut through any caulk or sealant between the backsplash and the wall.

2 Detach any mounting hardware, located underneath the countertop inside the vanity.

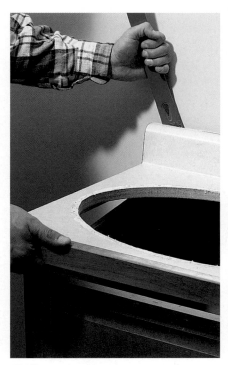

3 Remove the countertop from the vanity, using a pry bar if necessary.

4 Turn off the main water supply, then remove the shutoff valves, preserving as much of the supply pipe as possible. Cap the supply pipes or install new shutoff valves after the vanity is removed, then turn the water supply back on.

5 Remove the screws or nails (usually driven through the back rail of the cabinet) that anchor the vanity to the wall.

6 Cut through any caulk or sealant between the vanity and wall, using a utility knife, then pry the vanity away from the wall.

Shower pipe

Faucet body

Shutoff valves

Supply pipes

Disconnect the faucet through the access panel, usually located on the wall surface behind or next to the tub faucet and drain. (If the tub does not have an access panel, add one, as directed on page 179.) Turn off the shutoff valves, then cut the shower pipe above the faucet body. Disconnect or cut off the supply pipes above the shutoff valves.

Removing Bathtubs & Showers

Bathtubs and showers are heavy and bulky fixtures, so they pose special problems for removal. Unless the tub or shower has unique salvage value, cut or break the unit into pieces for easy removal and disposal. This technique allows one person to handle most of the disposal chores. Always wear eye protection and heavy gloves when cutting or breaking apart fixtures.

For most tubs and showers, you need to remove at least 6" of wall surface around the tub or shower pan to gain access to fasteners holding it to the wall studs. Maneuvering a tub out of an alcove also is easier when the wall surfaces are removed. If you are replacing the entire wall surface, do all the demolition work before removing the tub.

Everything You Need
Tools: reciprocating saw, channel-type pliers, screwdriver, hacksaw, adjustable wrench, flat pry bar, wrecking bar, hammer, masonry chisel, wire cutter, eye protection, utility knife.
Materials: 2 × 4 or 1 × 4 lumber, rag.

How to Remove Handles & Spouts

1 Shut off the water supply, then remove the faucet handles by prying off the covers and unscrewing the mounting screws.

2 Remove the tub spout by inserting a screwdriver into the spout and twisting counterclockwise until it unscrews from the stub-out that extends from the wall plumbing.

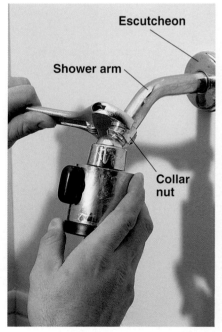

Escutcheon

Shower arm

Collar nut

3 Unscrew the collar nut to remove the showerhead. Loosen the escutcheon, then twist the shower arm counterclockwise to unscrew it from the wall plumbing.

How to Remove a Bathtub Drain

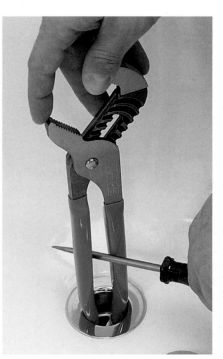

1 Remove the drain plug. Most bathtub plugs are connected to drain plug linkage that is lifted out along with the plug.

Spring-mounted drain plugs: Remove the plug by unscrewing it from the drain crosspiece.

2 Disconnect the drain assembly from the tub by inserting a pair of pliers into the drain opening and turning the crosspiece counterclockwise. Insert a long screwdriver between the handles and use it to twist the pliers.

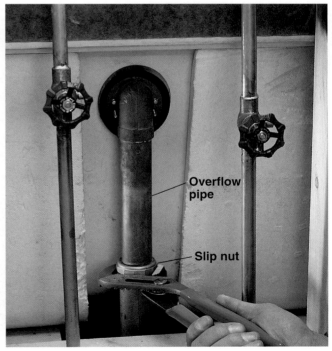

3 Remove the screws in the overflow coverplate (top photo). Remove the coverplate along with any attached drain plug (bottom photo).

4 Remove the overflow pipe by unscrewing the slip nut that holds it to the rest of the drain assembly, then lifting out the pipe. Stuff a rag into the waste pipe after the overflow pipe is removed to keep debris from entering the trap.

How to Remove a Shower Stall

1 After disconnecting the faucet handles, spout and shower-head (page 66), remove the shower curtain rod or shower door, molding or trim, and any other accessories.

2 Slice the caulking around each shower panel, using a utility knife. Remove any screws holding the panels together. NOTE: Tiled shower walls are removed in the same way as any ceramic tile wall (see page 74).

3 Pry shower panels away from the wall, using a flat pry bar. If the panels are still intact, cut them into small pieces for easier disposal, using a jig saw or a sharp utility knife.

Fabricated shower bases (fiberglass or plastic)**:** Slice the caulking between the base and the floor, then unscrew any fasteners holding the base to the wall studs. Pry the base from the floor with a wrecking bar.

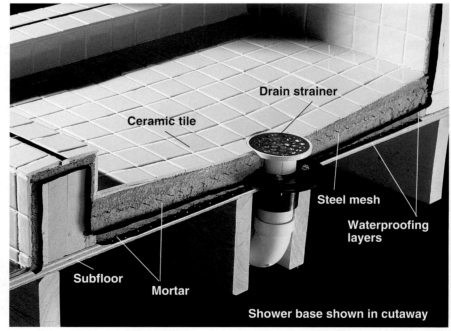

Drain strainer

Ceramic tile

Steel mesh

Waterproofing layers

Subfloor

Mortar

Shower base shown in cutaway

Ceramic-tile shower base: Remove the drain strainer, then stuff a rag into the drain opening. Wearing protective equipment, break apart a section of tile with a hammer and masonry chisel. Cut through any steel mesh reinforcement, using a wire cutter. Continue knocking tile and mortar loose until the waterproofing layers are exposed, then scrape off the layers with a long-handled floor scraper (page 74).

How to Remove a Bathtub

1 Use a reciprocating saw to cut away at least 6" of the wall surface above the tub on all sides. Before cutting into a wall, be sure faucet handles, spouts, and drains are all disconnected (pages 66 to 67).

2 Remove the fasteners that hold the tub flanges to the wall studs, then use a wrecking bar or a piece of 2 × 4 to pry the bathtub loose.

3 Lift the edge of the bathtub and slip a pair of soaped 1 × 4 runners beneath the tub apron. Pull the tub away from the wall, using the runners as skids. Have helpers when removing steel and cast-iron tubs.

4 Cut or break the bathtub into small pieces for easy disposal. Fiberglass, reinforced polymer, or pressed steel tubs can be cut with a reciprocating saw. Cast-iron and steel tubs should be carried out.

Removing Electrical Fixtures & Bathroom Accessories

Electrical fixtures and bathroom accessories should be disconnected and removed in the order that best suits your remodeling project.

Remove fragile accessories, like porcelain towel rods and vanity lights, early in the project so they are not damaged, but leave electrical receptacles and light fixtures in place as long as possible to provide light and power for tools. Store accessories in a safe place if you are planning to reuse them.

Everything You Need

Tools: screwdrivers, neon circuit tester.

Materials: rags, wire connectors, duct tape.

Remove shower lights and other fixtures before removing wall and ceiling surfaces. If you plan to reinstall the shower light, take care not to lose or damage the waterproof gasket that fits between the light cover and the ceiling. Remove the metal canister for recessed light fixtures after the wiring is disconnected and the ceiling surface is removed.

Tips for Removing Accessories

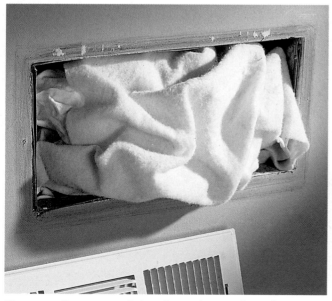

Remove the coverplates from ductwork and vent fan units, then stuff them with rags to keep debris and dust from circulating.

Unscrew the mounting plates holding surface-mounted towel rods, toilet-paper holders, and other bathroom accessories.

How to Remove Electrical Fixtures

Grounding screw

1 Shut off the electrical power to the bathroom circuits at the main service panel.

2 Loosen the mounting screws, then remove the bases and coverplates from lights and other electrical fixtures. Be careful not to touch the wires until they have been tested for power.

3 Test the circuit wires for power, using a neon circuit tester. Touch one probe to a grounding screw, and the other to each circuit wire connection. If the circuit tester light glows, turn off the main circuit breaker, and retest.

4 When you are sure the power is off, disconnect the fixture or receptacle from the circuit wires.

5 Use wire connectors to cap bare wire ends. If more than one circuit cable enters the electrical box, group the wires by color, and cap wires of the same color together.

6 Cover the electrical box with duct tape to keep out dust and debris during demolition.

Cutting ceramic tile walls into small sections for removal is easier than chipping away individual tiles. Use a reciprocating saw to cut through the wall surfaces. For general safety, shut off electrical power and water supply lines, and check for pipes and wires before cutting into any wall. Be careful not to cut through studs.

Removing Wall & Floor Surfaces

Removing and replacing wall and floor surfaces has two main benefits. First, access to wall cavities makes it much easier to update or expand the bathroom's plumbing and electrical systems. Second, removing surfaces lets you check the framing members behind the walls and under the floors for water damage and warping.

Do not try to install a new wall surface, such as ceramic tile, over old plaster or drywall. This practice may seem to save time, but by concealing possible structural problems inside the walls, it actually may create more work in the long run.

Damaged framing members may be concealed by water-damaged wall or floor surfaces. If any portion of a wall surface shows peeling, discoloration, or bowing, remove the entire surface to examine the framing. Repair or reinforce any damaged framing members before installing new wall surfaces.

Everything You Need

Tools: level, reciprocating saw, long-handled floor scraper, pry bar, masonry chisel, maul, circular saw, wrecking bar, heat gun, putty knives, utility knife.

Materials: trisodium phosphate (TSP), tubing.

Tips for Removing Wall & Floor Surfaces

Inspect the walls and floors for signs of warping or water damage before you remove the surfaces. Drag a long straightedge across the floor or wall to help detect valleys and bulges in the surface, which indicate that your wall or floor may have structural problems (see pages 76 to 79).

Pry off trim and molding. Loosen long pieces of trim a little at a time to prevent splintering. Use blocking between the pry bar and the wall to increase leverage. Label trim pieces as they are removed so you can reattach them properly.

Wear protective equipment when removing old wall and floor surfaces. Protective equipment should include a particle mask, eye protection, hearing protection, long-sleeved shirt, heavy gloves, and sturdy shoes.

Use a masonry chisel and maul to chip away ceramic floor tile. Chipping away tiles makes it easier to cut the mortar bed and any underlayment into small sections for removal (page 74).

How to Remove Ceramic Wall Tile

1 Knock a small starter hole into the bottom of the wall, using a maul and masonry chisel. Be sure the floor is covered with a heavy tarp, and the electricity and water are shut off.

2 Begin cutting out small sections of the wall by inserting a reciprocating saw with a bimetal blade into the hole, and cutting along grout lines. Be careful when sawing near pipes and wiring.

3 Cut the entire wall surface into small sections, removing each section as it is cut. Be careful not to cut through studs.

How to Remove Ceramic Floor Tile

Ceramic tile set in adhesive: Chip away the tile, using a maul and masonry chisel, then use a long-handled floor scraper to scrape away the tile fragments and old adhesive residue. A floor sander may be used to create a smooth finish on the subfloor.

Ceramic tile set in mortar: Chip away tile, using a maul and masonry chisel. Cut the old subfloor into small sections, using a circular saw with an old carbide blade. Pry up individual sections of floor with a wrecking bar. NOTE: If the old tile was laid on underlayment, raise the blade of the saw so it cuts through the underlayment and mortar, but not the subfloor.

74

How to Remove Vinyl Floor Tiles

1 Soften the flooring adhesive by warming the tiles with a heat gun. Wear eye protection and gloves.

2 Pry up tiles with a putty knife or a drywall knife, then use the knife to scrape the old adhesive residue off the underlayment or the subfloor.

3 Remove stubborn tile adhesive with a long-handled floor scraper.

How to Remove Sheet-vinyl Flooring

1 Remove the baseboards, then cut the old flooring into 10"-wide strips, using a utility knife or a flooring knife. Cut through both the flooring and the backing.

2 Remove the flooring strip by strip. Wrap one end around a rolling pin or piece of tubing, then roll up the strip of flooring material.

3 Scrape away any remaining backing or adhesive, using a long-handled floor scraper. When needed, use a trisodium phosphate (TSP) solution to loosen the residue. Wear rubber gloves.

Framing Bathrooms

Many bathroom fixtures require special framework. Common framing projects include shower or bathtub alcoves, bathtub and whirlpool decks, frames for recessed cabinets, and cross braces for supporting plumbing fixtures or grab bars. Complete all framing work before you install new fixtures and surface materials.

In bathrooms, the structural elements of floors and walls are prone to water damage. Inspect the framing members and subfloors carefully, especially if wall or floor surfaces show signs of discoloration, cracking or peeling. Locate the source of any damage, such as a leaky pipe, and correct the problem before you replace or reinforce damaged wood.

If several framing members are warped, bowed, or deteriorated, your house may have a serious structural problem. Have a building inspector or a licensed building contractor evaluate the damage.

If you're removing a loadbearing wall or creating a new or enlarged opening in one, use temporary supports to shore up the ceiling while the work is being done (page 78). Keep in mind that all exterior walls are loadbearing. Temporary supports are not necessary for removing non-loadbearing (partition) walls.

This section shows:

- Framing Partition Walls (pages 80 to 83)
- Framing Doors & Windows (pages 84 to 87)

Use 2 × 6 lumber to build new plumbing walls that contain drain and supply pipes, called "wet walls." The extra thickness allows you to cut notches or drill holes for drain pipe without weakening the weight-bearing capacity of the wall.

The Steel Framing Alternative

Lumber is not the only material available for framing walls. Metal studs and tracks are also a choice for new construction. Steel-framed walls can be installed faster than wood stud walls—the parts are attached by crimping and screwing the flanges—and the channels are precut to accommodate electrical and plumbing lines. Steel framing is also lighter in weight, easy to recycle, fireproof, and comparable in price to lumber. If you are interested in using steel framing for a new wall in a wood-framed home, consult a professional for information about electrical, plumbing, and loadbearing safety precautions. Steel framing is available at most home centers.

Tips for Framing Bathrooms

Cut notches or drill holes in 2 × 4 wall studs to make room for plumbing pipes, then attach 2 × 2 furring strips to each stud in the wall. The strips provide a nailing surface for wall coverings and add strength to the wall.

Build a framed chase to provide space for new plumbing pipes, such as a new main waste-vent stack. In a two-story house, stack chases one over the other on each floor in order to run plumbing from the basement to the attic. Once plumbing is completed and inspected, the chase is covered with wallboard and finished to match the room.

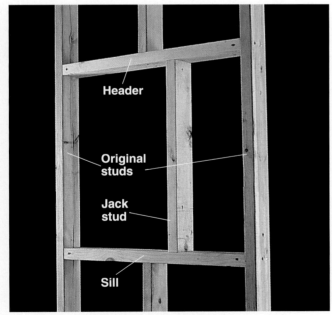

Frame an opening for a recessed cabinet by cutting away wall studs with a reciprocating saw or handsaw, then installing a header, sill, and jack studs as needed. Follow the cabinet manufacturer's specifications for rough-opening size.

Create access panels so you will be able to service fixture fittings and shutoff valves located inside the walls. Frame an opening between studs, then trim the opening with wood moldings. Cover it with a removable plywood panel the same thickness as the wall surface, then finish it to match the surrounding walls.

(continued next page)

Tips for Framing Bathrooms (continued)

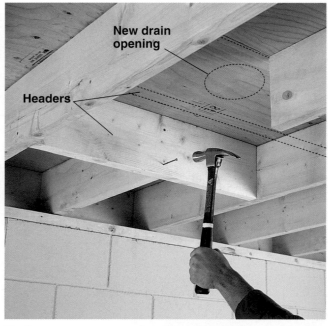

If the subfloor around the toilet drain is damaged, cut out the damaged area, exposing some nailing surface on the joists that border the cutout. Measure the drain hole, then cut and install a plywood patch the same thickness as the subfloor. Install new underlayment before laying new floor covering.

To frame a new opening for a toilet, you may need to cut away a section of a floor joist and nail headers in place. Use lumber with the same dimensions as the floor joists for the headers. Always support the floor joist from below while you cut and install headers (below, left).

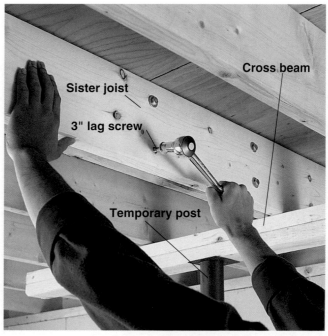

Install a support post and cross beam below a sagging bathroom floor. Adjust the post to rough height, using metal pins, then position the post so it is plumb. Raise post by turning the threaded base plate; pressure will hold the post and beam in place. Raise no more than ¼" per week, until floor above is level. Building codes may restrict use of adjustable posts, so consult an inspector.

To reinforce floor joists, attach a sister joist alongside the existing joist, using 3" lag screws. The sister joist should run the full length of the original floor joist. Sister joists should be installed wherever existing joists are damaged, and may be required under floor areas that will support bathtubs or whirlpools. A temporary post and cross beam can be useful for holding joists while they are fastened together.

Basements in newer houses
often contain drain and water supply stub-outs for a sink, shower, and toilet. To finish the basement bathroom, frame around the existing stub-outs, and extend water supply pipes and drain pipes as needed. Floor drain stub-outs may be framed with 2 × 4s and buried under gravel fill (photo below), or may extend through the concrete floor (page 141).

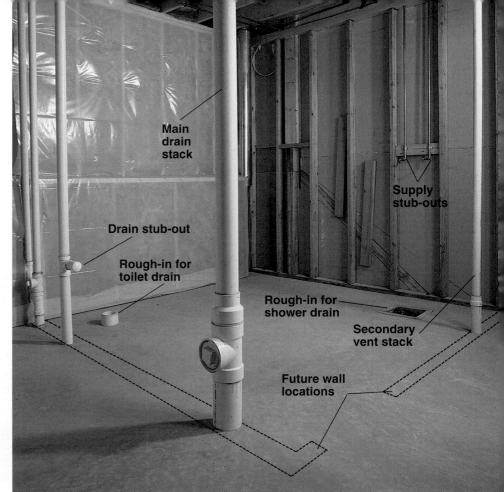

Main drain stack

Supply stub-outs

Drain stub-out

Rough-in for toilet drain

Rough-in for shower drain

Secondary vent stack

Future wall locations

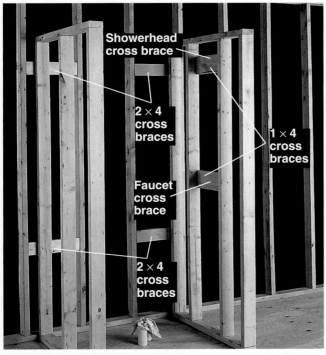

Showerhead cross brace

2 × 4 cross braces

1 × 4 cross braces

Faucet cross brace

2 × 4 cross braces

Build a shower alcove using 2 × 4 partition walls. Several 2 × 4 cross braces between existing studs help anchor the shower alcove and any nailing strips that will be added for attaching wall surfaces. The 1 × 4 cross braces within the alcove frame help anchor the faucet and showerhead. See page 144 for framing a shower alcove.

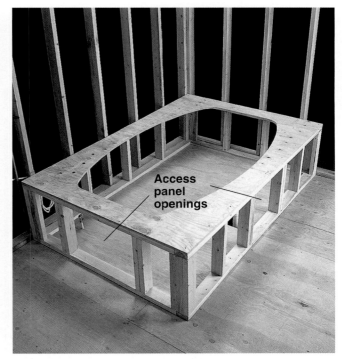

Access panel openings

Build a frame for a drop-in bathtub or whirlpool using short 2 × 4 stud walls topped with a plywood deck. The hole in the deck should be slightly smaller than the tub rim flanges. The deck frame should include extra studs to frame access panel openings. See pages 168 to 171 for directions on building a deck for a whirlpool tub.

A typical partition wall consists of top and bottom plates and 2 × 4 studs spaced 16" on center. Use 2 × 6 lumber for walls that will hold large plumbing pipes (inset).

Framing Partition Walls

Non-loadbearing, or partition, walls are typically built with 2 × 4 lumber and are supported by ceiling or floor joists or by blocking between the joists. For basement walls that sit on bare concrete, use pressure-treated lumber for the bottom plates.

In remodeling projects it is generally much easier to build a wall in place, rather than to build a complete wall on the floor and tilt it upright, as in new construction. The build-in-place method allows for variations in floor and ceiling levels.

If the wall will include a door or other opening, see pages 84 to 87 before laying out the wall. NOTE: After the walls are framed and the mechanical rough-ins are completed, be sure to install metal protector plates where pipes and wires run through framing members (see page 129).

Everything You Need

Tools: measuring tape, hammer, combination square, chalk line, circular saw, framing square, plumb bob, powder-actuated nailer, T-bevel.

Materials: 2 × 4 lumber, blocking lumber, common nails (8d, 16d), concrete fasteners.

Variations for Fastening Top Plates to Joists

When a new wall is perpendicular to the ceiling or floor joists above, attach the top plate directly to the joists, using 16d nails.

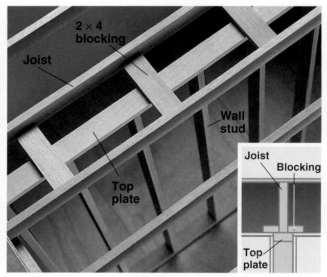

When a new wall falls between parallel joists, install 2 × 4 blocking between the joists every 24". The blocking supports the new wall's top plate and provides backing for the ceiling wallboard. If the new wall is aligned with a parallel joist, install blocks on both sides of the wall, and attach the top plate to the joist (inset).

Variations for Fastening Bottom Plates to Joists

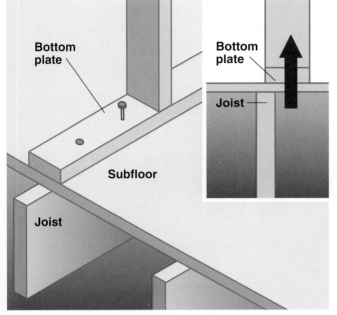

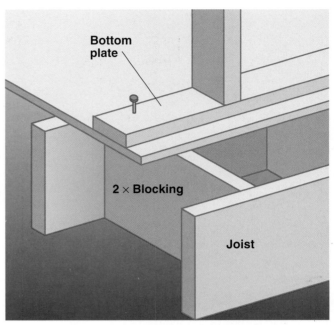

If a new wall is aligned with a joist below, install the bottom plate directly over the joist or off-center over the joist (inset). Off-center placement allows you to nail into the joist but provides room underneath the plate for pipes or wiring to go up into the wall.

If a new wall falls between parallel joists, install 2 × 6 or larger blocking between the two joists below, spaced 24" on center. Nail the bottom plate through the subfloor and into the blocking.

How to Frame a Partition Wall

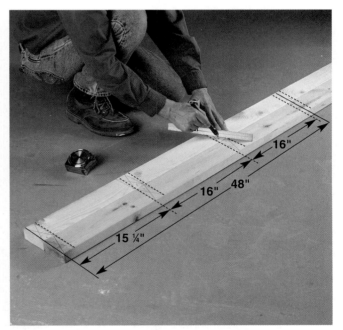

1 Mark the location of the leading edge of the new wall's top plate, then snap a chalk line through the marks across the joists or blocks. Use a framing square, or take measurements, to make sure the line is perpendicular to any intersecting walls. Cut the top and bottom plates to length.

2 Set the plates together with their ends flush. Measure from the end of one plate, and make marks for the location of each stud. The first stud should fall 15¼" from the end; every stud thereafter should fall 16" on center. Thus, the first 4 × 8-ft. wallboard panel will cover the first stud and "break" in the center of the fourth stud. Use a square to extend the marks across both plates. Draw an "X" at each stud location.

(continued next page)

3 Position the top plate against the joists, aligning its leading edge with the chalk line. Attach the plate with two 16d nails driven into each joist. Start at one end, and adjust the plate as you go to keep the leading edge flush with the chalk line.

4 To position the bottom plate, hang a plumb bob from the side edge of the top plate so the point nearly touches the floor. When it hangs motionless, mark the point's location on the floor. Make plumb markings at each end of the top plate, then snap a chalk line between the marks. Position the bottom plate along the chalk line, and use the plumb bob to align the stud markings between the two plates.

5 Fasten the bottom plate to the floor. On concrete, use a pow- der-actuated nailer or masonry screws, driving a pin or screw every 16". On wood floors, use 16d nails driven into the joists or sleepers below.

6 Measure between the plates for the length of each stud. Cut each stud so it fits snugly in place but is not so tight that it bows the joists above. If you cut a stud too short, see if it will fit somewhere else down the wall.

7 Install the studs by toenailing them at a 60° angle through the sides of the studs and into the plates. At each end, drive two 8d nails through one side of the stud and one more through the center on the other side.

How to Frame Corners (shown cut away)

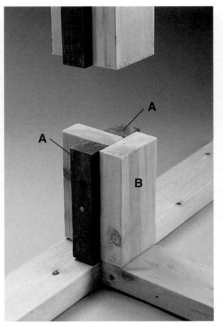

L-corners: Nail 2 × 4 spacers (A) to the inside of the end stud. Nail an extra stud (B) to the spacers. The extra stud provides a surface to attach wallboard at the inside corner.

T-corner meets stud: Fasten 2 × 2 backers (A) to each side of the side-wall stud (B). The backers provide a nailing surface for wallboard.

T-corner between studs: Fasten a 1 × 6 backer (A) to the end stud (B) with wallboard screws. The backer provides a nailing surface for wallboard.

How to Frame an Angled Partition Wall in an Attic

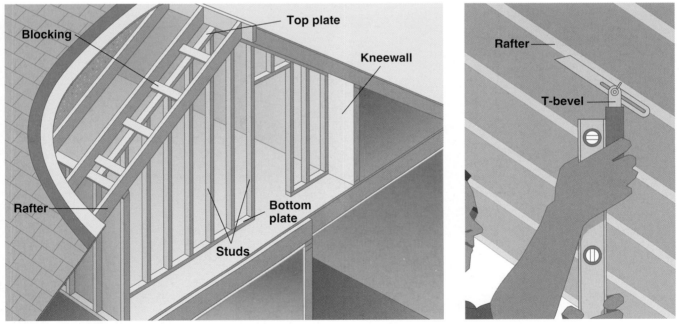

Full-size attic partition walls typically run parallel to the rafters and have sloping top plates that extend down to knee walls on either side. To build one, cut the top and bottom plates, and mark the stud locations on the bottom plate only. Nail the top plates in place, and use a plumb bob to position the bottom plate, as with a standard wall. Use the plumb bob again to transfer the stud layout marks from the bottom to the top plate. To find the proper angle for cutting the top ends of the studs, set a level against the top plate (or rafter) and hold it plumb. Then, rest the handle of a T-bevel against the level, and adjust the T-bevel blade to follow the plate. Transfer the angle to the stud ends, and cut them to length.

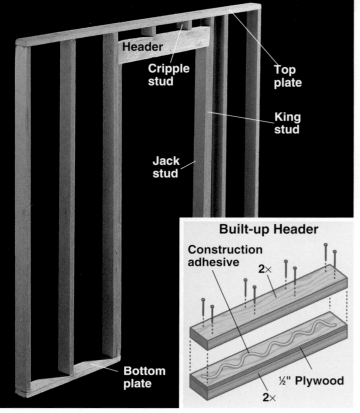

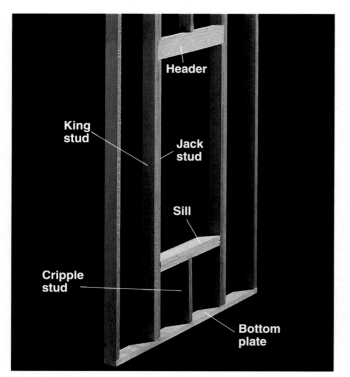

Door frames for prehung doors start with king studs that attach to the top and bottom plates. Inside the king studs, jack studs support the header at the top of the opening. Cripple studs continue the wall-stud layout above the opening. In non-loadbearing walls, the header may be a 2 × 4 laid flat or a built-up header (inset). The dimensions of the framed opening are referred to as the rough opening.

Window frames, like door frames, have full-length king studs, as well as jack studs that support the header. They also have a sill that defines the bottom of the rough opening.

Framing Doors & Windows

To lay out and build a door or window frame, you'll need the actual dimensions of the door or window unit you will be installing. Follow the manufacturer's specifications for rough opening size.

In new walls, build the door frames along with the rest of the wall. The project shown on pages 85 to 86 demonstrates framing a rough opening for an interior prehung door in a new, non-load-bearing partition wall. These same techniques can be used when framing a rough opening for linen closet doors. However, large closet openings, such as for double bifold or by-pass doors, need a built-up header: two 2 × 4s set on edge and nailed together with a strip of ½"-thick plywood in between. This provides additional strength to support the weight of the doors.

Because exterior walls are loadbearing, window frames are required by code to have built-up headers to carry the weight from above. The required size for the header is set by local building codes and varies according to the width of the rough opening. Hire a contractor to build window frames in loadbearing gable walls and in the second story of a balloon frame house. If you aren't certain what type of wall you have, consult a professional.

When framing a rough opening in a finished wall, remove enough of the wall material so there is one additional stud bay on either side of the opening. (This provides you with space to work.) Also leave at least 6" of wall material at the ceiling to provide a surface for taping the joint between the new wall material and the existing surface.

All loadbearing walls must be supported until the header is in place. If you will be removing more than one wall stud when framing a rough opening in a non-loadbearing wall, make temporary supports to carry the structural load until the header is installed.

Everything You Need

Tools: tape measure, hammer, framing square, circular saw, handsaw, 4-ft. level, pry bar, nippers, plumb bob, combination square.

Materials: door or window unit, 2× lumber, common nails (8d, 10d, 16d), ½"-thick plywood, construction adhesive.

How to Frame a Rough Opening for an Interior Prehung Door

King stud marking

Door unit width

Extra ½"

Extra ½"

King stud marking

Jack stud marking

Jack stud marking

1 To mark the layout for the studs that make up the door frame, measure the width of the door unit along the bottom. Add 1" to this dimension to calculate the width of the rough opening (the distance between the jack studs). This gives you a ½" gap on each side for adjusting the door frame during installation. Mark the top and bottom plates for the jack and king studs.

2 After you've installed the top and bottom plates (pages 80 to 83), cut the king studs. Check for plumb, then toenail them in place at the appropriate markings, using 8d nails.

3 Measure the full length of the door unit, then add ½" to the height of the rough opening. Using that dimension, measure up from the floor and mark the king studs. Cut a 2 × 4 header to fit between the king studs. Position the header flat, with its bottom face at the marks, and secure it to the king studs with 16d nails.

4 Cut and install a cripple stud above the header, centered between the king studs. Install any additional cripples required to maintain the 16"-on-center layout of the standard studs in the rest of the wall.

(continued next page)

How to Frame a Rough Opening for an Interior Prehung Door (continued)

5 Cut the jack studs to fit snugly under the header. Fasten them in place by nailing down through the header, then drive 10d nails through the faces of the jack studs and into the king studs, spaced 16" apart.

6 Saw through the bottom plate so it's flush with the inside faces of the jack studs. Remove the cut-out portion of the plate. NOTE: If the wall will be finished with wallboard, hang the door after the wallboard is installed.

How to Frame a Window Opening

1 Prepare the project site, and remove the interior wall surfaces (pages 72 to 74). Measure and mark the rough opening width on the bottom plate, then mark the locations of the jack studs and king studs on the bottom plate. Where practical, use the existing studs as king studs.

2 Measure and cut king studs, as needed, to fit between the bottom plate and the top plate. Position the king studs and toenail them to the bottom plate with 10d nails. Check the king studs with a level to make sure they are plumb, then toenail them to the top plate with 10d nails.

3 Measuring from the floor, mark the rough opening height on one of the king studs. This line marks the bottom of the window header. For most windows, the recommended rough opening is ½" taller than the height of the window unit.

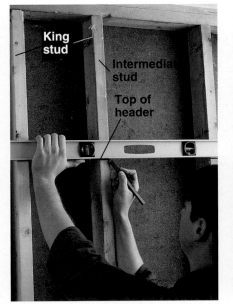

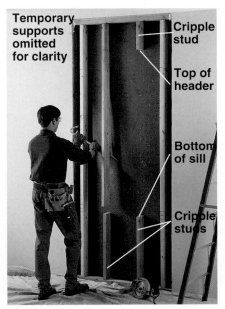

4 Measure and mark where the top of the window header will fit against the king stud. The header size depends on the distance between the king studs. Use a level to extend the lines across the intermediate studs to the opposite king stud.

5 Measure down from the bottom header line, and outline the rough double sill on the king stud. Use a level to extend the lines across the intermediate studs to the opposite king stud. Use a circular saw to cut through the intermediate studs along the lines that mark both the bottom of the rough sill and the top of the header. (Do not cut the king studs.)

6 On each stud, make a cut about 3" above the sill cut. Knock out the 3" pieces, then tear out the intermediate studs inside the rough opening, using a pry bar. Use nippers to clip away any exposed nails. Cut two jack studs to reach from the bottom plate to the bottom header lines on the king studs, then nail them to the king studs with 10d nails driven every 1".

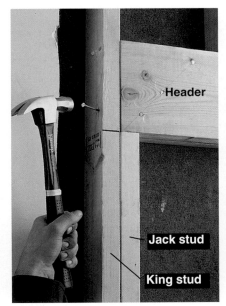

7 Build a header to fit between the king studs on top of the jack studs, using two pieces of 2× lumber sandwiched around ½" plywood (page 84).

8 Position the header on the jack studs, using a hammer if necessary. Attach the header to the king studs, jack studs, and cripple studs, using 10d nails.

9 Build the rough sill to reach between the jack studs by nailing together a pair of 2 × 4s. Position the rough sill on the cripple studs, and nail it to the jack studs and cripple studs with 10d nails. When you're ready to install the window, remove the exterior wall surface.

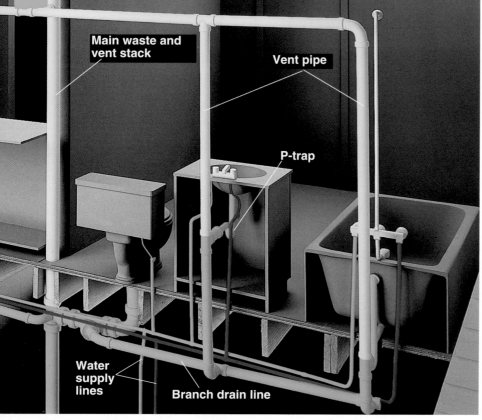

A bathroom plumbing system includes supply pipes that carry water to the fixtures, and drain pipes that carry waste water to branch drains and to the main waste and vent stack. Branch drain lines that are longer than 3 ft., 6" require a vent pipe that loops back to the main drain stack. Vent pipes equalize pressure in the drain lines, preventing the creation of a partial vacuum that may siphon standing water from drain traps. Without standing water in the drain traps, dangerous sewer gases may enter your house.

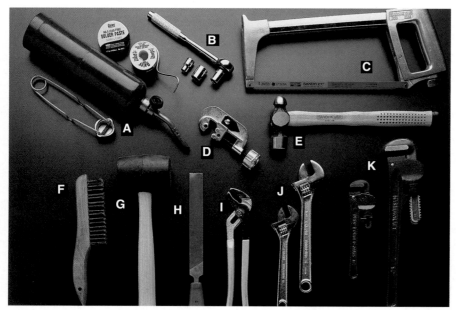

Plumbing tools include: Propane torch with striker, solder paste, and lead-free solder (A), ratchet wrench with sockets (B), hacksaw (C), tubing cutter (D), ball peen hammer (E), wire brush (F), rubber mallet (G), file (H), channel-type pliers (I), adjustable wrenches (J), and pipe wrenches (K). You will use these tools extensively during remodeling projects and when making future repairs. Specialty and power tools for plumbing projects can be rented from rental centers.

Plumbing Bathrooms

A home plumbing system is divided into two parts: the supply system and the drain-waste-vent system. Most major bathroom remodeling projects require changes or additions to both of these systems.

The supply system is made up of a series of pipes that deliver hot and cold water to the bathroom fixtures. The water in these supply pipes is pressurized, which moves it through the system.

Supply pipes have small diameters, usually ½" to 1", and are joined with strong, watertight fittings. The supply lines are generally located inside wall cavities or strapped to the undersides of floor joists.

The drain-waste-vent (DWV) system uses gravity to draw waste water down vertical and sloped pipes, and into a municipal sewer system or septic tank. Drain pipes are larger in diameter than supply pipes, ranging from 1¼" to 4", to allow waste water to pass easily. Drain pipe slope is governed by local building codes, but typically is ¼" per foot.

Each drain requires a curved section of pipe, called a trap, that holds standing water to prevent sewer gases from entering the house. The standing water is flushed away and replaced every time the drain is used.

For waste water to flow freely, a vent system is used to bring outdoor air into the drain system to lower the pressure in the pipes, usually through a rooftop vent stack. Inadequately vented lines can hinder drain function, and allow sewer gas backup.

Tips for Plumbing Bathrooms

Use masking tape to mark the locations of fixtures and pipes on the walls and floors. Read the layout specifications that come with each sink, tub, or toilet, then mark the drain and supply lines accordingly. Position the fixtures on the floor, and outline them with tape. Measure and adjust until the arrangement is comfortable to you and meets minimum clearance specifications. If you are working in a finished room, prevent damage to wallpaper or paint by using self-adhesive notes to mark the walls.

Consider the location of cabinets when roughing in the water supply and drain stub-outs. You may want to temporarily position the cabinets in their final locations before completing the drain and water supply runs.

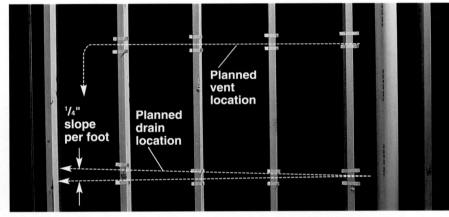

Plan drain lines in walls so they slope down toward the main drain stack or branch drain at a rate of ¼" per foot. Fixtures located more than 3 ft., 6" from the branch drain or drain stack must also be connected to a vent pipe that joins the main stack or exits through the roof.

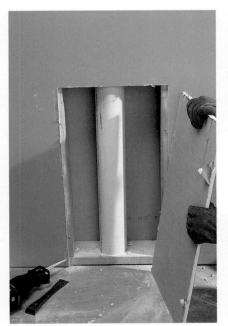

Remove a section of wall, if necessary, to gain access to existing plumbing lines. Remove enough wall surface to reveal half of the stud face at each side of the opening, providing a nailing surface so the wall can be patched easily when plumbing work is ccmpleted.

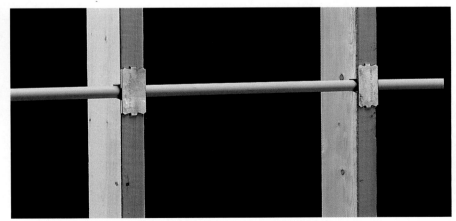

Protect pipes from punctures, if they are less than 1¼" from front face of wall studs, by attaching metal protector plates to the framing members.

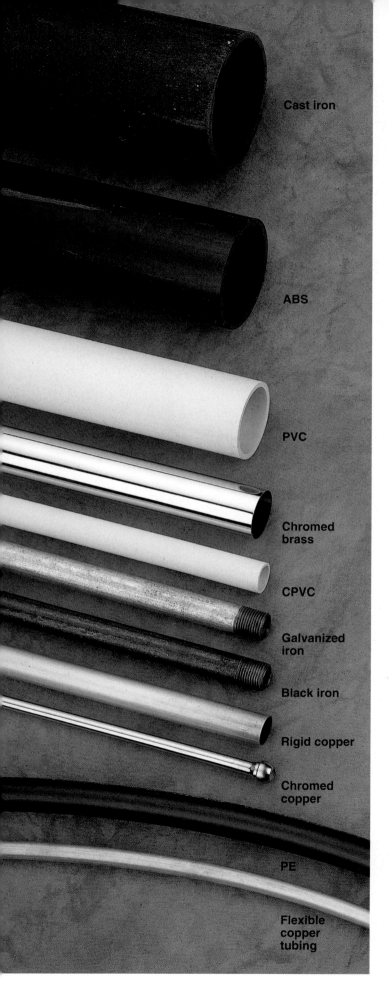

Cast iron

ABS

PVC

Chromed brass

CPVC

Galvanized iron

Black iron

Rigid copper

Chromed copper

PE

Flexible copper tubing

Plumbing Materials

Recognizing the different types of piping used in plumbing systems is important for troubleshooting and crucial when purchasing supplies or making repairs. The materials used in home plumbing systems are closely regulated by building codes, so look for product standard codes and check local plumbing regulations prior to making purchases.

Cast iron is commonly used for drain-waste-vent (DWV) purposes. Though it is the strongest piping, it's very heavy and somewhat difficult to join and install. Its thickness helps contain the noise inherent in drain systems.

Plastic piping is often used for water supply pipes where permitted by local code. It's inexpensive, easy to handle, doesn't corrode or rust, and has insulating properties. Plastic pipe is available in four types: acrylonitrile butadiene (ABS) and polyvinyl chloride (PVC) are used exclusively in DWV systems, chlorinated polyvinyl chloride (CPVC) is suitable for water supply lines, and polyethylene (PE) is used for outdoor water supply pipes.

Brass, and the more expensive but attractive chromed brass, are durable plumbing materials used for drains, valves, and shutoffs.

Galvanized iron, suitable for supply and DWV purposes, is rarely used today because it corrodes and is difficult to install.

Copper is considered the best choice for water supply lines and parts of some DWV systems. It resists scale deposits, maintains water flow and pressure, is lightweight, and is easily installed. Copper is more expensive than plastic.

Fittings come in many sizes, but the basic shapes are standard to all metal and plastic pipes. In general, fittings used to connect DWV pipes have gradual bends for a smooth flow of waste water from drains. Because water in supply lines moves under pressure, the bends in water supply fittings can be sharper, conserving space.

Note: When pipes of different metals touch each other, a process called galvanic action can lead to premature corrosion. Use only brackets and straps made of the same material as your pipes. To join dissimilar metals, such as galvanized iron and copper, you must use dielectric fittings.

Standard Fittings

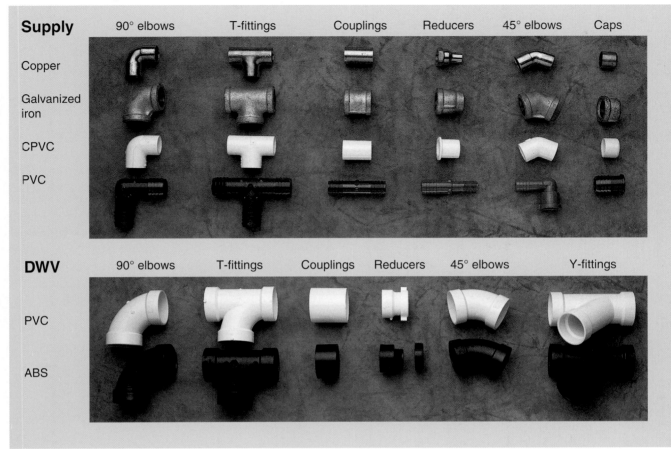

Supply	90° elbows	T-fittings	Couplings	Reducers	45° elbows	Caps
Copper						
Galvanized iron						
CPVC						
PVC						

DWV	90° elbows	T-fittings	Couplings	Reducers	45° elbows	Y-fittings
PVC						
ABS						

Transition Fittings

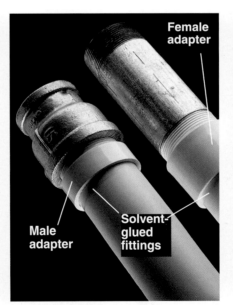

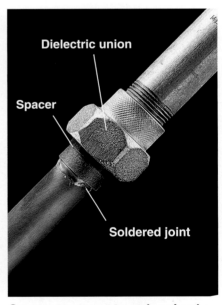

Connect plastic to cast iron with banded couplings. Rubber sleeves cover the ends of the pipes for a watertight joint. See pages 108 to 109 for installing banded couplings.

Connect plastic to threaded metal pipes with male and female threaded adapters. Glue a plastic adapter to the plastic pipe with solvent-based glue. Wrap the threads of the pipe with Teflon tape, then screw the metal pipe directly to the adapter.

Connect copper to galvanized iron with a dielectric union. Attach the threaded end of the union to the iron pipe and solder the other end to the copper pipe. A dielectric union has a plastic spacer that prevents corrosion caused by galvanic action.

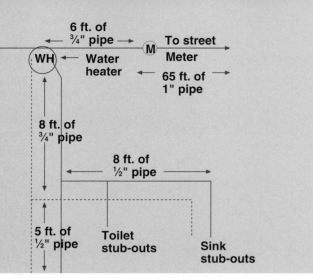

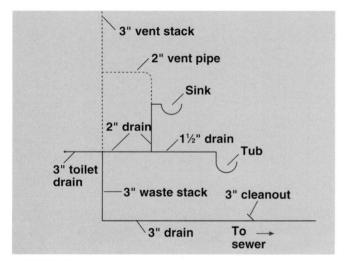

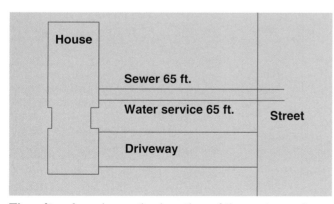

The supply riser diagram shows the length of the hot and cold water pipes and the relation of the fixtures to one another. The inspector will use this diagram to determine the proper size for the new water supply pipes in your system.

A DWV diagram shows the routing of drain and vent pipes in your system. Indicate the lengths of drain pipes and the distances between fixtures. The inspector will use this diagram to determine if you have properly sized the drain traps, drain pipes, and vent pipes.

The site plan shows the location of the water main and sewer main with respect to your yard and home. The distances from your foundation to the water main and from the foundation to the main sewer should be indicated on the site map.

Plumbing Codes & Permits

The Plumbing Code is the set of regulations that building officials and inspectors use to evaluate your project plans and the quality of your work. Codes vary from region to region, but most are based on the National Uniform Plumbing Code, a highly technical, difficult-to-read manual. More user-friendly code handbooks are available at bookstores and libraries. These handbooks are based on the National Uniform Plumbing Code, but they are easier to read and include diagrams and photos.

Sometimes these handbooks discuss three different plumbing zones in an effort to accommodate state variations in regulations. Remember that local plumbing code always supersedes national code. Your local building inspector can be a valuable source of information and may provide you with a convenient summary sheet of the regulations that apply to your project.

As part of its effort to ensure public safety, your community building department requires a permit for most plumbing projects. When you apply for a permit, the building official will want to review three drawings of your plumbing project: a site plan, a water supply diagram, and a drain-waste-vent diagram. If the official is satisfied that your project meets code requirements, you will be issued a plumbing permit, which is your legal permission to begin work. As your project nears completion, the inspector will visit your home to check your work.

Note: The diagrams and charts shown on pages 92 through 94 are for general reference only. The listed specifications may not conform to all building codes; check with your local building department regarding regulations in your area.

Fixture Supply Pipe & Trap Sizes

Fixture	Unit Rating	Min. branch pipe size	Min. supply tube size	Min. trap size
Toilet	3	1/2"	3/8"	N/A
Vanity Sink	1	1/2"	3/8"	1 1/4"
Shower	2	1/2"	3/8"	2"
Bathtub	2	1/2"	1/2"	1 1/2"

To determine the minimum size of supply pipes and fixture drain traps, you must know the fixture's unit rating, a unit of measure assigned by the plumbing code. NOTE: Branch pipes are the water supply lines that run from the distribution pipes toward the individual fixtures. Supply tubes carry water from the branch pipes to the fixtures.

Maximum Hole & Notch Sizes

Framing member	Maximum hole size	Maximum notch size
2 × 4 loadbearing stud	1 7/16" diameter	7/8" deep
2 × 4 non-loadbearing stud	2 1/2" diameter	1 7/16" deep
2 × 6 loadbearing stud	2 1/4" diameter	1 3/8" deep
2 × 6 non-loadbearing stud	3 5/16" diameter	2 3/16" deep
2 × 6 joists	1 1/2" diameter	7/8" deep
2 × 8 joists	2 3/8" diameter	1 1/4" deep
2 × 10 joists	3 1/16" diameter	1 1/2" deep
2 × 12 joists	3 3/4" diameter	1 7/8" deep

The maximum hole and notch sizes that can be cut into framing members for running pipes is shown above. Where possible, use notches rather than bored holes to ease pipe installation. When boring holes, there must be at least 5/8" of wood between the edge of a stud and the hole, and at least 2" between the edge of a joist and the hole. Joists can be notched only in the end one-third of the overall span; never in the middle one-third of the joist. When two pipes are run through a stud, the pipes should be stacked one over the other, never side by side.

Sizes for Horizontal & Vertical Drain Pipes

Pipe size	Maximum fixture units for horizontal branch drain	Maximum fixture units for vertical drain stacks
1 1/4"	1	2
1 1/2"	3	4
2"	6	10
2 1/2"	12	20
3"	20	30
4"	160	240

Drain pipe sizes are determined by the load on the pipes, as measured by the total fixture units. Horizontal drain pipes less than 3" in diameter should slope 1/4" per foot toward the main drain. Pipes 3" or more in diameter should slope 1/8" per foot. NOTE: Horizontal or vertical drain pipes for a toilet must be 3" or larger.

Pipe Support Intervals

Type of pipe	Vertical support interval	Horizontal support interval
Copper	6 ft.	10 ft.
ABS	4 ft.	4 ft.
CPVC	3 ft.	3 ft.
PVC	4 ft.	4 ft.
Galvanized Iron	12 ft.	15 ft.
Cast Iron	5 ft.	15 ft.

Minimum intervals for supporting pipes are determined by the type of pipe and its orientation in the system. Use only brackets and supports made of the same (or compatible) materials as the pipes. Remember that the measurements shown above are minimum requirements; many plumbers install pipe supports at closer intervals.

Tip: Drain Cleanouts

Drain cleanouts make your DWV system easier to service. In most areas, the plumbing code requires that you place cleanouts at the end of every horizontal drain run. Where horizontal runs are not accessible, removable drain traps will suffice as cleanouts.

Wet Venting

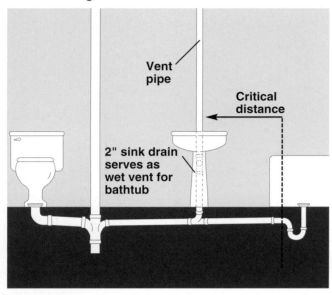

Wet vents are pipes that serve as a vent for one fixture and a drain for another. The sizing of a wet vent is based on the total fixture units it supports (page 93): a 3" wet vent can serve up to 12 fixture units; a 2" wet vent is rated for 4 fixture units; a 1½" wet vent, for only 1 fixture unit. NOTE: The distance between the wet-vented fixture and the wet vent itself must be no more than the maximum critical distance.

Vent Pipe Sizes, Critical Distances

Size of fixture drain	Minimum vent pipe size	Maximum trap-to-vent distance
1¼"	1¼"	2½ ft.
1½"	1¼"	3½ ft.
2"	1½"	5 ft.
3"	2"	6 ft.
4"	3"	10 ft.

Vent pipes are usually one pipe size smaller than the drain pipes they serve. Code requires that the distance between the drain trap and the vent pipe fall within a maximum "critical distance," a measurement that is determined by the size of the fixture drain. Use this chart to determine both the minimum size for the vent pipe and the maximum critical distance.

Auxiliary Venting

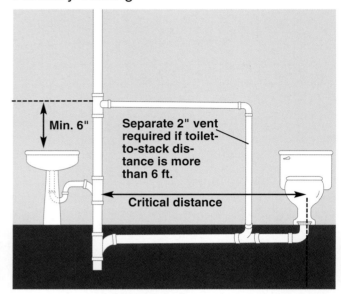

Fixtures must have auxiliary vents if the distance to the main waste-vent stack exceeds the critical distance. A toilet, for example, should have a separate vent pipe if it is located more than 6 ft. from the main waste-vent stack. This secondary vent pipe should connect to the stack or an existing vent pipe at a point at least 6" above the highest fixture on the system.

Vent Pipe Orientation to Drain Pipe

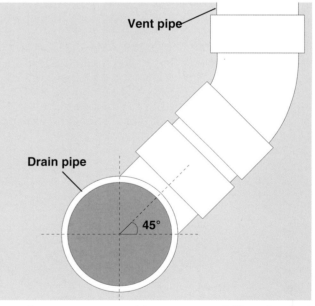

Vent pipes must extend in an upward direction from drains, no less than 45° from horizontal. This ensures that waste water cannot flow into the vent pipe and block it. At the opposite end, a new vent pipe should connect to an existing vent pipe or main waste-vent stack at a point at least 6" above the highest fixture draining into the system.

Testing New Plumbing Pipes

When the building inspector comes to review your new bathroom plumbing, he or she may require that you perform a pressure test on the DWV and water supply lines. The inspection and test should be performed after the system is completed, but before the new pipes are covered with wallboard. To ensure that the inspection goes smoothly, perform your own preliminary test, so you can locate and repair any problems before the inspection.

The DWV system is tested by blocking off the new drain and vent pipes, then pressurizing the system with air to see if it leaks. At the fixture stub-outs, the DWV pipes can be capped off or plugged with test balloons designed for this purpose. The air pump, pressure gauge, and test balloons required to test the DWV system can be obtained at tool rental centers.

Testing the water supply lines is a simple matter of turning on the water and examining the joints for leaks. If you find a leak, drain the pipes, disassemble and resolder the faulty joints.

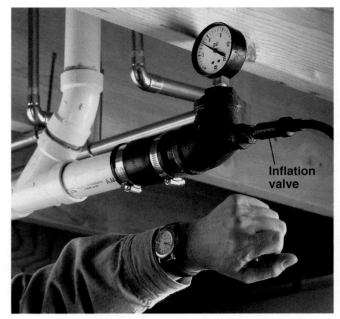

A pressure gauge and air pump are used to test DWV lines. The system is blocked off at each fixture and at points near where the new drain and vent pipes connect to the main stack. A weenie—a special test balloon with an air gauge and inflation valve—is inserted at a cleanout valve. An air pump is attached to the weenie, and the pipe is pressurized to 5 pounds per square inch (psi). To pass inspection, the system must hold this pressure for 15 minutes.

Testing New DWV Pipes

Insert test balloons into test T-fittings at the top and bottom of new DWV lines, blocking the pipes entirely. NOTE: Ordinary T-fittings installed near the bottom of drain lines and near the top of vent lines are generally used for test fittings. Use large balloons for toilet drains, and inflate them with an air pump.

Cap off the remaining fixture drains by solvent-gluing test caps onto the stub-outs. If the DWV system loses air when pressurized, check joints for leaks by rubbing soapy water over the fittings and looking for active bubbles. Cut out problem joints from the existing fitting and solvent-glue a new fitting in place, using couplings and short lengths of pipe.

After the DWV system has been inspected and approved by a building official, remove the test balloons and close the test T-fittings by solvent-gluing caps onto the open lines. Remove test caps by knocking them loose with a hammer.

Working with Copper Pipe

Copper is the ideal material for water supply pipes. It resists corrosion and has smooth surfaces that allow good water flow. Copper pipes are available in several diameters, but most home water supply systems use ½" or ¾" pipe. Copper pipe is manufactured in rigid and flexible forms.

Rigid copper, sometimes called hard copper, is approved for home water supply systems by all local codes. It comes in three wall-thickness grades: Types M, L, and K. Type M is thin and inexpensive, which makes it a good choice for do-it-yourself home plumbing.

Rigid Type L usually is required by codes for commercial plumbing. Because it is strong and solders easily, it may be preferable for home use. Type K has the heaviest wall thickness and is used for underground water service lines.

Flexible copper, also called soft copper, comes in two wall-thickness grades: Types L and K. Both are approved for most home water supply systems, although flexible Type L is used primarily for gas service lines. Because it is bendable and resists mild frosts, Type L may be installed as part of a water supply system in unheated indoor areas, such as crawlspaces. Type K is used for underground water service lines.

Copper pipes are usually connected with soldered fittings. Correctly soldered fittings are strong and trouble-free. Copper pipe can also be joined with compression fittings. They are more expensive than soldered joints but allow pipes or fixtures to be repaired or replaced readily. Flare fittings are used with flexible copper pipes, usually as a gas-line fitting; it's best to leave these to professionals.

Many bathroom remodeling projects involve separating existing joints to extend supply lines or remove defective pipes; this isn't difficult, but it's important to work carefully.

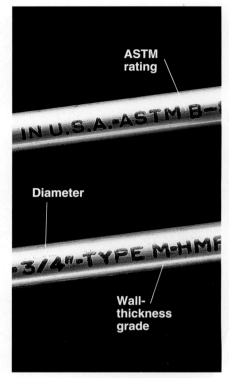

Check the grade stamp information for pipe diameter, wall-thickness grade, and stamp of approval from the American Society for Testing and Materials (ASTM). Type M pipe is identified by red lettering, Type L by blue lettering.

Tips for Working with Copper Pipe

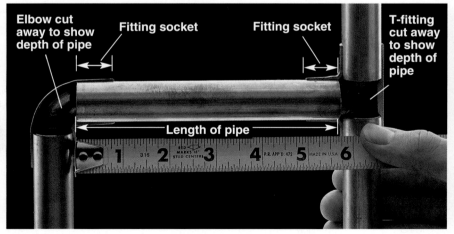

Determine the length of copper pipe needed by measuring between the bottom of the copper fitting sockets (fittings shown here cut away). Mark the length on the pipe with a felt-tipped pen.

Bend flexible copper pipe with a coil-spring tubing bender to avoid kinks. Use a bender that matches the outside pipe diameter; slip it over the pipe with a twisting motion, and bend slowly into the correct angle, but not more than 90°.

96

Copper Pipe & Fitting Chart

Fitting Method	Rigid Copper Type M	Rigid Copper Type L	Rigid Copper Type K	Flexible Copper Type L	Flexible Copper Type K	General Comments
Soldered	yes	yes	yes	yes	yes	Inexpensive, strong, and trouble-free fitting method. Requires some skill.
Compression	yes	not recommended		yes	yes	Easy to use. Allows pipes or fixtures to be repaired or replaced readily. More expensive than solder. Best used on flexible copper.
Flare	no	no	no	yes	yes	Use only with flexible copper pipes. Usually used as a gas-line fitting. Requires some skill.

How to Take Apart Soldered Joints

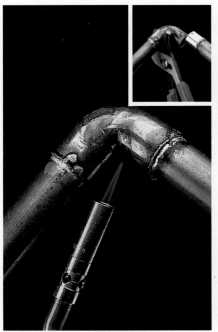

1 Turn off the water at the main shutoff valve and drain the pipes by opening the highest and lowest faucets in the house. Light a propane torch (page 100) and hold the flame tip to the fitting until the solder becomes shiny and begins to melt. Separate the pipes from the fitting with channel-type pliers (inset). Discard the old fittings—they should not be reused.

2 Remove the old solder by heating the ends of the pipe with the propane torch. Carefully wipe away the melted solder with a dry rag. Work quickly, but cautiously. The pipes will be hot.

3 Allow the pipes to cool, then use an emery cloth to polish the ends down to the bare metal. Any residual solder or metal burrs left on the pipe may cause the new joint to leak.

Cutting & Soldering Copper Pipe

Protect wood from the heat of the torch flame while soldering, using a double layer (two 18" × 18" pieces) of 26-gauge sheet metal available at hardware stores or home centers.

Everything You Need

Tools: tubing cutter with reaming tip (or hacksaw and round file), wire brush, flux brush, propane torch, spark lighter.

Materials: copper pipe, copper fittings (or brass valve), emery cloth, soldering paste (flux), lead-free solder, dry rag.

The best way to cut rigid and flexible copper pipe is with a tubing cutter. A tubing cutter makes a smooth, straight cut—an important first step toward making a watertight joint. Remove any metal burrs on the cut edges with a reaming tool or round file.

Copper also can be cut with a hacksaw, which is useful in tight areas where a tubing cutter won't fit. Since it is more difficult to be accurate with a hacksaw, take care to make smooth, straight cuts.

To form a watertight seal, start with copper pipes and fittings that are clean and dry. Practice soldering scrap pipe before starting your project. Protect flammable surfaces with a double layer of 26-gauge sheet metal or a heat-absorbent pad (photo, left).

A soldered pipe joint, also called a sweated joint, is made by heating a copper or brass fitting with a propane torch until the fitting is just hot enough to melt metal solder. The heat draws the solder into the gap between the fitting and the pipe to form a watertight seal. A fitting that is overheated or unevenly heated will not draw in solder. The tip of the torch's inner flame produces the most heat.

Tips for Soldering Copper Pipe

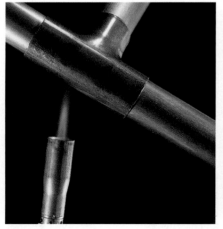

Use caution when soldering copper. Allow pipes and fittings time to cool before handling them.

Keep joints dry when soldering existing water pipes by plugging the pipe ends with bread. Bread absorbs moisture that would ruin the soldering process and cause pinhole leaks. The bread dissolves when the water is turned back on.

Prevent accidents by shutting off the propane torch immediately after use; make sure the valve is completely closed.

How to Cut & Solder Copper Pipe

1 Place a tubing cutter over the pipe, then tighten the handle so the pipe rests on both rollers, and the cutting wheel is on the marked line. Turn the tubing cutter one rotation to score a continuous straight line around the pipe.

2 Rotate the tubing cutter in the opposite direction, tightening the handle slightly after every two rotations, until the cut is complete.

3 Remove sharp metal burrs from the inside edge of the cut pipe, using the reaming point on the tubing cutter or a round file.

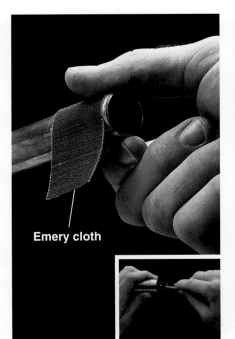

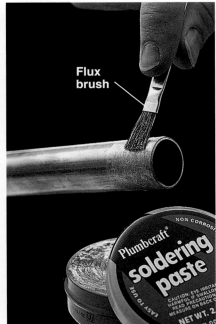

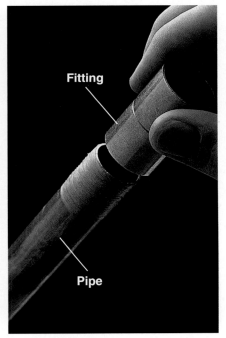

4 Clean the end of each pipe by sanding it with emery cloth. The ends must be free of dirt and grease to ensure that the solder forms a good seal. Also clean inside each fitting with a wire brush or emery cloth (inset).

5 Apply a thin layer of soldering paste (flux) to the end of each pipe, using a flux brush. Cover about 1" of the end of the pipe with the paste.

6 Assemble each joint by inserting the pipe into the fitting so it is tight against the bottom of the fitting sockets. Twist the fitting slightly to spread the soldering paste.

(continued next page)

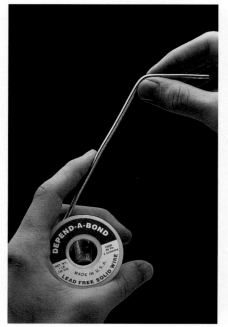

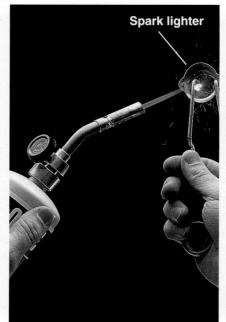

Spark lighter

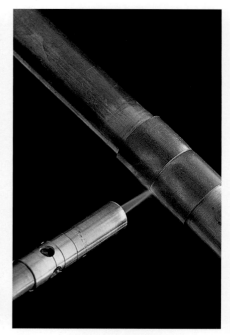

7 Prepare the wire solder by unwinding 8" to 10" of wire from the spool. Bend the first 2" of the wire to a 90° angle.

8 Light a propane torch by opening the valve and striking a spark lighter next to the torch nozzle until the gas ignites. Adjust the torch valve until the inner portion of the flame is 1" to 2" long.

9 Hold the flame tip against the middle of the fitting for 4 to 5 seconds, until the soldering paste begins to sizzle.

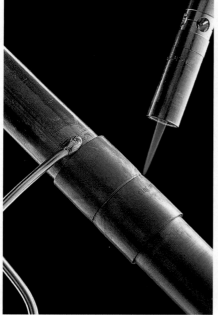

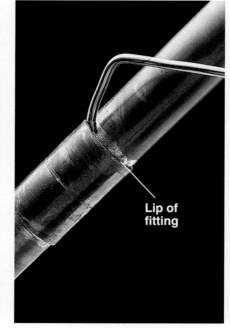

Lip of fitting

10 Heat the other side of the copper fitting to ensure that the heat is distributed evenly. Touch the solder to the pipe. If the solder melts, the joint is ready to be soldered.

11 Remove the torch and quickly push ½" to ¾" of solder into each joint. Capillary action fills the joint with liquid solder. A correctly soldered joint shows a thin bead of solder around the lip of the fitting.

12 Carefully wipe away excess solder with a dry rag. (The pipes will be hot.) When all the joints have cooled, turn on the water and check for leaks. If a joint leaks, drain the pipes, disassemble and clean the pipe and fittings, then resolder the joint.

Using Compression Fittings

When cramped or poorly ventilated spaces make it difficult or unsafe to solder, compression fittings are a good choice. They're also appropriate for connections that may need to be taken apart at a later date. Because they're easy to disconnect, compression fittings often are used to install supply tubes and fixture shutoff valves (page 242).

Compression fittings work well with flexible copper pipe, which is soft enough to allow the compression ring to seat snugly, creating a watertight seal. They are also used to make connections with Type M rigid copper pipe.

Compression fittings are available in unions, 90° elbows, tees, straight and angled shutoff valves, and hose bibs. They usually have flat sides that can be gripped with an adjustable wrench.

When measuring copper pipe for compression fittings, add ½" for the length of the pipe that must fit inside the valve. As with all plumbing joints, smooth, straight cuts are vital to forming watertight seals. Cut pipe with a tubing cutter or a hacksaw and remove any metal burrs on the cut edges, using a reaming tool or round file.

Compression fittings tend to cross thread, so check the fittings for leaks after the assembly. To ensure a watertight seal, cover compression rings with pipe joint compound before assembling the fittings.

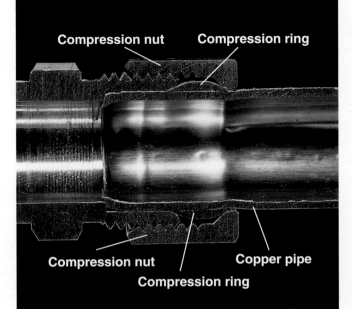

A compression fitting (shown here cut away) has a compression ring and a compression nut, which forms a tight seal by forcing the ring against the inner portion of the fitting.

Everything You Need

Tools: tubing cutter or hacksaw, adjustable wrenches.

Materials: brass compression fittings, pipe joint compound.

How to Join Two Copper Pipes with a Compression Union Fitting

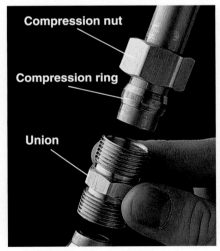

1 Slide the compression nuts and rings over the ends of the pipes. Place the threaded union between the pipes.

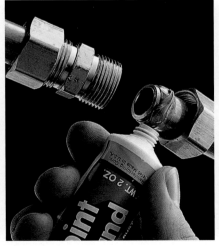

2 Apply a layer of pipe joint compound to the compression rings, then screw the compression nuts onto the threaded union. Hand-tighten the nuts.

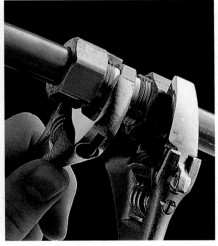

3 Hold the center of the union fitting with an adjustable wrench. Use another wrench to tighten each compression nut one complete turn. Turn on the water. If the fitting leaks, gently tighten the nuts.

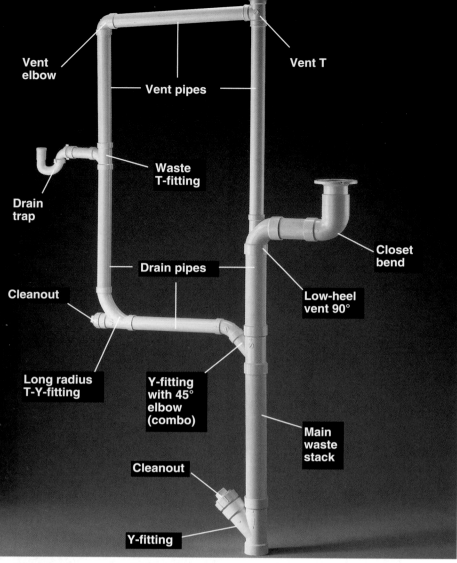

Labels on the image:
- Vent elbow
- Vent pipes
- Vent T
- Waste T-fitting
- Drain trap
- Drain pipes
- Closet bend
- Cleanout
- Low-heel vent 90°
- Long radius T-Y-fitting
- Y-fitting with 45° elbow (combo)
- Main waste stack
- Cleanout
- Y-fitting

Working with Plastic Pipe

Drain-waste-vent (DWV) fittings come in a variety of shapes to serve different functions within the plumbing system. Bends in the vent pipes can be very sharp, but drain pipes should use fittings with a noticeable sweep. Fittings used to direct falling waste water from a vertical to a horizontal pipe should have bends that are even more sweeping. Your local plumbing code may require that you install cleanout fittings where vertical drain pipes meet horizontal runs.

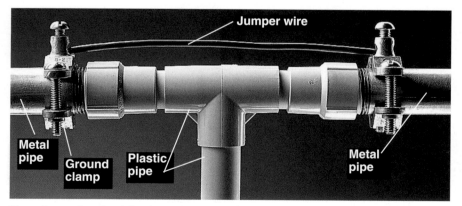

Labels on the image:
- Jumper wire
- Metal pipe
- Ground clamp
- Plastic pipe
- Metal pipe

Your home's electrical system may be grounded through metal water pipes. When adding plastic pipes to a metal plumbing system, make sure the electrical ground circuit remains intact. Use ground clamps and jumper wires (available at hardware stores) to bypass the plastic transition and complete the electrical ground circuit. Make sure the clamps are firmly attached to bare metal on both sides of the plastic pipe.

Plastic pipes and fittings are lightweight, inexpensive, and easy to use. They are available in rigid and flexible forms.

ABS and PVC are rigid plastics used in drain-waste-vent (DWV) systems. PVC resists chemical damage and heat better than ABS, and is approved for above-ground use by all plumbing codes; some codes still require cast-iron pipe for main drains running under concrete slabs.

CPVC is also a rigid plastic, and is used for hot and cold water supply lines.

Flexible plastics are used for water supply pipes. Although PB is restricted in finished construction by building codes (PB fittings were found to leak), it can be used for exposed supply tubes, such as beneath a sink. PE is typically used in outdoor plumbing.

Plastic pipes can be joined to iron or copper pipes with transition fittings (page 91), but different types of plastic should not be joined. For example, if your drain pipes are ABS plastic, use only ABS pipes and fittings when making repairs.

Prolonged exposure to sunlight eventually can weaken plastic plumbing pipe, so do not install or store plastics in areas that receive constant, direct sunlight.

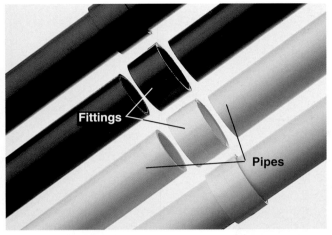

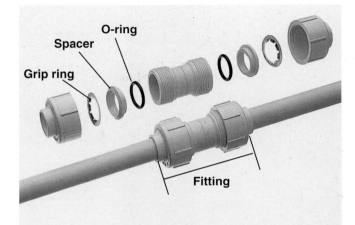

Solvent-glued fittings are used on rigid plastic pipes. The solvent dissolves a thin layer of plastic and bonds the pipe and fitting together.

Plastic compression fittings (or grip fittings) are used to join CPVC pipe. Some types have a rubber O-ring, instead of a compression ring, that makes the watertight seal.

Plastic Pipe Grade Stamps

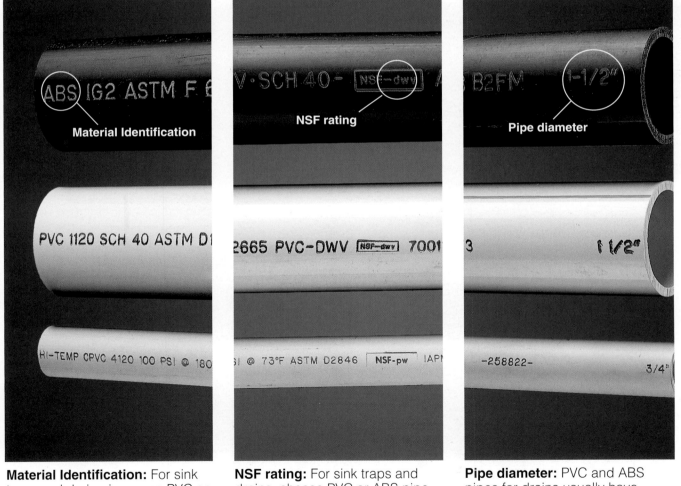

Material Identification: For sink traps and drain pipes, use PVC or ABS pipe. For water supply pipes, use CPVC pipe.

NSF rating: For sink traps and drains, choose PVC or ABS pipe that has a DWV rating from the NSF. For water supply pipes, choose CPVC pipe that has a PW rating.

Pipe diameter: PVC and ABS pipes for drains usually have an inside diameter of 1¼" to 4". CPVC pipes for water supply usually have an inside diameter of ½" or ¾".

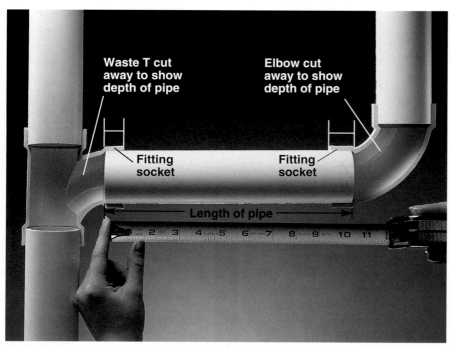

Find the length of plastic pipe needed by measuring between the bottoms of the fitting sockets (fittings shown here cut away). Mark the length on the pipe with a felt-tipped pen.

Everything You Need

Tools: tubing cutter (or saw), felt-tipped pen, utility knife, jig saw or hole saw, drill, hammer.

Materials: plastic pipe and fittings, emery cloth, petroleum jelly, plastic-pipe primer, solvent glue, rag, masking tape, 1 × 4 lumber, pipe straps, metal protecter plates.

Fitting & Installing Plastic Pipe

Rigid ABS, PVC, or CPVC pipes can be cut with a tubing cutter or saw. Make sure all cuts are level and straight to ensure watertight joints.

CPVC pipes are joined using compression fittings (page 103). Rigid ABS and PVC plastics are joined using plastic fittings and primer and solvent glue specifically made for the pipe material being joined. All-purpose or universal solvents may be used on all types of rigid plastic pipe. Solvent glue hardens in about 30 seconds, so test-fit all plastic pipe and fittings before gluing the first joint. For best results, the pipe and fittings should be dulled with an emery cloth and liquid primer before being joined.

Liquid solvent glues and primers are toxic and flammable. Always provide adequate ventilation when fitting plastics, and store the products away from heat.

Cutting Rigid Plastic Pipe

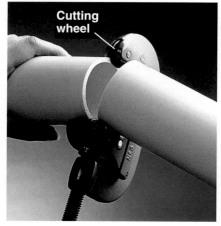

Tubing cutter: Tighten the tool around the pipe so the cutting wheel is on the marked line. Rotate the tool around the pipe, tightening the screw every two rotations, until the pipe snaps.

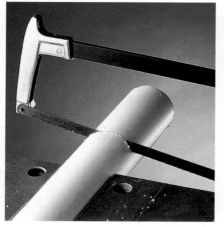

Hacksaw: Clamp the plastic pipe in a gripping bench or a vise. Keep the hacksaw blade straight while sawing. TIP: To draw a straight cutting line, wrap a sheet of paper around the circumference of the pipe and trace along the edge.

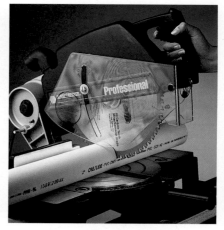

Miter saw: Make straight cuts on all types of plastic pipe with a power miter saw or hand miter box. With a hand miter box, use a hacksaw rather than a backsaw.

How to Fit Rigid Plastic Pipe with Solvent Glue

1 Measure and cut the pipe to length. Remove rough burrs on the cut ends, using a utility knife.

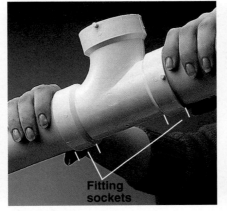

2 Test-fit all pipes and fittings. The pipes should fit tightly against the bottom of the fitting sockets.

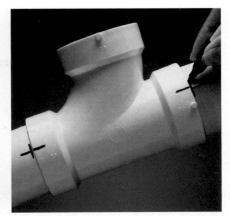

3 Make alignment and depth marks across each pipe joint, using a felt-tipped pen. Disassemble the pipes.

4 Clean the ends of the pipes and the fitting sockets, using an emery cloth.

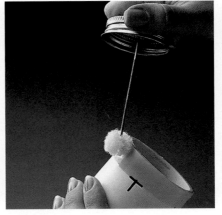

5 Apply plastic-pipe primer to one end of a pipe.

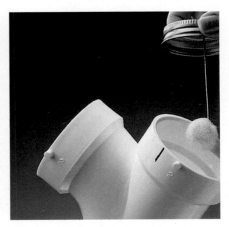

6 Apply plastic-pipe primer inside the fitting socket.

7 Apply a thick coat of solvent glue to the end of the pipe, and a thin coat to the inside surface of the fitting socket. Work quickly—solvent glue hardens in about 30 seconds.

8 Quickly position the pipe and fitting so the alignment marks are offset by about 2" and the end of the pipe fits flush against the bottom of the socket.

9 Twist the pipe until the marks are aligned. Hold the pipe in place for about 20 seconds, then wipe away any excess glue with a rag. Let the joint dry undisturbed for 30 minutes.

How to Install Drain Pipe for a Sink

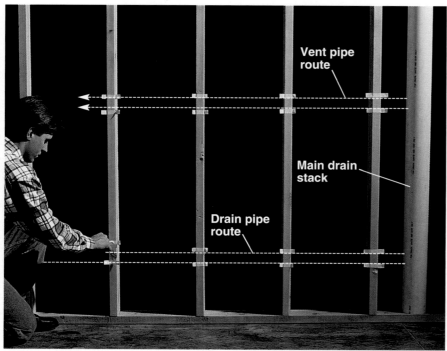

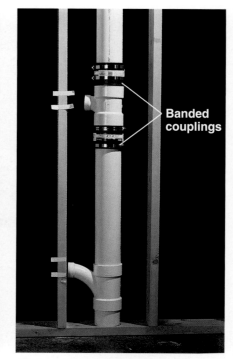

1 Mark the route for the new drain pipe on the wall studs, using masking tape. Drain pipe should slope down toward the main drain stack at a rate of ¼" per 12". If the new drain line is over 42" long, a separate vent pipe is required (pages 92 to 94). Install a 1 × 4 cross brace between studs where the drain stub-out will be located.

2 Install transition fittings for connecting new plastic pipes to existing drain pipes. Use banded couplings to make connections to the main drain stack.

3 Cut notches or holes in the framing members along the marked route for the pipes (page 93).

4 Cut and test-fit new pipes and fittings. When satisfied with the layout, make alignment marks and solvent-glue the pieces together permanently (page 105). After the joints have set at least 30 minutes, anchor the pipe to the cross braces, using pipe straps.

5 Attach metal protector plates across the front of framing members to protect the pipes from punctures.

How to Install Plastic Water Supply Pipes for a Sink

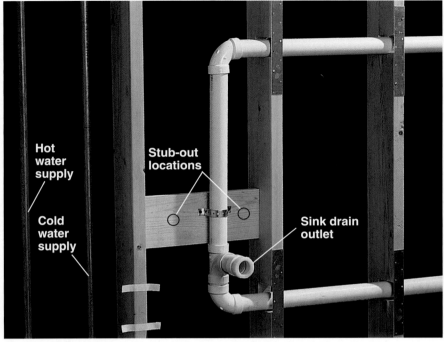

Hot water supply

Cold water supply

Stub-out locations

Sink drain outlet

1 Mark the location of new water supply pipes on the wall studs, using masking tape. Water supply stub-outs generally are centered around the drain outlet, spaced about 8" apart. The stub-out for the hot water line should be on the left side of the drain stub-out, and the cold water line should be on the right. Shut off the main water supply, and turn on faucets to drain the plumbing lines.

2 Drill holes through the centers of the framing members to hold the new plastic water supply pipes. New pipes must not be larger in diameter than the existing water supply pipes.

T-fitting

3 Cut out sections of the existing supply pipes, using a pipe cutter, and install T-fittings for connecting the new plastic pipes.

4 Cut and test-fit the plastic supply pipes and fittings. When you are satisfied with the pipe layout, solvent-glue the pieces together.

5 Attach the new pipes to the cross brace, using pipe straps, then attach the shutoff valves to the ends of the pipes. (Some shutoff valves are solvent-glued, others use compression fittings.)

Working with Cast-Iron Pipe

Cast-iron pipe is rarely installed today, but years ago it was commonly used within DWV systems. It can be identified by its dark color, rough surface, and large size—usually 3" or more in diameter.

Cast-iron pipe is often joined with hubbed fittings (step 1, below), made by inserting the straight end of one pipe into the flared, or hubbed, end of another pipe. The joints are sealed with packing material (called oakum) and lead.

Hubbed fittings sometimes develop leaks, and pipes can rust through. Replace a leaky fitting with a section of plastic pipe, and connect a new drain pipe to a cast-iron stack using a plastic waste fitting.

Banded couplings are special fittings used to connect new plastic pipe to existing cast iron. They have a neoprene sleeve that seals the joint and stainless steel bands and screw clamps that hold the pipes together. These couplings come in different styles, so check the local plumbing code to determine which types are approved in your area.

The best way to cut cast-iron pipe is with a rental tool called a snap cutter. Before you cut, have a professional inspect the pipe and recommend the best method for cutting it.

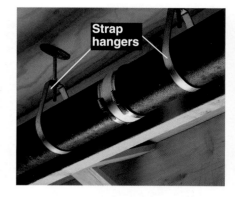

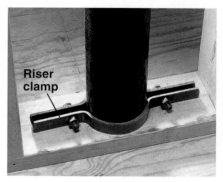

Install supports for cast-iron pipe before cutting. Support horizontal pipe with strap hangers every 5 ft. and at every joint connection (top). Support vertical pipe at every floor level and above every cut, using riser clamps (bottom).

Everything You Need

Tools: chalk, adjustable wrench, snap cutter, hacksaw, ratchet wrench, screwdriver.

Materials: riser clamps or strap hangers, wood blocks, 2½" drywall screws, banded couplings, plastic pipe.

Replacing a Section of Cast-iron Pipe

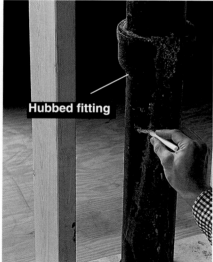

1 Use chalk to mark cutting lines on the cast-iron pipe. If you're replacing a leaky hubbed fitting, mark at least 6" above and below the fitting.

2 Support the lower section of pipe by installing a riser clamp flush against the bottom plate or floor. Install a riser clamp 6" to 12" above the section being replaced. Attach wood blocks to the studs with 2½" drywall screws, so that the riser clamp rests securely on the tops of the blocks.

3 Wrap the chain of the snap cutter around the pipe so the cutting wheels align with the chalk line. Tighten the chain and then snap the pipe according to the tool manufacturer's directions.

108

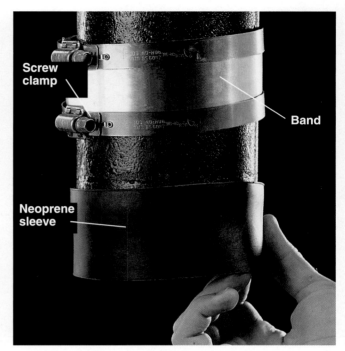

4 Make a second cut at the other chalk line, and remove the section of pipe. Cut a length of PVC or ABS plastic pipe 1" shorter than the section of cast-iron pipe that has been cut away (page 104).

5 Slip a band and neoprene sleeve of a banded coupling onto each end of the cast-iron pipe. Make sure the cast-iron pipe is seated snugly against the rubber separator ring molded into the interior of the sleeve (step 6).

6 Fold back the end of each neoprene sleeve until the molded separator ring on the inside of the sleeve is visible. Position the new plastic pipe so it is aligned with the cast-iron pipes.

7 Roll the ends of the neoprene sleeves over the new plastic pipe.

8 Slide the bands over the neoprene sleeves and tighten the screw clamps with a ratchet wrench or screwdriver.

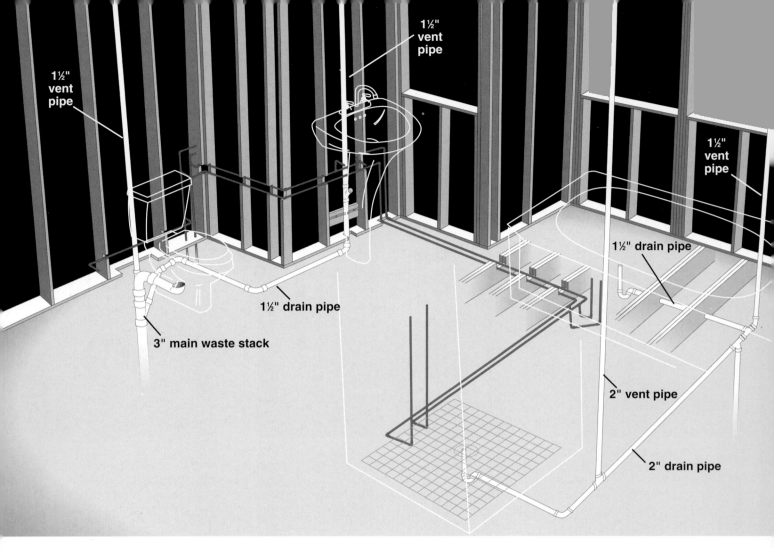

Plumbing a Master Bathroom

A large bathroom has more plumbing fixtures and consumes more water than any other room in your house. For this reason, a master bath has special plumbing needs.

Frame bathroom "wet walls" with 2 × 6 studs to provide plenty of room for running 3" pipes and fittings. If your bathroom includes a heavy whirlpool tub, you will need to strengthen the floor by installing sister joists alongside the existing floor joists underneath the tub (page 78). Follow local building code requirements concerning allowable sizes for holes and notches cut into framing members. See the chart on page 93.

For convenience, this project is divided into the following sequences:

- How to Install DWV Pipes for the Toilet & Sink (pages 111 to 113)
- How to Install DWV Pipes for the Tub & Shower (pages 114 to 115)
- How to Connect Drain Pipes & Vent Pipes to the Main Waste-Vent Stack (page 116)
- How to Install Water Supply Pipes (page 117)

Our demonstration bathroom is a second-story master bath. We are installing a 3" vertical drain pipe to service the toilet and the vanity sink, and a 2" vertical pipe to handle the tub and shower drains. The branch drains for the sink and bathtub are 1½" pipes; the shower requires a 2" pipe. Each fixture has its own vent pipe extending up into the attic, where they are joined together and connected to the main stack.

How to Install DWV Pipes for the Toilet & Sink

1 Use masking tape to outline the locations of the fixtures and pipe runs on the subfloor and walls. Mark the location for a 3" vertical drain pipe on the bottom plate in the wall behind the toilet. Mark a 4½"-diameter circle for the toilet drain on the subfloor.

2 Cut out the drain opening for the toilet, using a jig saw. Mark and remove a section of flooring around the toilet area, large enough to provide access for installing the toilet drain and for running drain pipe from the sink. Make cuts using a circular saw with blade set to the thickness of the subfloor.

3 If a floor joist interferes with the toilet drain, cut away a short section of the joist and box-frame the area with double headers. (Check local building code regarding the construction and fastening requirements for double headers.) The framed opening should be just large enough to install the toilet and sink drains.

4 To create a path for the vertical 3" drain pipe, cut a 4½" × 12" notch in the bottom plate of the wall behind the toilet. Make a similar cutout in the double wall plate at the bottom of the joist cavity. From the basement, locate the point directly below the cutout by measuring from a reference point, such as the main waste-vent stack.

5 Mark the location for the 3" drain pipe on the basement ceiling, then drill a small test hole up through the center of the marked area. Direct the beam of a bright flashlight up into the hole, then return to the bathroom and look down into the wall cavity. If you can see light, return to the basement and cut a 4½"-diameter hole centered over the test hole.

(continued next page)

Low-heel vent 90° fitting

Y-fitting

7 Lower the pipe so the bottom end slides through the opening in the basement ceiling. Support the pipe with vinyl pipe strap wrapped around the low-heel vent 90° fitting and screwed to framing members.

6 Measure and cut a length of 3" drain pipe to reach from the bathroom floor cavity to a point flush with the bottom of the ceiling joists in the basement. Solvent-glue a 3" × 3" × 1½" Y-fitting to the top of the pipe, and a low-heel vent 90° fitting above the Y. The branch inlet on the Y should face toward the sink location; the front inlet on the low-heel should face forward. Carefully lower the pipe into the wall cavity.

8 Use a length of 3" pipe and a 4" × 3" reducing elbow to extend the drain out to the toilet location. Make sure the drain slopes at least ⅛" per foot toward the wall, then support it with pipe strap attached to the joists. Solvent-glue a short length of pipe into the elbow, so it extends at least 2" above the subfloor. After the new drains are pressure tested, this stub-out will be cut flush with the subfloor and fitted with a toilet flange.

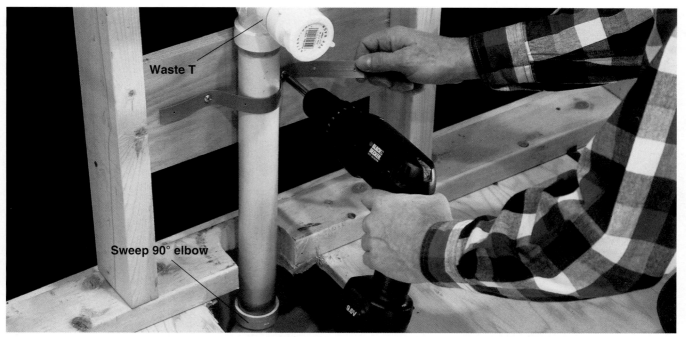

9 Notch out the bottom plate and subfloor below the sink location. Cut a length of 1½" plastic drain pipe, then solvent-glue a waste T to the top of the pipe and a sweep 90° elbow to the bottom. NOTE: The distance from the subfloor to the center of the waste T should be 14" to 18". The branch of the T should face out, and the discharge on the elbow should face toward the toilet. Adjust the pipe so the top edge of the elbow nearly touches the bottom of the bottom plate. Anchor it with pipe strap and a 1× backing board nailed between studs.

10 Dry-fit lengths of 1½" drain pipe and elbows to extend the sink drain to the 3" drain pipe behind the toilet. Use a right-angle drill to bore holes in joists, if needed. Make sure the horizontal drain pipe slopes at least ¼" per foot toward the vertical drain. When satisfied with the layout, solvent-glue the pieces together and support the drain pipe with vinyl pipe straps attached to the joists.

11 In the top plates of the walls behind the sink and toilet, bore ½"-diameter holes up into the attic. Insert pencils or dowels into the holes, and tape them in place. Enter the attic and locate the pencils, then clear away insulation and cut 2"-diameter holes for the vertical vent pipes. Cut and install 1½" vent pipes running from the toilet and sink drain at least 1 foot up into the attic.

How to Install DWV Pipes for the Tub & Shower

1 On the subfloor, use masking tape to mark the locations of the tub and shower, the water supply pipes, and the tub and shower drains, according to your plumbing plan. Use a jig saw to cut out a 12"-square opening for each drain, and drill 1"-diameter holes in the subfloor for each water supply riser.

2 When installing a large whirlpool tub, cut away the subfloor to expose the full length of the joists under the tub, then nail, screw, or bolt a sister joist against each existing joist. Make sure both ends of each joist are supported by loadbearing walls (page 78).

2" inlet for shower drain

1½" inlet for tub drain

3 In a wall adjacent to the tub, establish a route for a 2" vertical waste-vent pipe running from the basement. This pipe should be no more than 3½ ft. from the bathtub trap. Then, mark a route for the horizontal drain pipe running from the bathtub drain to the waste-vent pipe location. Cut 3"-diameter holes through the centers of the joists for the bathtub drain.

4 Cut and install a vertical 2" drain pipe running from basement to the joist cavity adjoining the tub location, using the same technique as for the toilet drain (steps 4 to 6, pages 111 to 112). At the top of the drain pipe, use assorted fittings to create branch inlets for the bathtub and shower drains, and a 1½" top inlet for a vent pipe running to the attic.

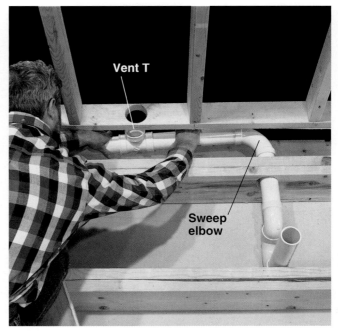

5 Dry-fit a 1½" drain pipe running from the bathtub drain location to the vertical waste-vent pipe in the wall. Make sure the pipe slopes ¼" per foot toward the wall. When satisfied with the layout, solvent-glue the pieces together and support the pipe with vinyl pipe straps attached to the joists.

6 Dry-fit a 2" drain pipe from the shower drain to the vertical waste-vent pipe near the tub. Install a solvent-glued trap at the drain location, cut a hole in the bottom plate, and insert a 2" × 2" × 1½" vent T within 5 ft. of the trap. Make sure the drain is sloped ¼" per foot downward, away from the shower drain. When satisfied with the layout, solvent-glue the pipes together.

7 Cut and install vertical vent pipes for the bathtub and shower, extending up through the wall plates and at least 1 foot into the attic. These vent pipes will be connected in the attic to the main waste-vent stack. In our project, the shower vent is a 2" pipe, while the bathtub vent is a 1½" pipe.

How to Connect Drain Pipes to the Main Waste-Vent Stack

1 In the basement, cut into the main stack and install the fittings necessary to connect the 3" toilet-sink drain and the 2" bathtub-shower drain. In our project, we created an assembly made of a waste T-fitting with an extra side inlet and two short lengths of pipe, then inserted it into the existing stack using banded couplings (pages 108 to 109). Position the T-fittings so the drain pipes have the proper downward slope toward the stack. NOTE: If your stack is cast iron, install supports before cutting into the pipe (page 108).

2 Dry-fit Y-fittings with 45° elbows onto the vertical 3" and 2" drain pipes. Position the horizontal drain pipes against the fittings, and mark them for cutting. When satisfied with the layout, solvent-glue the pipes together, then support the pipes every 4 ft. with vinyl pipe straps. Solvent-glue cleanout plugs on the open inlets on the Y-fittings.

How to Connect Vent Pipes to the Main Waste-Vent Stack

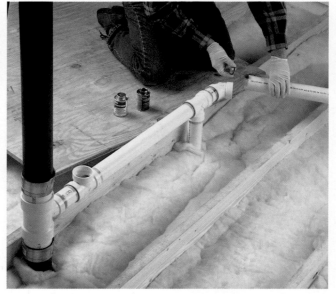

1 In the attic, cut into the main waste-vent stack and install a vent T-fitting, using banded couplings. The side outlet on the vent T should face the new 2" vent pipe running down to the bathroom. Attach a test T-fitting to the vent T. NOTE: If your stack is cast iron, make sure to adequately support it before cutting into it (page 108).

2 Use elbows, vent T-fittings, reducers, and lengths of pipe as needed to link the new vent pipes to the test T-fitting on the main waste-vent stack. Vent pipes can be routed in many ways, but you should make sure the pipes have a slight downward angle to prevent moisture from collecting in the pipes. Support the pipes every 4 ft.

How to Install Copper Water Supply Pipes

1 After shutting off the water, cut into existing supply pipes and install T-fittings for new branch lines. Notch out studs and run copper pipes to the toilet and sink locations. Use an elbow and threaded female fitting to form the toilet stub-out. Once satisfied with the layout, solder the pipes in place (pages 98 to 100).

2 Cut 1" × 4" notches around the wall, and extend the supply pipes to the sink location. Install reducing T-fittings and female threaded fittings for the sink faucet stub-outs. Position the stub-outs about 18" above the floor, spaced 8" apart. When satisfied with the layout, solder the joints, then insert 1× blocking behind the stub-outs and strap them in place.

3 Extend the water supply pipes to the bathtub and shower. In our project, we removed the subfloor and notched the joists to run ¾" supply pipes from the sink to a whirlpool bathtub, then to the shower. At the bathtub, we used reducing T-fittings and elbows to create ½" risers for the tub faucet. Solder caps onto the risers; after the subfloor is replaced, the caps will be removed and replaced with shutoff valves.

4 At the shower location, use elbows to create vertical risers where the shower wet wall will be constructed. The risers should extend at least 6" above floor level. Support the risers with a 1× backer board attached between joists. Solder caps onto the risers; after the shower stall is constructed, the caps will be removed and replaced with shutoff valves.

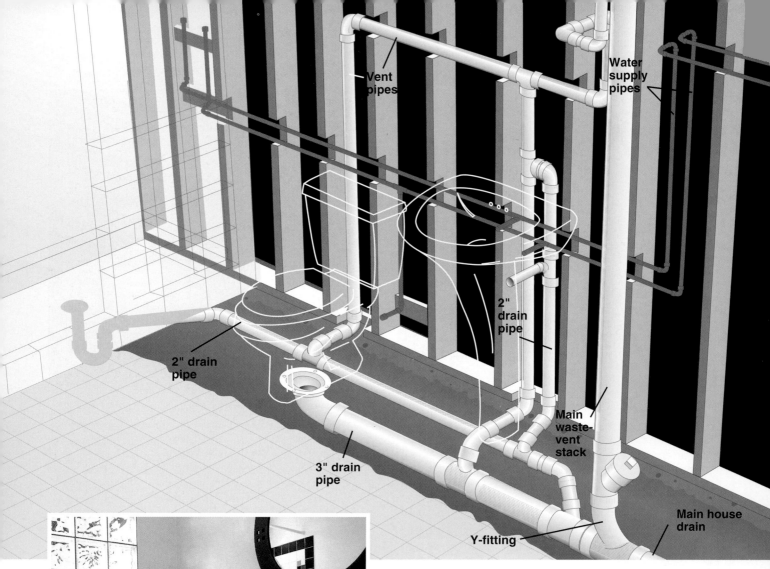

Vent pipes

Water supply pipes

2" drain pipe

2" drain pipe

3" drain pipe

Main waste-vent stack

Y-fitting

Main house drain

Plumbing rough-ins for our demonstration bathroom include a 2" drain pipe for the shower and sink, and a 3" drain for the toilet. The drain pipes converge at a Y-fitting joined to the existing main drain. The shower, toilet, and sink have individual vent pipes that meet inside the wet wall. From there, a single vent extends up to the attic, where it joins the main waste-vent stack.

Plumbing a Basement Bath

Unless your basement already has bathroom stub-outs in place, completing the rough-ins usually requires breaking up a portion of the concrete floor and digging a trench for the fixture drains. To simplify this process, it's best to arrange the fixtures in a line along one wall. Also consider the location of the bathroom: The fixtures must be close enough to the main drain tie-in that the drain lines maintain a ¼" per foot downward slope.

In some basements, the main house drain does not extend through the basement floor, but instead makes a turn above the floor and begins its run out to the city sewer. In this situation, a basement bathroom requires a sewage ejector to collect the waste from each fixture and pump it up to the main drain.

For this project you will need a jackhammer, concrete, and concrete working tools in addition to the standard plumbing tools. Jackhammers can be rented at your local rental center.

How to Plumb a Basement Bath

1 Outline a 24"-wide trench on the concrete where new branch drains will run to the main drain. (In our project, we ran the trench parallel to an outside wall, leaving a 6" ledge for framing a wet wall.) Use a masonry chisel and hand maul to break up concrete near the stack.

2 Use a circular saw and masonry blade to cut along the outline, then break the rest of the trench into convenient chunks with a jackhammer. Remove any remaining concrete with a chisel. Excavate the trench to a depth about 2" deeper than the main drain. At vent locations for the shower and toilet, cut 3" notches in the concrete all the way to the wall.

3 Cut the 2 × 6 framing for the wet wall that will hold the pipes. Use pressure-treated lumber for the bottom plate. Cut 3" notches in the bottom plate for the pipes, then secure the plate to the floor with construction adhesive and masonry fasteners. Install the top plate, then attach studs.

4 Assemble a 2" horizontal drain pipe for the sink and shower, and a 3" drain pipe for the toilet. The 2" drain pipe includes a solvent-glued trap for the shower, a vent T, and a waste T for the sink drain. The toilet drain includes a toilet bend and a vent T. Use elbows and straight lengths of pipe to extend the vent and drain pipes to the wet wall. Make sure the vent fittings angle upward from the drain pipe at least 45°.

(continued next page)

5 Use pairs of stakes with vinyl pipe straps slung between them to cradle drain pipes in the proper position (inset). The drain pipes should be positioned so they slope ¼" per foot down toward the main drain.

6 Assemble the fittings required to tie the new branch drains into the main drain. In our project, we will be cutting out the cleanout and sweep on the main waste-vent stack in order to install a new assembly that includes a Y-fitting to accept the two new drain pipes.

7 Support the main waste-vent stack before cutting. Use a 2 × 4 for a plastic stack, or riser clamps (page 108) for a cast-iron stack. Using a reciprocating saw, or snap cutter for cast iron, cut into the main drain as close as possible to the stack.

8 Cut into the stack above the cleanout and remove the pipe and fittings. Wear rubber gloves, and have a bucket and plastic bags ready, as old pipes and fittings may be coated with messy sludge.

3" × 3" × 2" reducing Y

9 Test-fit, then solvent-glue the new cleanout and reducing Y assembly into the main drain. Support the weight of the stack by adding sand underneath the Y, but leave plenty of space around the end for connecting the new branch pipes.

10 Working from the reducing Y, solvent-glue the new drain pipes together. Be careful to maintain proper slope of the drain pipes when gluing. Be sure the toilet and shower drains extend at least 2" above the floor level.

11 Check for leaks by pouring fresh water into each new drain pipe. If no leaks appear, cap or plug the drains with rags to prevent sewer gas from leaking into the work area as you complete the installation.

(continued next page)

12 Run 2" vent pipes from the drains up the inside of the wet wall. Notch the studs and insert a horizontal vent pipe, then attach the vertical vent pipes with an elbow and vent T-fitting. Test-fit all pipes, then solvent-glue them in place.

13 Route the vent pipe from the wet wall to a point below a wall cavity running from the basement to the attic. NOTE: If there is an existing vent pipe in the basement, you can tie into this pipe rather than run the vent to the attic.

14 If you are running vent pipes in a two-story home, remove sections of wall surface as needed to bore holes for running the vent pipe through wall plates. Feed the vent pipe up into the wall cavity from the basement.

15 Wedge the vent pipe in place while you solvent-glue the fittings. Support the vent pipe at each floor with vinyl pipe straps. Do not patch the walls until your work has been reviewed by an inspector.

16 Cut into the main stack in the attic, and install a vent T-fitting, using banded couplings. (If the stack is cast iron make sure to support it adequately above and below the cuts, as demonstrated on pages 108 and 109.) Attach a test T-fitting to the vent T, then join the new vent pipe to the stack, using elbows and lengths of straight pipe as needed.

17 Shut off the main water supply, cut into the water supply pipes as near as possible to the new bathroom, and install T-fittings. Install full-bore control valves on each line, then run ¾" branch supply pipes down into the wet wall by notching the top wall plate. Extend the pipes across the wall by notching the studs.

18 Use reducing T-fittings to run ½" supplies to each fixture, ending with female threaded adapters. Install backing boards, and strap the pipes in place. Attach metal protector plates over notched studs to protect pipes. After having your work approved by a building inspector, fill in around the pipes with dirt or sand, then mix and pour new concrete to cover the trench. Trowel the surface smooth, and let the cement cure for 3 days before installing fixtures.

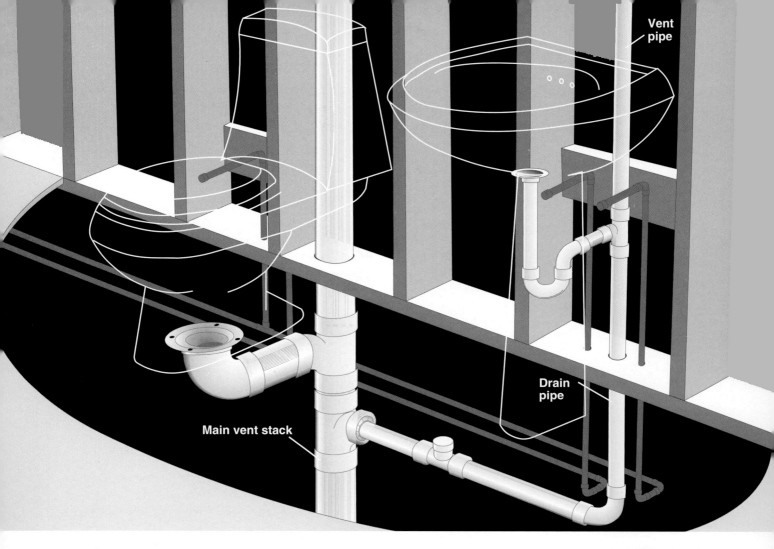

Vent pipe

Drain pipe

Main vent stack

Plumbing a Half Bath

A first-story half bath is easy to install when located behind a kitchen or existing bathroom, because you can take advantage of accessible supply and DWV lines. It is possible to add a half bath on an upper story or in a location distant from existing plumbing, but the complexity and cost of the project may be increased considerably.

Be sure that the new fixtures are adequately vented. In the project overview shown here, the pedestal sink is vented with a pipe that runs up the wall a few feet before turning to join the main stack. However, if there are higher fixtures draining into the main stack, you would be required to run the vent up to a point at least 6" above the highest fixture before splicing it into the main stack or an existing vent pipe. When the toilet is located within 6 ft. of the stack, as in our design, it requires no additional vent pipe.

The techniques for plumbing a half bath are similar to those used for a master bath. Refer to pages 110 to 117 for more detailed information.

In our demonstration half bath, the toilet and sink are close to the main stack for ease of installation, but are spaced far enough apart to meet minimum allowed distances between fixtures. Check local code for any restrictions in your area. Generally, there should be at least 15" from the center of the toilet drain to a side wall or fixture, and a minimum of 21" of space between the front edge of the toilet and the opposing wall.

How to Plumb a Half Bath

1 Locate the main waste-vent stack in the wet wall, and remove the wall surface behind the planned location for the toilet and sink. Cut a 4½"-diameter hole for the toilet flange (centered 12" from the wall, for most toilets). Drill two ¾" holes through the bottom plate for sink supply lines and one hole for the toilet supply line. Drill a 2" hole for the sink drain.

2 In the basement, cut away a section of the stack and insert two waste T-fittings. The top fitting should have a 3" side inlet for the toilet drain; the bottom fitting requires a 1½" reducing bushing for the sink drain. Install a toilet bend and 3" drain pipe for the toilet, and install a 1½" drain pipe with a sweep elbow for the sink.

3 Tap into water distribution pipes with ¾" × ½" reducing T-fittings, then run ½" copper supply pipes through the holes in the bottom plate to the sink and toilet. Support all pipes at 4-ft. intervals with strapping attached to joists.

4 Attach drop ear elbows to the ends of the supply pipes, and anchor them to blocking installed between studs. Run a vertical vent pipe from the waste T-fitting up the wall to a point at least 6" above the highest fixture on the main stack. Then, route the vent pipe horizontally and splice it into the vent stack with a vent T.

Bathrooms require at least two circuits, one 20-amp, GFCI-protected receptacle circuit, and one circuit for lighting fixtures.

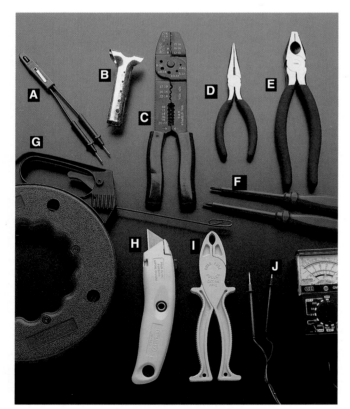

Electrical tools include: neon circuit tester (A), cable ripper (B), combination tool (C), needlenose pliers (D), linesman's pliers (E), insulated screwdrivers (F), fish tape (G), utility knife (H), fuse puller (I), continuity tester (J). These basic electrical tools are simple, inexpensive, and widely available. You will need them for many home improvement projects.

Wiring Bathrooms

If your bathroom remodeling project will require new electrical circuits to be installed, you will need to understand how a standard household circuit works.

Household circuits carry electricity along a regular route from the main service panel, through the house, and back to the service panel. For the circuit to function properly, this loop must remain uninterrupted.

Current travels outward to electrical devices on "hot" wires and returns along "neutral" wires. The two kinds of wires are color coded: hot wires are black or red, and neutral wires typically are white or light gray.

For safety, most circuits also include a bare copper or green insulated grounding wire. The grounding wire helps reduce the chance of electrical shock and carries any excess current in the case of a short circuit or overload.

Circuits are rated according to the amount of power they can carry without overheating. If the devices on a circuit try to draw more power than that amount, the fuse or circuit breaker is triggered and automatically shuts down the circuit.

Usually, several switches, receptacles, fixtures, or appliances are connected to each circuit, and a loose connection at any device can cause electricity to flow outside the circuit wires. The resulting reduction in resistance, called a short circuit, triggers the circuit breaker or fuse, and the circuit shuts down.

After passing through the electrical devices, current returns to the service panel along a neutral circuit wire. There it merges with a main circuit wire and leaves the house on a neutral service line that returns it to the transformer on the utility pole.

Before working with your home's wiring, always shut off the electrical power at the main service panel, and test for power (page 71) at the bathroom before beginning your project.

In this section:

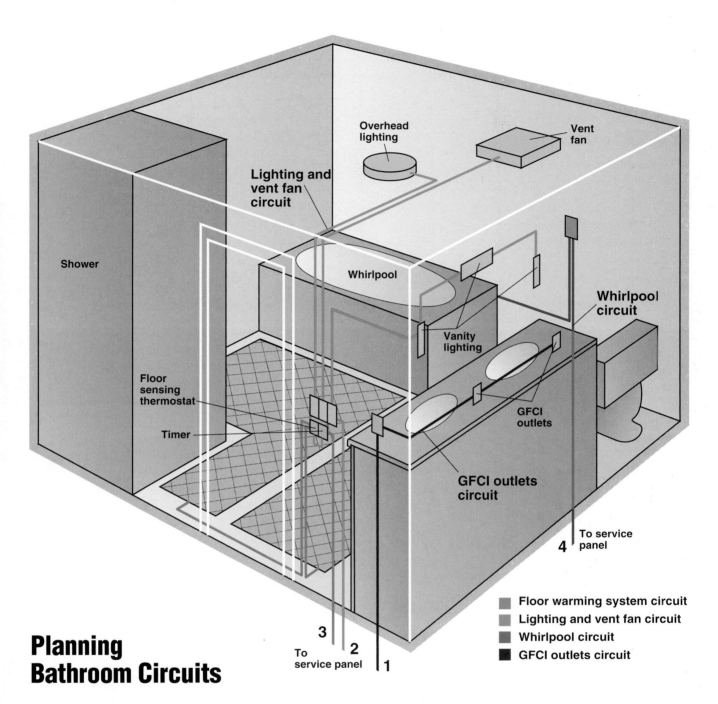

Overhead lighting

Vent fan

Lighting and vent fan circuit

Shower

Whirlpool

Vanity lighting

Whirlpool circuit

Floor sensing thermostat

Timer

GFCI outlets

GFCI outlets circuit

To service panel 4

3

To service panel 2

1

- ▨ Floor warming system circuit
- ▨ Lighting and vent fan circuit
- ▨ Whirlpool circuit
- ■ GFCI outlets circuit

Planning Bathroom Circuits

Careful planning of a bathroom wiring project ensures you will have plenty of power for present and future needs. Consider all possible ways a space might be used, and plan for enough electrical service to meet peak needs.

Draw a circuit map for each new electrical circuit in your bathroom. Bathrooms require at least two circuits, one 20-amp, GFCI-protected receptacle circuit for small appliances, and one 15-amp or 20-amp circuit for general lighting fixtures. Vent fans with only light fixtures usually can be wired into the general lighting circuit, but units with built-in heat lamps or blowers require separate circuits. When drawing a circuit map, include all the lights, switches, receptacles, and fixtures connected to each circuit.

The circuits for the master bathroom shown above start at the main service panel in the basement. *Circuit 1* controls the bathroom's receptacles. *Circuit 2* runs the light fixtures and vent fan. *Circuit 3* provides power to the floor-warming system. *Circuit 4* feeds the whirlpool. Circuits 1, 3, and 4 are GFCI-protected circuits. Circuits 3 and 4 also are dedicated circuits, meaning each serves only one device or fixture.

After all the new bathroom circuits are installed and connected, be sure to label each circuit at the main service panel, and store the completed circuit maps near the service panel for future reference.

See the circuit maps on page 128 for a closer look at typical wiring layouts for bathrooms.

How to Wire Common Bathroom Circuits

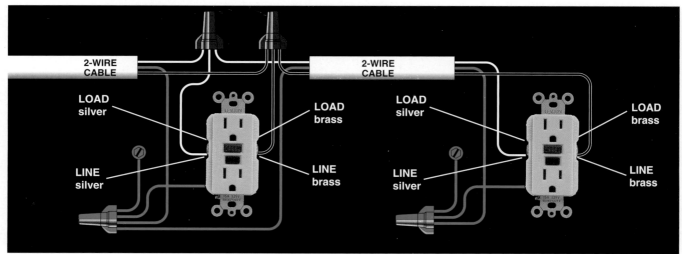

GFCI Receptacle Circuit: Wire GFCI receptacles on a dedicated 20-amp circuit, using this circuit map. To prevent "nuisance tripping" caused by normal power surges, GFCIs should be connected only at the LINE screw terminal, so they protect a single location, not the fixtures on the LOAD side of the circuit. This circuit is for all the general-use receptacles in the bathroom—no lighting outlets or bathroom fixtures can be connected to it.

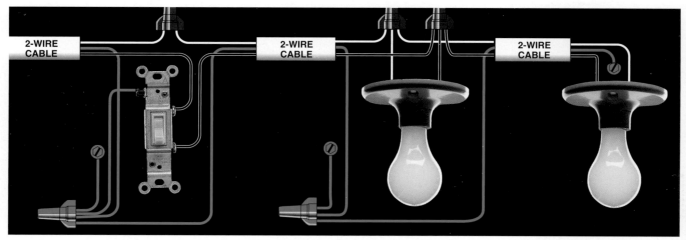

General Lighting Circuit: Use this layout to provide power for light fixtures. The circuit can be wired with a single switch to control a number of linked light fixtures, or multiple switches to control specific fixtures (see below).

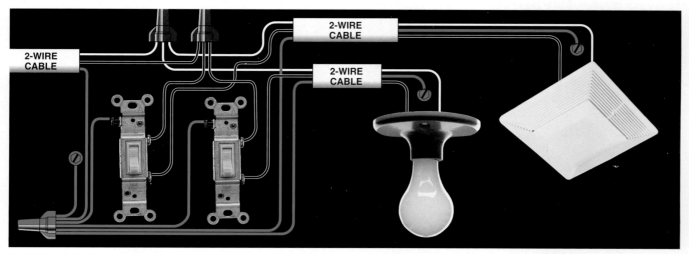

Switched Fixture Circuit: Use one double-gang box to house two switches run by the same circuit. A single feed cable provides power to both switches; each switch controls a separate electrical fixture or series of fixtures. A similar layout with two feed cables can be used to place switches from different circuits in the same box.

Wiring Codes & Permits

To ensure public safety, your community requires that you get a permit to install new wiring and have the completed work reviewed by an appointed inspector. Electrical inspectors use the National Electrical Code (NEC) as the primary authority for evaluating wiring, but they also follow the local Building Code and Electrical Code standards.

As you begin planning new circuits, call or visit your local electrical inspector and discuss the project with him or her. The inspector can tell you which of the national and local code requirements apply to your job, and may give you a packet of information summarizing these regulations. Later, when you apply to the inspector for a work permit, he or she will expect you to understand the local guidelines as well as a few basic National Electrical Code requirements.

The National Electrical Code is a set of standards that provides minimum safety requirements for wiring installations. It is revised every three years.

In addition to being the final authority of code requirements, inspectors are electrical professionals with years of experience. Although they have busy schedules, most inspectors are happy to answer questions and help you design well-planned circuits.

As with any project, if you are uncomfortable working with electricity hire a professional electrician to complete new wiring installations and connections.

The bathroom requirements listed below are for general information only. Contact your local electrical inspector for specific wiring regulations:

- A separate 20-amp receptacle circuit for small appliances is required.
- All receptacles must be GFCI protected.
- Light fixtures and switches must be on a separate circuit. (A minimum 15-amp circuit.)
- All fixture and appliance switches must be grounded.
- There must be at least one ceiling-mounted light fixture.
- Whirlpools and other large fixtures or appliances are required to be on a dedicated circuit.

The manufacturers of some home spa fixtures, such as saunas and whirlpools, may specify that a certified electrician make the electrical connections for their product. Make sure to follow these directions, as doing otherwise may result in the warranty being voided.

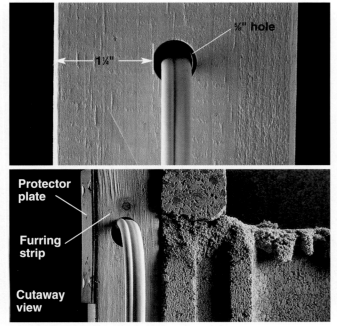

Cables must be protected against damage by nails and screws by at least 1¼" of wood (top). When cables pass through 2 × 2 furring strips (bottom), protect the cables with metal protector plates.

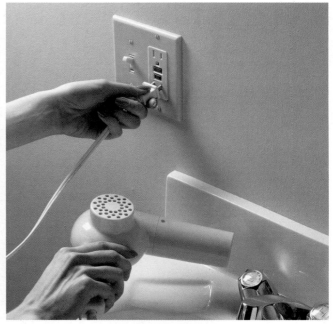

Kitchen and bathroom receptacles must be protected by a GFCI (page 135). Also, all outdoor receptacles and general-use receptacles in an unfinished basement or crawlspace must be protected by a GFCI.

129

Label the cables entering each box to indicate their destinations. In boxes with complex wiring configurations, also tag the individual wires to simplify the final hookups. After all cables are installed, your rough-in work is ready to be reviewed by an electrical inspector.

Installing Electrical Boxes & Cables

Install electrical boxes for all devices only after your wiring plan has been approved by an inspector. Use your plan as a guide and follow electrical code guidelines when laying out box positions. Some electrical fixtures, like recessed lights and exhaust fans, have their own wire connection boxes; install these along with the other electrical boxes.

After your boxes are installed, run all of the non-metallic (NM) cables. Start each new circuit near the service panel or subpanel, and run them to the first boxes in the circuit. Also run any branch cables between boxes on the same circuit. Schedule a rough-in inspection after the cables are run. When the rough-in wiring has been approved, you can close up the walls and install the electrical devices. Finally, make cable connections at the service panel or subpanel yourself (pages 136 to 137), or hire an electrician to complete the task.

Everything You Need
Tools: screwdrivers, drill, ⅝" and 1" bits, bit extender, needlenose pliers, fish tape, cable ripper, combination tool.
Materials: electrical boxes, NM cable, cable clamps and staples, cable lubricant, masking and electrical tape, grounding pigtails, wire connectors.

Tips for Installing Electrical Boxes

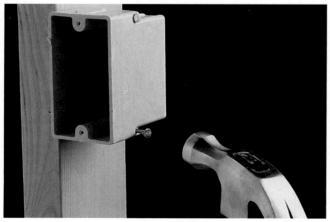

Position each box against a stud so the front face will be flush with the finished wall. For example, if you will be installing ½" drywall, position the box so it extends ½" past the front edge of the stud. Anchor the box by driving the mounting nails into the stud.

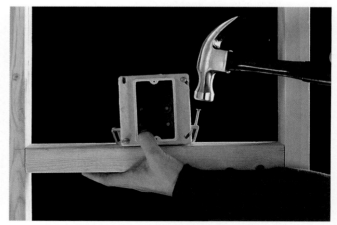

To install a switch box between studs, first install a cross block between the studs, with the top edge 46" above the floor. Position the box on the cross block so the front face will be flush with the finished wall, and drive the mounting nails into the cross block.

How to Install NM Cable in New Framing

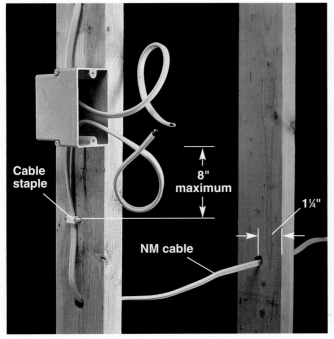

1 Anchor NM sheathed cable to framing members with cable staples driven no more than 4 ft. apart, and within 8" of electrical boxes. Run cable through the framing members by drilling ⅝" holes, set back at least 1¼" from the front of the framing members.

2 Open one knockout for each cable that will enter the box. You can open the knockouts as you install the boxes or wait until you run cable to each box. Open a knockout by striking inside the scored lines of the knockout with a screwdriver and hammer. Then, use the screwdriver to break off any sharp edges that might damage the vinyl sheathing of the cable.

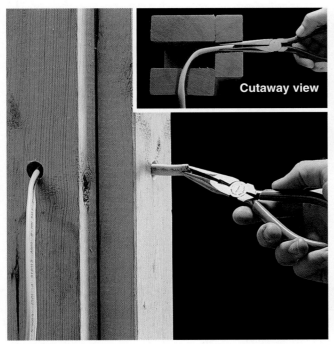

At corners, drill intersecting holes in adjoining faces of studs. Form a slight L-shaped bend in the end of the cable at corners and insert it into one hole. Retrieve the cable through the other hole, using needlenose pliers (inset).

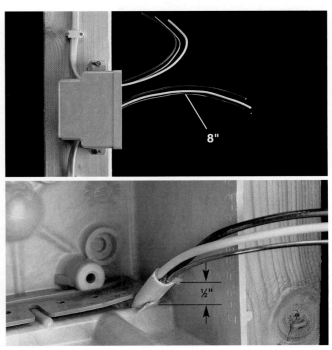

3 Extend wire at least 8" beyond the front face of electrical boxes (top photo). Cables should have at least ½" of outer sheathing extending intact into the box (bottom photo). The sheathing protects the cable wires from possible damage caused by the clamp.

131

How to Install NM Cable in Finished Walls

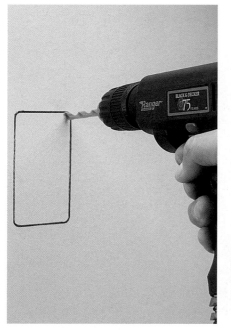

1 Position a retrofit electrical box at the box location, then outline it with a pencil. Drill a pilot hole at one corner of the outline, then complete the cutout with a drywall saw or jig saw.

2 Plan a route for running cable between electrical boxes. Where cable must cross framing members, cut an access opening in the wall or ceiling surface, then cut a notch into the framing member with a wood chisel.

3 Insert a fish tape (a semi-rigid wire used to pull cables) through the access hole (top photo), and extend it until it pokes out of the cutout for the new electrical box (bottom photo).

Cutaway view

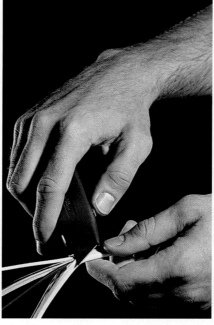

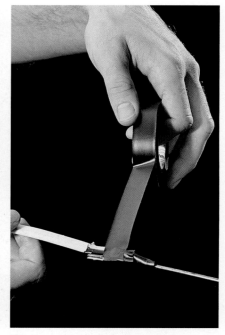

VARIATION: If there is access to ceiling joists above the cutout area, drill a 1" hole down through the top plate and into the wall cavity, using a spade bit. Extend a fish tape through the hole and to the nearest wall cutout.

4 Trim back 2" of outer insulation from the end of the NM cable, then insert the wires through the loop at the tip of the fish tape.

5 Bend the wires against the cable, then use electrical tape to bind them tightly. Apply cable-pulling lubricant to the taped end of the fish tape.

6 Use the fish tape to pull the cable through the remaining access openings until the entire cable run has been completed.

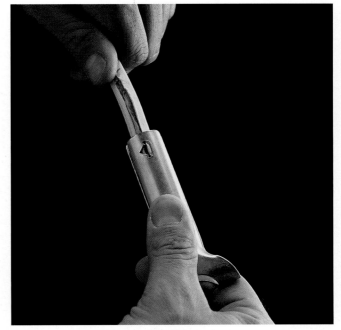

7 Cut cable so at least 18" remains at each end of the cable run, then use a cable ripper to strip back 12" of sheathing from each end.

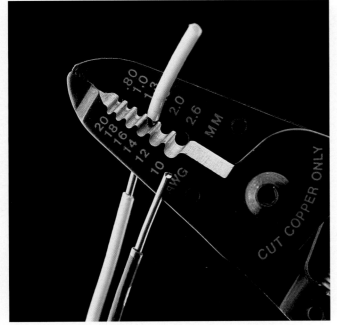

8 Use a wire stripper to remove ¾" of insulation from the end of each wire, at both ends of the cable run.

9 Insert cables into the retrofit box, then tighten the cable clamp. Insert the retrofit box into the cutout, flush against the wall surface. Tighten the mounting screw in the rear of the box. This causes the bracket on the back side of the box to draw the "plaster ears" of the mounting flange tight against the wall surface. Patch any access opening in the wall.

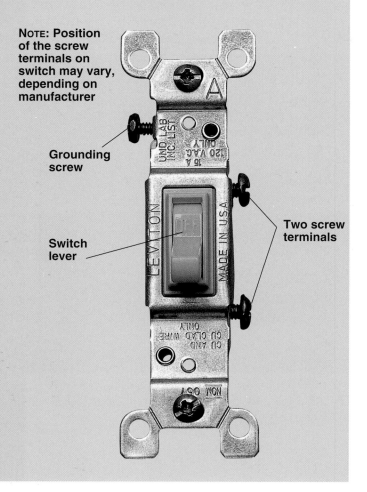

NOTE: Position of the screw terminals on switch may vary, depending on manufacturer

Grounding screw

Switch lever

Two screw terminals

Connecting Switches

A single-pole switch is the most common type of wall switch used in bathrooms. It usually has ON-OFF markings on the switch lever and is used to control a set of lights, an appliance, or a receptacle from a single location. A single-pole switch has two screw terminals and a grounding screw. When installing a single-pole switch, check to make sure the ON marking shows when the switch lever is in the up position.

In a correctly wired single-pole switch, a hot circuit wire is attached to each screw terminal. However, the color and number of wires inside the switch box will vary, depending on the location of the switch along the electrical circuit.

If two cables enter the box, then the switch lies in the middle of the circuit. In this installation, both of the hot wires attached to the switch are black.

If only one cable enters the box, then the switch lies at the end of the circuit. In this installation (sometimes called a switch loop), one of the hot wires is black, but the other hot wire usually is white. A white hot wire should be coded with black tape or paint.

Typical Single-pole Switch Installations

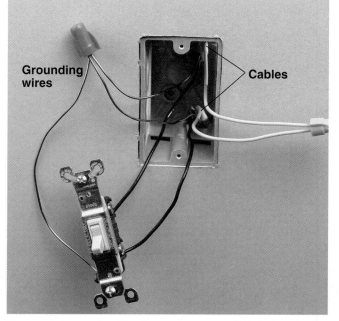

Grounding wires

Cables

Two cables enter the box when a switch is located in the middle of a circuit. Each cable has a white and a black insulated wire, plus a bare copper grounding wire. The black wires are hot and are connected to the screw terminals on the switch. The white wires are neutral and are joined together with a wire connector. Grounding wires are pigtailed to the switch.

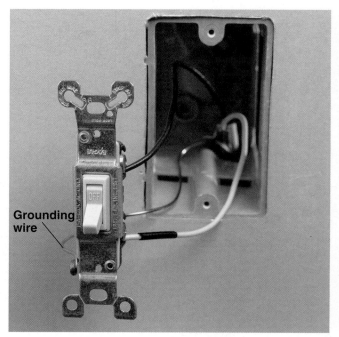

Grounding wire

One cable enters the box when a switch is located at the end of a circuit. The cable has a white and a black insulated wire, plus a bare copper grounding wire. In this installation, both of the insulated wires are hot. The white wire may be labeled with black tape or paint to identify it as a hot wire. The grounding wire is connected to the switch grounding screw.

Connecting GFCI Receptacles

The ground-fault circuit-interrupter (GFCI) receptacle protects against electrical shock caused by a faulty appliance, or a worn cord or plug. It senses small changes in current flow and can shut off power in as little as $\frac{1}{40}$ of a second.

GFCIs are required in bathrooms, kitchens, garages, crawl spaces, unfinished basements, and outdoor receptacle locations. Consult your local codes for any requirements regarding the installation of GFCI receptacles. Most GFCIs use standard screw terminal connections, but some have wire leads and are attached with wire connectors. Because the body of a GFCI receptacle is larger than a standard receptacle, small crowded electrical boxes may need to be replaced with more spacious boxes.

The GFCI receptacle may be wired to protect only itself (single location), or it can be wired to protect all receptacles, switches, and light fixtures from the GFCI "forward" to the end of the circuit (multiple locations). See the circuit maps on page 128.

Because the GFCI is so sensitive, it is most effective when wired to protect a single location. The more receptacles any one GFCI protects, the more susceptible it is to "phantom tripping," shutting off power because of tiny, normal fluctuations in current flow.

How to Connect a GFCI Receptacle

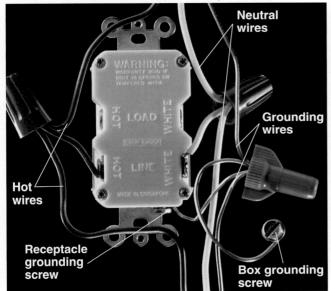

A GFCI wired for single-location protection (shown from the back) has hot and neutral wires connected only to the screw terminals marked LINE. A GFCI connected for single-location protection may be wired as either an end-of-run or middle-of-run configuration (page 128).

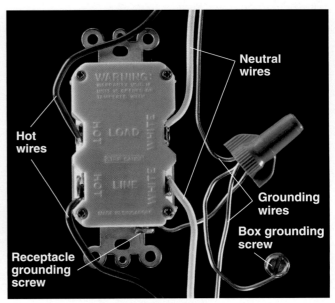

A GFCI wired for multiple-location protection (shown from the back) has one set of hot and neutral wires connected to the LINE pair of screw terminals, and the other set connected to the LOAD pair of screw terminals. A GFCI receptacle connected for multiple-location protection may be wired only as a middle-of-run configuration.

Setscrew terminals

Neutral bus bar

Test for current before touching any parts inside a circuit breaker panel. With the main breaker turned off but all the other breakers turned on, touch one probe of a neon tester to the neutral bus bar, and touch the other probe to each setscrew on one of the double-pole breakers (not the main breaker). If the tester does not light for either setscrew, it is safe to work in the panel.

Connecting Circuit Breakers

The last step in a wiring project is connecting circuits at the breaker panel. After this is done, the work is ready for the final inspection.

Circuits are connected at the main breaker panel, if it has enough open slots, or at a circuit breaker subpanel. When working at a subpanel, make sure the feeder breaker at the main panel has been turned OFF, and test for power (photo, left) before touching any parts in the subpanel.

Make sure the circuit breaker amperage does not exceed the "ampacity" of the circuit wires you are connecting to it. Also be aware that circuit breaker styles and installation techniques vary according to manufacturer. Use breakers designed for your type of panel.

NOTE: Hire a professional to complete any projects you are uncomfortable completing yourself.

Everything You Need

Tools: screwdriver, hammer, pencil, combination tool, cable ripper, neon circuit tester, pliers.

Materials: cable clamps, single- and double-pole circuit breakers.

How to Connect Circuit Breakers

1 Shut off the main circuit breaker in the main circuit breaker panel (if you are working in a sub-panel, shut off the feeder breaker in the main panel). Remove the panel coverplate, taking care not to touch the parts inside the panel. Test for power (photo, top).

2 Open a knockout in the side of the circuit breaker panel, using a screwdriver and hammer. Attach a cable clamp to the knockout.

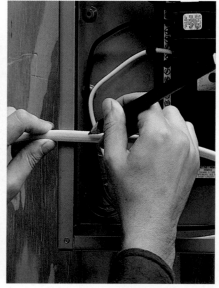

3 Hold a cable across the front of the panel near the knockout, and mark the sheathing about ½" inside the edge of the panel. Strip the cable from the marked line to the end, using a cable ripper. (There should be 18" to 24" of excess cable.) Insert the cable through the clamp and into the service panel, then tighten the clamp.

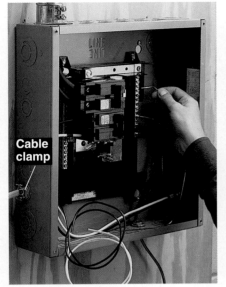

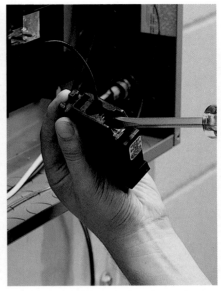

4 Bend the bare copper grounding wire around the inside edge of the panel to an open setscrew terminal on the grounding bus bar. Insert the wire into the opening on the bus bar, and tighten the setscrew. Fold any excess wire around the inside edge of the panel.

5 For 120-volt circuits, bend the white circuit wire around the outside of the panel to an open setscrew terminal on the neutral bus bar. Clip away any excess wire, then strip ½" of insulation from the wire, using a combination tool. Insert the wire into the terminal opening, and tighten the setscrew.

6 Strip ½" of insulation from the end of the black circuit wire. Insert the wire into the setscrew terminal on a new single-pole circuit breaker, and tighten the setscrew.

7 Slide one end of the circuit breaker onto the guide hook, then press it firmly against the bus bar until it snaps into place. (Breaker installation may vary, depending on the manufacturer.) Fold excess black wire around the inside edge of the panel.

8 **120/240-volt circuits (top):** Connect the red and black wires to a double-pole breaker. Connect the white wire to the neutral bus bar and the grounding wire to the grounding bus bar.
240-volt circuits (bottom): Attach the white and black wires to the double-pole breaker, tagging the white wire with black tape. There is no neutral bus bar connection on this circuit.

9 Remove the appropriate breaker knockout on the panel coverplate to make room for the new circuit breaker. A single-pole breaker requires one knockout, while a double-pole breaker requires two knockouts. Reattach the coverplate, and label the new circuit on the panel index.

Bathroom Remodeling Projects

Select showers, bathtubs, and spas first when planning your new bathroom. These fixtures, available in a limited range of colors and styles, set the tone for an entire room. Sinks, cabinets, tile, and accessories are available in many styles and colors, and can be matched easily to a new tub or whirlpool.

Installing Showers, Bathtubs & Spas

Installing and hooking up plumbing for bathtubs and showers is a fairly simple job. Whirlpools and saunas are more complicated because they also require electrical hookups, as well as structural frames.

The most difficult task when installing tubs, showers, and spas is moving the bulky fixtures and materials up stairways and through narrow doorways. With a two-wheel dolly and a little help, however, the job is much easier. Measure your doorways and hallways to make sure that any large fixture you buy will fit through them.

If you do not plan to remove and replace your

wall surfaces, you still should cut away at least 6" of wall surface above a tub or whirlpool to allow easier access during installation.

This chapter contains the follow projects:

- Building Showers (pages 142 to 147)
- Building a Custom-tiled Shower Base
  (pages 148 to 153)
- Building a Glass Block Shower
  (pages 154 to 159)
- Installing Bathtubs (pages 160 to 163)
- Installing Bathtub Surrounds (pages 164 to 165)
- Installing Whirlpools (pages 166 to 171)
- Installing a Sauna (pages 172 to 177)

Tips for Installing Showers, Bathtubs & Spas

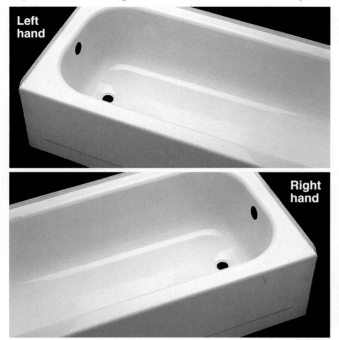

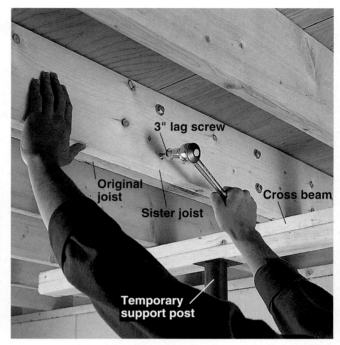

Choose the correct tub for your plumbing setup. Alcove-installed tubs with only one side apron are sold as either "left-hand" or "right-hand" models, depending on the location of the predrilled drain and overflow holes in the tub. To determine which type you need, face into the alcove and check whether the tub drain is on your right or your left.

Install extra floor support if the floor joists below the planned shower, bathtub, or spa location are damaged, too small, or spaced too far apart. Generally, you should attach additional sister joists under the tub area if your current joists are 2 × 10 or smaller, or if they are more than 16" apart. If you are unsure about structural support issues, contact a building inspector or a professional contractor.

Add fiberglass insulation around the body of a bathtub to reduce noise and conserve heat. Before setting the tub in position, wrap unfaced batting around the tub, and secure it with string or twine. For showers, deck-mounted whirlpools, and saunas, insulate between the framing members.

Chisel out mortar around plumbing stub-outs set into basement floors, to make room for drain fittings that slip over the drain pipe. Use a hand maul and masonry chisel, directing the blows away from the pipe, until you have exposed the pipe about 1" below floor level. Wear eye protection and heavy gloves.

Building Showers

Showers can be built in a number of ways, from a number of materials, as discussed on pages 24 to 25. One of the easiest ways to build a shower is to frame an alcove and line it with prefabricated panels. Though water-resistant drywall is the standard backer for prefab panels, always check the manufacturer's recommendations. Some building codes also require a waterproof membrane between the studs and the backer material.

The type of shower base you use will affect the installation sequence. Some bases are made to be installed after the backer; others should be installed first. If your base is going in after the wall surface, be sure to account for the thickness of the surface material when framing the alcove.

Everything You Need

Tools: circular saw, drill, plumbing tools (page 88), hacksaw, channel-type pliers, trowel, level.

Materials: 2 × 4 and 1 × 4 lumber, 16d and 8d nails, plumbing supplies, shower base, rag, dry-set mortar, soap.

Ceramic tile for custom showers is installed the same way as ceramic wall tile. Ceramic shower accessories are mortared in place during the tile installation.

Anti-scald Valves

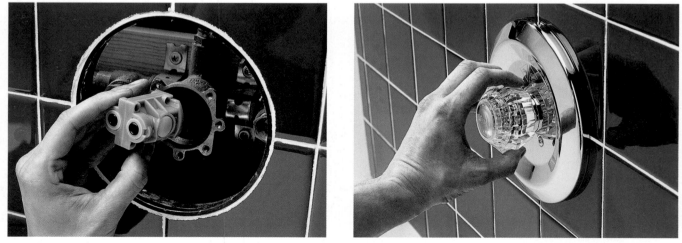

Anti-scald valves are safety devices that protect against sudden water temperature changes. They are required by most building codes for faucets in showers and combination tub-showers. Once installed, faucets with anti-scald valves look like standard faucets.

Anatomy of a Shower

Shower stalls are available in many different sizes and styles, but the basic elements are the same. Most shower stalls have a shower alcove, a supply system, and a drain system.

Shower alcove: The alcove is the frame for the stall, with 2 × 4 walls built to fit around a shower base and blocking to secure the plumbing. The base sets into a mortar bed for support, and water-resistant drywall or cementboard covers the alcove walls.

The supply system: The shower arm extends from the wall, where an elbow fitting connects it to the shower pipe. The pipe runs up from the faucet, which is fed by the hot and cold water supplies.

The drain system: The drain cover attaches to the drain tailpiece. A rubber gasket on the tailpiece slips over the drain pipe, leading to the P-trap and the branch drain.

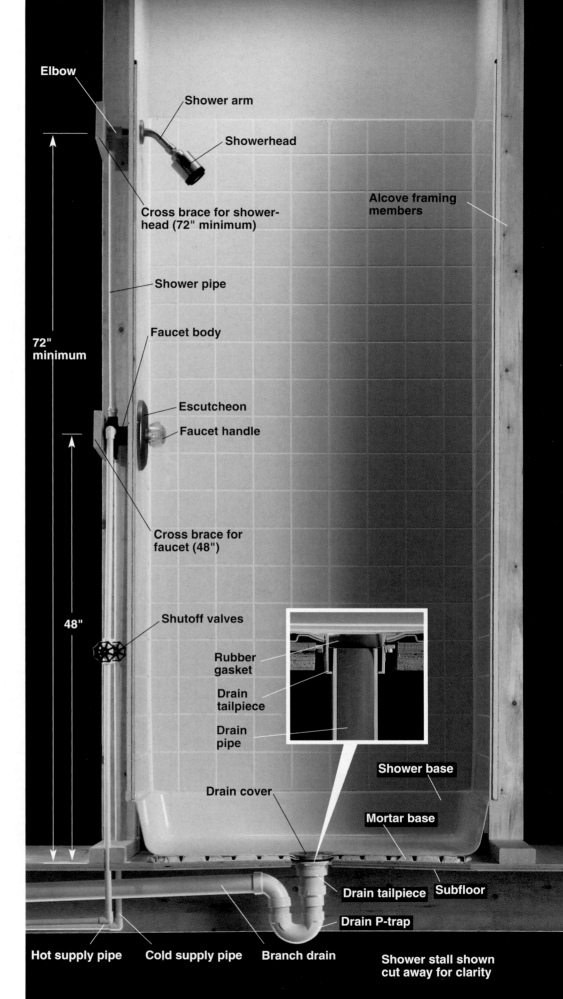

Elbow

Shower arm

Showerhead

Alcove framing members

Cross brace for shower-head (72" minimum)

Shower pipe

Faucet body

72" minimum

Escutcheon

Faucet handle

Cross brace for faucet (48")

48"

Shutoff valves

Rubber gasket

Drain tailpiece

Drain pipe

Shower base

Mortar base

Drain cover

Drain tailpiece   Subfloor

Drain P-trap

Hot supply pipe   Cold supply pipe   Branch drain   Shower stall shown cut away for clarity

How to Frame a Shower Alcove

1 Measure the shower base and mark its dimensions on the floor. Measure from center of drain pipe to ensure that drain will be centered in the shower alcove. Install blocking between studs in existing walls to provide a surface for anchoring the alcove walls.

2 Build 2 × 4 alcove walls just outside the marked lines on the floor. Anchor the alcove walls to the existing wall and the subfloor. If necessary, drill holes or cut notches in the bottom plate for plumbing pipes.

3 In the stud cavity that will hold the shower faucet and shower-head, mark reference points 48" and 72" above the floor to indicate the location of the faucet and the showerhead. For taller users, you may want to install the shower-head higher than 72".

4 Attach 1 × 4 cross braces between studs to pro-vide surfaces for attaching the showerhead and the faucet. Center the cross braces on the marked reference points, and position them flush with the back edge of the studs to provide adequate space for the faucet body (inset) and showerhead fittings.

5 Following the manufacturer's directions, assemble the plumbing pipes and attach the faucet body and showerhead fitting to the cross braces. (See pages 102 to 107 for information on working with plastic plumbing pipes.)

How to Install a Shower Base

1 Trim the drain pipe in the floor to the height recommended by the manufacturer (usually near or slightly above floor level). Stuff a rag into the drain pipe, and leave it in until you are ready to make the drain connections.

2 Prepare the shower drain piece as directed by the manufacturer, and attach it to the drain opening in the shower base (see inset photo, page 143). Tighten locknut securely onto drain tailpiece to ensure a waterproof fit.

3 Mix a batch of dry-set mortar, then apply a 1" layer to the subfloor, covering the shower base area. Mortar stabilizes and levels the shower base.

4 Apply soap to the outside of the drain pipe in the floor, and to the inside of the rubber gasket in the drain tailpiece. Set the shower base onto the drain pipe, and press down slowly until the rubber gasket in the drain tailpiece fits snugly over the drain pipe.

5 Press the shower base down into the dry-set mortar, carefully adjusting it so it is level. If directed by manufacturer, anchor the shower base with screws driven through the edge flanges and into the wall studs. Let mortar dry for 6 to 8 hours.

How to Install a Shower Panel Kit

1 Attach the shower dome, if included with the shower panel kit, to the walls of the shower alcove. Refer to the manufacturer's directions for the exact installation height for the dome.

2 Screw the mounting strips for the shower door frame to both sides of the shower opening.

3 Make a template for marking the pipe hole locations in the shower panels, using the panel kit shipping carton or heavy paper. Mark holes for the showerhead and the faucet handle(s).

4 Lay the template over the shower panel, and drill out holes with a hole saw. Cut larger holes with a jig saw. For more accurate cuts, use plywood to support the panel near the cutout area.

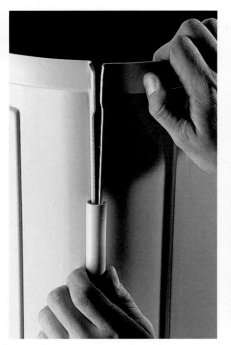

5 Assemble the shower panels according to the manufacturer's directions. Most shower panels are joined together with clips or interlocking flanges before they are installed.

6 Apply heavy beads of panel adhesive to the walls of the shower alcove, and to the mounting strips for the door frame.

7 Slide the shower panels into the alcove, and press them against the walls. Pull the panels away from the walls for about 1 minute to allow the adhesive to begin to set, then press the panels back in place.

8 Wedge lengths of lumber covered with scraps of carpeting or rags between the shower panels to hold them in place until the adhesive has set completely. Allow the panel adhesive to dry for at least 24 hours before removing the braces.

9 Attach the faucet handle(s), shower arm, and showerhead (pages 240 to 243), then caulk the seams between the panels and around the base, using tub & tile caulk.

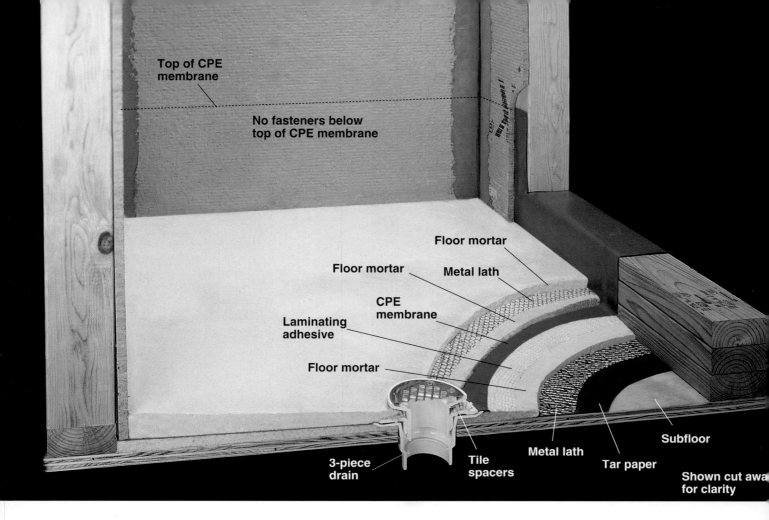

Top of CPE membrane

No fasteners below top of CPE membrane

Floor mortar

Floor mortar

Metal lath

CPE membrane

Laminating adhesive

Floor mortar

3-piece drain

Tile spacers

Metal lath

Tar paper

Subfloor

Shown cut awa for clarity

Building a Custom-Tiled Shower Base

A custom-tiled shower base offers you great flexibility in the location and size of your shower. Building the base is quite simple, though it does require time and some knowledge of basic masonry techniques because the base is formed primarily using mortar.

A custom shower base is built in three layers to ensure proper water drainage: the pre pan, the shower pan, and the shower floor. A mortar pre pan is first built on top of the subfloor, establishing a slope toward the drain of ¼" for every 12" of shower floor. Next, a waterproof chlorinated polyethylene (CPE) membrane forms the shower pan, providing a watertight seal for the shower base. Finally, a second mortar bed reinforced with wire mesh is installed for the shower floor, providing a surface for tile installation. If water penetrates the tiled shower floor, the shower pan and sloped pre pan will redirect it to the weep holes of the 3-piece drain.

One of the most important steps in building a custom shower base is testing the shower pan after installation (step 13). This allows you to locate and fix any leaks to prevent costly damage.

The materials needed to build a tiled shower base can be found at most home centers or at a tile specialty store. Be sure to contact your local building department regarding code restrictions and to secure the necessary permits.

Everything You Need

Tools: tape measure, circular saw, hammer, utility knife, stapler, 2-ft. level, mortar mixing box, trowel, wood float, felt-tip marker, ratchet wrench, expandable stopper, drill, tin snips, torpedo level, tools for installing tile (pages 184, 202).

Materials: 2 x 4 and 2 x 10 framing lumber, 16d galvanized common nails, 15# building paper, staples, 3-piece shower drain, PVC primer, PVC cement, galvanized finish nails, galvanized metal lath, thick-bed floor mortar ("deck mud"), latex mortar additive, laminating adhesive, CPE waterproof membrane & preformed dam corners, CPE membrane solvent glue, CPE membrane sealant, cementboard and materials for installing cementboard (page 182), materials for installing tile (pages 184, 202).

How to Build a Custom-Tiled Shower Base

1 After framing-in the shower alcove (page 144), cut three 2 × 4s to size for the curb and fasten them to the floor joists and the studs at the shower threshold with 16d galvanized common nails. Also cut 2 × 10 lumber to size and install in the stud bays around the perimeter of the shower base.

Curb

2 Staple 15# building paper to the subfloor of the shower base. Disassemble the 3-piece shower drain and glue the bottom piece to the drain pipe with PVC cement (page 105). Partially screw the drain bolts into the drain piece, and stuff a rag into the drain pipe to prevent mortar from falling into the drain.

Reference line

3 Mark the height of the bottom drain piece on the wall farthest from the center of the drain. Measure from the center of the drain straight across to that wall, then raise the height mark ¼" for every 12" of shower floor to slope the pre pan toward the drain. Trace a reference line at the height mark around the perimeter of the entire alcove, using a level.

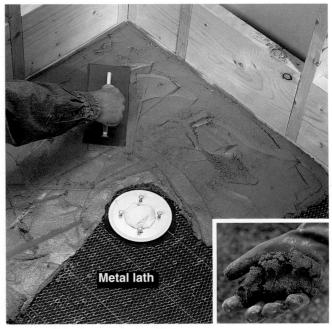

Metal lath

4 Staple galvanized metal lath over the building paper; cut a hole in the lath ½" from the drain. Mix floor mortar (or "deck mud") to a fairly dry consistency, using a latex additive for strength; mortar should hold its shape when squeezed (inset). Trowel the mortar onto the subfloor, building the pre pan from the flange of the drain piece to the height line on the perimeter of the walls.

(continued next page)

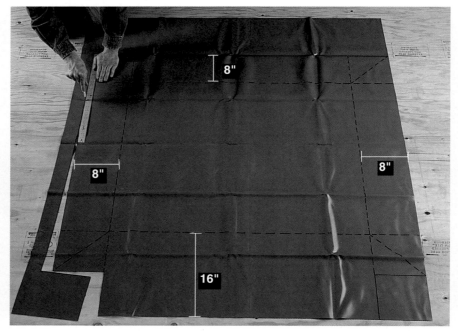

5 Continue using the trowel to form the pre pan, checking the slope using a level and filling any low spots with mortar. Finish the surface of the pre pan with a wood float until it is even and smooth. Allow the mortar to cure overnight.

6 Measure the dimensions of the shower floor, and mark it out on a sheet of CPE waterproof membrane, using a felt-tipped marker. From the floor outline, measure out and mark an additional 8" for each wall and 16" for the curb end. Cut the membrane to size, using a utility knife and straightedge. Be careful to cut on a clean, smooth surface to prevent puncturing the membrane.

7 Measure to find the exact location of the drain and mark it on the membrane, outlining the outer diameter of the drain flange. Cut a circular piece of CPE membrane roughly 2" larger than the outline, then use CPE membrane solvent glue to weld it in place to reinforce the seal at the drain.

8 Coat the pre pan, curb, and perimeter blocking with laminating adhesive and a notched trowel, then apply CPE sealant around the drain. Fold the membrane along the floor outline, folding the corners as shown in step 9. Set the membrane over the pre pan so the reinforced drain seal is centered over the drain bolts.

9 Working from the drain to the walls, carefully smooth out any bubbles from under the membrane. Tuck the membrane tight into each corner, folding the extra material into triangular flaps. Apply CPE solvent glue to one side, press the flap flat, then staple it in place (inset). Staple the top edge of the membrane to the blocking; do not staple below the top of the curb, on the curb itself.

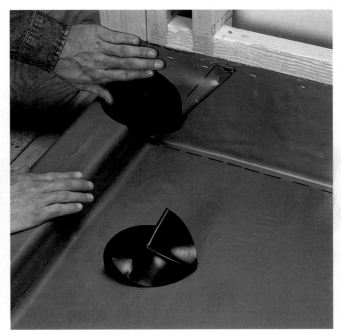

10 At the shower curb, cut the membrane along the studs so it can be folded over the curb. Solvent-glue a dam corner at each inside corner of the curb. Do not fasten the dam corners with staples.

11 At the reinforced drain seal on the membrane, locate and mark the drain bolts. Press the membrane down around the bolts, then use a utility knife to carefully cut a slit just large enough for the bolts to poke through. Push the membrane down over the bolts.

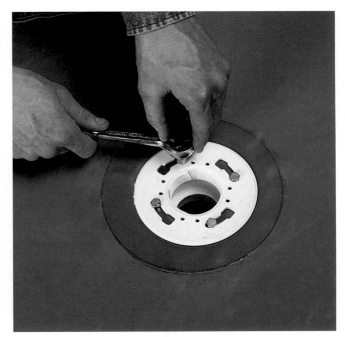

12 Use a utility knife to carefully cut away only enough of the membrane to expose the drain and allow the middle drain piece to fit in place. Remove the drain bolts, then position the middle drain piece over the bolt holes. Reinstall the bolts, tightening them evenly and firmly to create a watertight seal.

(continued next page)

13 Test the shower pan for leaks overnight. Place a balloon tester (inset) in the drain below the weep holes, and fill the pan with water, to 1" below the top of the curb. Mark the water level and let the water sit overnight. If the water level remains the same, the pan holds water. If the level is lower, locate and fix leaks in the pan using patches of membrane and CPE solvent.

14 Install cementboard on the alcove walls (pages 182 to 183), using ¼" wood shims to lift the bottom edge off the CPE membrane. To prevent puncturing the membrane, do not use fasteners in the lower 8" of the cementboard. Cut a piece of metal lath to fit around the three sides of the curb. Bend the lath so it tightly conforms to the curb. Pressing the lath against the top of the curb, staple it to the outside face of the curb. Mix enough mortar for the two sides of the curb.

15 Overhang the front edge of the curb with a straight 1× board, so it is flush with the outer wall material. Apply mortar to the mesh with a trowel, building to the edge of the board. Clear away excess mortar, then use a torpedo level to check for plumb, making adjustments as needed. Repeat for the inside face of the curb. NOTE: The top of the curb will be finished after tile is installed (step 19). Allow the mortar to cure overnight.

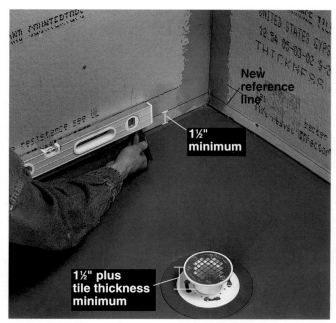

New reference line

1½" minimum

1½" plus tile thickness minimum

16 Attach the drain strainer piece to the drain, adjusting it to a minimum of 1½" above the shower pan. On one wall, mark 1½" up from the shower pan, then use a level to draw a reference line around the perimeter of the shower base. Because the pre pan establishes the ¼" per foot slope, this measurement will maintain that slope.

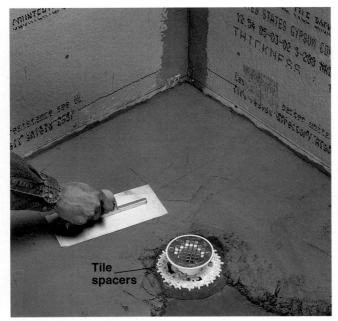

17 Spread tile spacers over the weep holes of the drain to prevent mortar from plugging the holes. Mix the floor mortar, then build up the shower floor to roughly half the thickness of the base. Cut metal lath to cover the mortar bed, keeping it ½" from the drain (see photo in next step).

18 Continue to add mortar, building the floor to the reference line on the walls. Use a level to check the slope, and pack mortar into low spots with a trowel. Leave space at the drain for the thickness of the tile. Float the surface using a wood float until it is smooth and slopes evenly to the drain. When finished, allow the mortar to cure overnight before installing the tiles.

19 After the floor has cured, draw reference lines and establish the tile layout, then mix a batch of thinset mortar and install the floor tile (pages 202 to 209). At the curb, cut the tiles for the inside to protrude ½" above the unfinished top of the curb, and the tiles for the outside to protrude ⅝" above the top, establishing a ⅛" slope so water drains back into the shower. Use a level to check the tops of the tiles for level as you work.

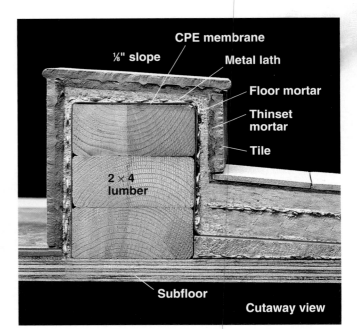

20 Mix enough floor mortar to cover the unfinished top of the curb, then pack it in place between the tiles, using a trowel. Screed off the excess mortar flush with the tops of the side tiles. Allow the mortar to cure, then install bullnose cap tile. Install the wall tile, then grout, clean, and seal all the tile (pages 184 to 190). After the grout has cured fully, run a bead of silicone caulk around all inside corners to create control joints.

Building a Glass Block Shower

A glass block shower is one of the most striking additions you can make to a bathroom. Glass block instantly adds a distinctive sparkle to a room, allowing light to flood shadowy corners. Mortared glass block is strong, easy to maintain, and impervious to water, making it a perfect shower material.

In this project we build our shower around a standard fiberglass shower base, modified to fit inside a concrete curb. Because glass block cannot be cut, it is crucial that the shower base fit the length of the glass block walls. For this project we used a 34" × 48" base to fit our shower design using 8" × 8" glass block. Other options for a glass block shower include building a custom-tiled shower base or using specially designed prefab shower bases built to hold and support glass block (see variations, page 159).

The key to any shower installation is making sure the base remains watertight. Concrete is a better option than wood for the curb in this project because it easily molds around the shower base, ensuring a tight fit, and it will not swell and produce gaps if water ever gets in. The curb is firmly anchored to the floor by pouring it over lag screws partially driven into the subfloor.

For best results when laying glass block, mix just enough mortar for about 30 minutes of work at a time. If possible, try to lay half of the courses on one day and finish on a second day. This will give the mortar in the first section time to harden, and will make the wall more stable as you climb higher.

The glass block wall is secured to the adjoining wall by means of metal panel anchors. Foam expansion strips between the glass block and the existing wall allow for some independent movement of each as the house settles.

Because of its weight (each block weighs 6 pounds), a glass block shower requires a sturdy foundation. A 4"-thick concrete basement floor should be strong enough, but a wood floor may need reinforcing (see Tip on page 155). Contact the local building department for requirements in your area. Also bear in mind that glass block products and installation techniques vary by manufacturer—ask a glass block retailer or manufacturer for advice about the best products and methods for your project.

Everything You Need

Tools: jig saw, straightedge, hammer, plumb bob, chalk line, drill, mixing box, socket wrench, paintbrush, wire cutter, rubber-ended trowel, level, jointing tool, sponge.

Materials: fiberglass shower base, dry-set mortar, 1 × 6 lumber, ½" × 2" filler strips, glass block (standard, corner, end), plastic sheeting, 4" lag screws, concrete, asphalt roofing cement, panel anchors, 2½" drywall screws, foam expansion strips, glass block mortar, glass block spacers, straight board, ladder-type reinforcement wire, 16-gauge wire, silicone caulk, mortar sealer.

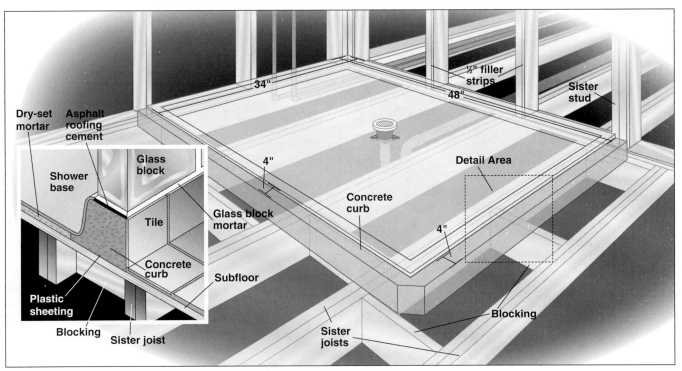

TIP: Install water supply and drain pipes before you begin the construction of the glass block shower. If you have to adjust the position of your base to fit the block wall (step 2), take this into account as you mark the location for the shower drain. While the floor is open for the plumbing, reinforce the floor joists beneath the shower by installing sister joists and blocking that are the same size as the existing joists. Add sister studs in the existing walls where the glass block will meet the walls.

How to Build a Glass Block Shower

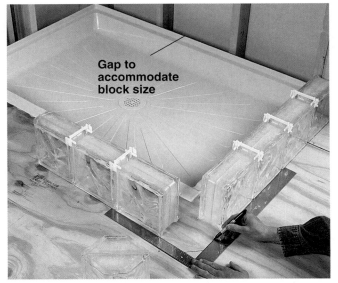

1 In order to create a watertight seal between the shower base, the concrete curb, and the glass block, use a jig saw to remove the front edge of the shower base threshold. Remove any vertical flange along the glass block side of the base, creating a smooth transition between the base and the curb. To ensure straight cuts, use a straightedge to guide your saw.

2 Set the shower base in place and dry-lay the first course of glass block and spacers. To allow for the wall material and expansion strips, include a gap between the stud wall and the first block. If there is space between the front block wall and the base, pull the base out from the wall slightly, so it is flush with the inside edge of the glass block, then mark reference lines for the curb outline. Attach ½" filler strips to the studs before you install the backerboard and wall material.

(continued next page)

How to Build a Glass Block Shower (continued)

Filler strips

3 Prepare the shower base drain for installation according to the manufacturer's directions. Mix a batch of dry-set mortar, then apply a 1" layer to the subfloor, covering the shower base area. Install the base onto the drain pipe. Press the base into the mortar and adjust it so it is level. Allow the mortar to dry for 6 to 8 hours (see page 145).

4 Build forms for the concrete curb from 1x lumber ripped even with the height of the shower base. Align the forms along the reference lines, check that they are level with the top edge of the base, then temporarily anchor them to the subfloor. Line the bottom of the forms with plastic to keep moisture from soaking into the subfloor. To provide anchoring for the curb, drive 4" lag screws 2" into the subfloor inside the forms, spaced every 12".

5 Mix a batch of concrete according to the manufacturer's directions. Pack the forms evenly with concrete. Rap the forms with a hammer to release air bubbles and settle the concrete. Run a 2 × 4 screed board over the forms to level off the concrete. Cover the curb with plastic and allow it to harden for two days, then remove the forms.

6 Wall material, such as solid-surface or fiberglass shower surrounds or ceramic tile, can be installed either before or after the glass block installation, but will go more quickly without the walls in the way. However, it is best to wait to tile around the outside of the curb until the finished flooring has been installed.

7 Spread a thick layer of asphalt roofing cement over the top of the dry curb, just up to the lip of the shower base. This will help to ensure a watertight seal between the curb and shower base and provide a smooth base for the mortar bed. When the asphalt has completely dried, you can begin laying block.

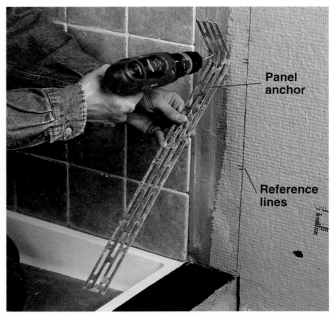

8 Mark plumb lines on the wall, straight up from the sides of the curb. Mark the finished height of each course along the lines. Fasten a panel anchor to the anchor stud at the top of every second course, using 2½" drywall screws. Cut foam expansion strips to size and adhere them to the wall between the anchors. NOTE: When installing the glass block, do not mortar between the blocks and the expansion strips.

9 Mix a batch of glass block mortar and lay a ⅜"-thick mortar bed along one side of the curb. Beginning at the corner, lay the first course. Use spacers at the mortar joint locations (follow the manufacturer's directions for modifying spacers for the corner blocks and the bottom and sides of the wall). Butter the leading edge of each block with enough mortar to fill the sides of both blocks. Make sure the faces of the block are plumb with the curb edge.

10 Lay the remainder of the course, plumbing and leveling each block as you work. Then check the entire course, using a flat board and a level. Tap the blocks into place using the rubber end of your trowel or a rubber mallet. At the top of the course, fill the joints with mortar. Then, lay a ¼" bed of mortar for the second course.

(continued next page)

11 Lay the block for the second course, this time starting at the wall. For the remaining courses, install the corner block last. Check each block for level and plumb as you work. Apply a half bed of mortar (⅛") over the second course. Press the panel anchor into the mortar. Repeat this process at each anchor location.

12 Add reinforcement wire in the same joints as the panel anchors, overlapping the anchors by 6". At the corners, cut the inner rail of the wire, bend the outer rail to follow the corner, then tie the inner rail ends together with 16-gauge wire. Cover the wire and panel anchor with another ⅛" mortar bed, then lay the next course of block.

13 Check the mortar after each course: when it is hard enough to resist light finger pressure (usually within 30 minutes), twist off the T-spacer tabs (inset) and pack mortar in the voids. Then, tool all of the joints with a jointing tool. Clean the glass block thoroughly, using a wet sponge and rinsing it often. Allow the surface to dry, then remove any cloudy residue with a clean, dry cloth.

14 Allow the mortar to dry for 24 hours, then run a thick bead of silicone caulk between the glass block and the shower base. Caulk the seams between the wall and the glass block, both inside and outside the shower. Install a door, if desired, according to the manufacturer's directions. After two weeks, apply a sealer to the mortar to prevent discoloration. NOTE: The shower can be used before sealing once the mortar has dried.

Installation Variation: Building a Floor-to-ceiling Glass Block Shower

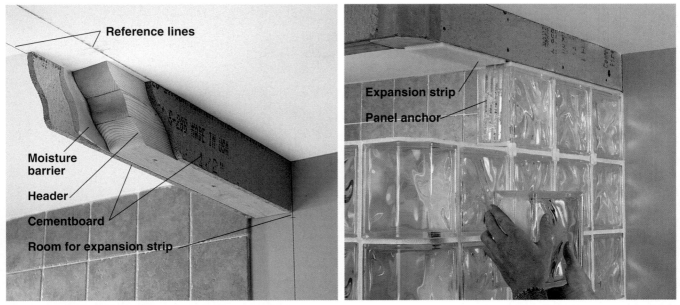

Reference lines

Expansion strip

Panel anchor

Moisture barrier

Header

Cementboard

Room for expansion strip

To extend your glass block shower to the ceiling, extend the plumb lines on the wall (step 8) onto the ceiling directly above your curb. Snap chalk lines to mark the location for the header. To determine the height of the header, measure from the final course mark on the wall to the ceiling and then subtract ⅜" for expansion. Build the header from pressure-treated 2 × 4s, ripped to 3" in width, stacked and fastened with construction adhesive and 2½" screws. Attach ½" cementboard to the sides of the header, including a moisture barrier on the shower side (left). As you install the final course of glass block, attach panel anchors to the header, running vertically between every other block along the top row (right). Install expansion strips above the final course. Do not mortar between the block and the expansion strips. Caulk the gap between the header and the final course of block. Finish by installing tile along the sides of the header.

Glass Block Shower Variations

A glass block wall can work any-where in the bathroom. Here, built between a tub and shower, glass block divides private areas while still bathing the room in light.

For a customized glass block shower, build a mortared and tiled shower base to fit your shower designs (pages 148 to 153).

Glass block shower kits include a prefab shower base with a built-in support for the glass block. In-stalled just like tradtional shower bases, they eliminate the need to modify the shower base and pour a concrete curb.

159

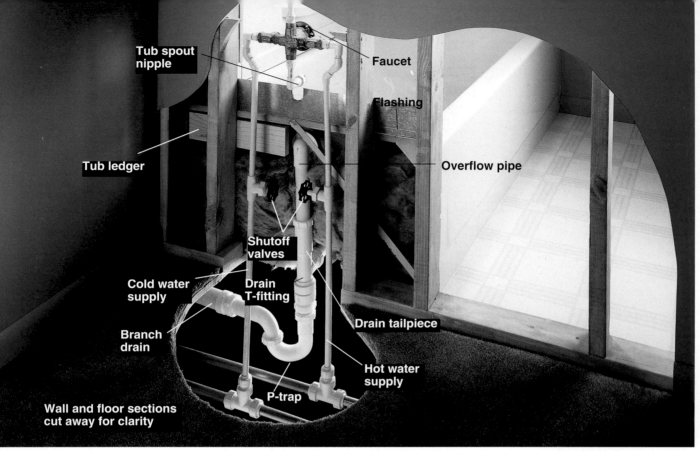

The supply system for a bathtub includes hot and cold supply pipes, shutoff valves, faucet, and a spout. Supply connections can be made before or after the tub is installed. The drain-waste-overflow system for a bathtub includes the overflow pipe, drain T-fitting, P-trap, and branch drain. The overflow pipe assembly is attached to the tub before installation.

Installing Bathtubs

As with showers, standard bathtubs are typically installed in an alcove. If you are building a new alcove, follow the tub manufacturer's specifications regarding its size. Tub alcoves can be finished with ceramic tile (pages 184 to 190) or prefabricated panels (pages 164 to 165).

Take care when handling a new bathtub, since the greatest risk of damaging it occurs during the installation. If the inside of your tub has a protective layer of removable plastic, leave it on until you've completed the installation. Also set a layer of cardboard into the bottom of the tub for added protection while you work.

Everything You Need

Tools: channel-type pliers, hacksaw, 4-ft. level, tape measure, saw, screwdriver, drill, adjustable wrench, hammer, trowel, caulk gun.

Materials: tub protector, shims, galvanized deck screws, drain-waste-overflow kit, lumber (1 × 3, 1 × 4, 2 × 4), galvanized roofing nails, galvanized flashing, tub & tile caulk, dry-set mortar, plumber's putty, soap.

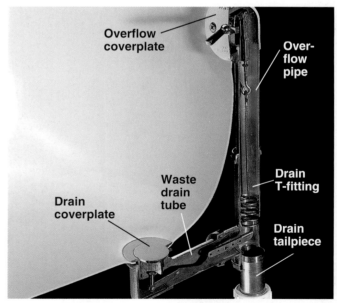

A drain-waste-overflow kit with a stopper mechanism must be attached to the tub before it is installed (page 162). Available in both brass and plastic types, most kits include an overflow coverplate, a height-adjustable overflow pipe, a drain T-fitting and tailpiece, a waste drain tube, and a drain coverplate that screws into the drain tube.

How to Install a Bathtub in an Alcove

1 Attach the faucet body and showerhead fittings to the water supply pipes, and secure the assemblies to 1 × 4 cross braces before installing the tub. Trim the drain pipe to the height specified by the drain-waste-overflow kit manufacturer.

2 Place a tub-bottom protector, which can be cut from the shipping carton, into the tub. Test-fit the tub by sliding it into the alcove so it rests on the subfloor, flush against the wall studs.

3 Check the tub rim with a level. If necessary, shim below the tub until it is level. Mark the top of the nailing flange at each stud. Remove the bathtub from the alcove.

4 Measure the distance from the top of the nailing flange to the underside of the tub rim (inset), and subtract that amount from the marks on the wall studs. Draw a line at that point on each wall stud.

(continued next page)

5 Cut ledger board strips from 1 × 4s, and attach them to the wall studs just below the marks for the underside of the tub rim (step 4), using galvanized deck screws. You may have to install the boards in sections to make room for any structural braces at the ends of the tub.

6 Adjust the drain-waste-overflow assembly to fit the drain and overflow openings. Attach the gaskets and washers as directed by the manufacturer, then position the assembly against the tub drain and overflow openings. Prop up the tub on 2 × 4s, if necessary.

7 Apply plumber's putty to the bottom of the drain coverplate flange, then insert the drain piece into the drain hole in the tub. Screw the drain piece into the waste drain tube, tightening until snug, then insert the pop-up drain plug. Insert the drain plug linkage into the overflow opening, and attach the overflow coverplate with long screws driven into the mounting flange on the overflow pipe. Adjust the drain plug linkage as directed by the manufacturer.

8 Use a trowel to apply a ½"-thick layer of dry-set mortar to the subfloor, covering the entire area where the tub will rest. Lay soaped 1 × 4 runners across the alcove so they rest on the back wall's bottom plate. The runners will allow you to slide the tub into the alcove without disturbing the mortar base.

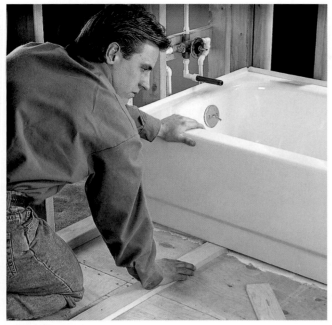

9 Slide the tub over the runners and into position, then remove the runners, allowing the tub to settle into the mortar. Press down evenly on the tub rims until they touch the ledger boards.

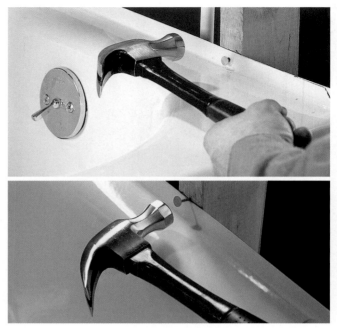

10 Before the mortar sets, nail the tub rim flanges to the wall studs. Attach the rim flanges either by drilling pilot holes into the flanges and nailing with galvanized roofing nails (top), or by driving roofing nails into the studs so the head of the nail covers the rim flange (bottom). After the rim flanges are secured, allow the mortar to dry for 6 to 8 hours.

11 Attach 4"-wide strips of galvanized metal roof flashing over the tub flange to help keep water out of the wall. Leave a ¼" expansion gap between the flashing and the tub rim. Nail the flashing to each wall stud, using 1" galvanized roofing nails.

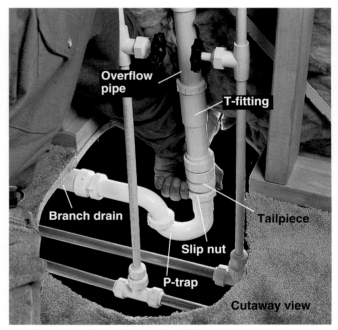

12 Adjust the drain tailpiece so the overflow assembly will fit into the P-trap (you may have to trim it with a hacksaw), then connect it, using a slip nut. Install the wall surfaces, then install the faucet handle and tub spout (page 243). Finally, caulk all around the bathtub.

Installing Bathtub Surrounds

Bathtub surrounds are designed and installed in the same way as shower surrounds. Though fiberglass and plastic fabricated enclosures, as well as custom ceramic tile, are traditional materials for surrounds, the use of solid-surface materials—materials common to sinks and countertops—are growing in popularity.

Solid-surface surrounds are available in kits with ¼" panels that are installed much the same as fiberglass enclosures. The panels can be fastened to any wall material—cementboard and greenboard are the most common in new construction. Walls must be free of debris and sealed with two coats of primer. Solid-surface panels can be installed over old tile, though you must chisel out any loose tiles, and install filler strips the same thickness as the tiles (usually ¼") to fill any gaps between the walls and panels.

Everything You Need

Tools: tape measure, 4-ft. level, jig saw, drill with a hole saw or spade bits, caulk gun.

Materials: solid-surface surround kit, sandpaper, pressure-sensitive tape, panel adhesive, tub & tile caulk, masking tape, 1× and 2× lumber.

How to Install a Solid-surface Bathtub Surround

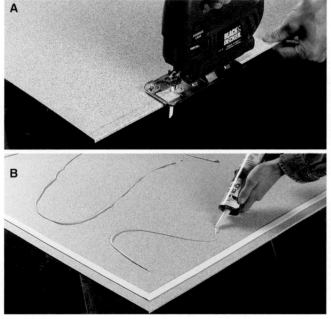

1 Begin panel installation with the back wall. Measure and mark the dimensions on the back side of the panel, then cut using a jig saw (photo A). Remove rough edges with fine or medium sandpaper. Test-fit the panel to ensure a proper fit. On the back side of the panel, apply pressure-sensitive tape 1" from each edge, then apply panel adhesive in the field (photo B). Keep the adhesive 1" from the tape edges.

2 Remove the backing of the pressure-sensitive tape. Lift the panel into position, tight into one corner, then firmly press the panel to the wall. Using your hands, smooth across the entire panel, applying pressure to ensure firm contact with the wall. Follow the same procedures to install the panel on the side wall, opposite the plumbing outlets.

3 For the wall with the plumbing outlets, measure and trim the panel to size. Measure the location of the plumbing outlets on the wall, then transfer the dimensions to the finished side of the panel. Drill holes ½" larger than the plumbing outlets, using a drill and a hole saw or spade bits. Place a scrap board beneath the cutout area to ensure a clean cut.

4 Test-fit the panel and make any necessary adjustments, then install, following the same procedures as with the first two panels. After all the panels are installed, seal each joint, seam, and edge with a bead of caulk.

5 Follow the manufacturer's instructions to install any trim. For corner molding, test fit each piece and trim to size, then apply a bead of panel adhesive down the corner joints and firmly press the moldings into position. Temporarily secure the molding with tape.

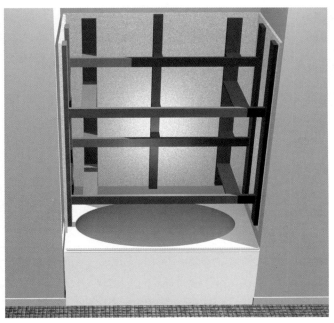

6 Use 1× and 2× lumber to construct temporary bracing to ensure a strong adhesive bond. Use soft cloth or carpet scraps to prevent the bracing from scratching the surround. Allow the adhesive to cure overnight, then remove the bracing. Wipe the surround clean with a damp cloth.

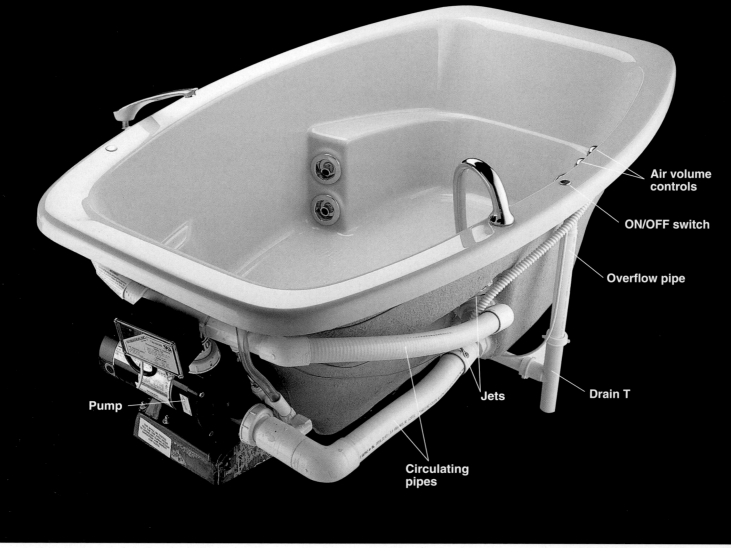

Air volume controls

ON/OFF switch

Overflow pipe

Drain T

Jets

Circulating pipes

Pump

A whirlpool circulates aerated water through jets mounted in the body of the tub. Whirlpool pumps move as much as 50 gallons of water per minute to create a relaxing "hydromassage" effect. The pump, pipes, jets, and most of the controls are installed at the factory, making the actual hookup in your home quite simple.

Installing Whirlpools

Installing a whirlpool is very similar to installing a bathtub, once the rough-in is completed. Completing a rough-in for a whirlpool requires that you install a separate GFCI-protected electrical circuit for the pump motor. Some building codes specify that a licensed electrician be hired to wire whirlpools; check with your local building inspector.

Select your whirlpool before you do rough-in work, because exact requirements will differ from model to model (pages 21 to 23). Select your faucet to match the trim kit that comes with your whirlpool. When selecting a faucet, make sure the spout is large enough to reach over the tub rim. Most whirlpools use "widespread" faucets because the handles and spout are separate, and can be positioned however you like,

even on opposite sides of the tub. Most building centers carry flex tube in a variety of lengths for connecting faucet handles and spout.

> ### Everything You Need
>
> Tools: framing square, circular saw, drill & spade bits, jig saw, hacksaw, trowel, screwdriver, staple gun, straightedge, utility knife, tiling tools, caulk gun.
>
> Materials: 2 × 4 lumber, 10d nails, ¾" exterior-grade plywood, galvanized deck screws, dry-set mortar, 12" wood spacer blocks, 8-gauge insulated wire, grounding clamp, paper-faced fiberglass insulation, cementboard, ceramic tile materials, silicone caulk.

Optional Whirlpool Accessories

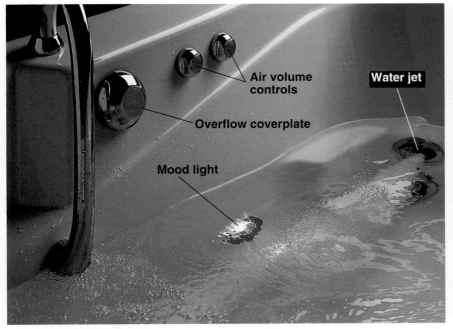

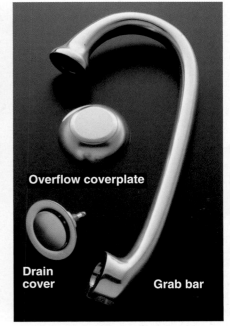

Mood lights are sold as factory-installed accessories by many manufacturers. Most are available with several filters to let you adjust the color to suit your mood. Mood lights are low-voltage fixtures wired through 12-volt transformers. Do not wire mood lights or other accessories into the electrical circuit that supplies the pump motor.

Trim kits for whirlpools are ordered at the time of purchase. Available in a variety of finishes, all of the trim pieces except the grab bar and overflow coverplate normally are installed at the factory.

Requirements for Making Electrical Hookups

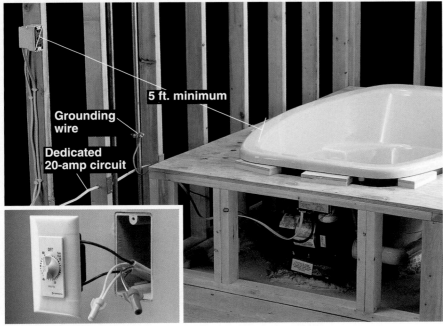

The electrical service for a whirlpool should be a dedicated 115- to 120-volt, 20-amp circuit. The pump motor should be grounded separately, normally to a metal cold water supply pipe. Most whirlpool motors are wired with 12/2 NM cable, but some local codes require the use of conduit. Remote timer switches (inset), located at least 5 ft. from the tub, are required by some codes, even for a tub with a built-in timer.

A GFCI circuit breaker at the main service panel is required with whirlpool installations. Hire an electrician to connect new circuits at your service panel if you are uncomfortable installing circuit cables on your own.

How to Install a Whirlpool

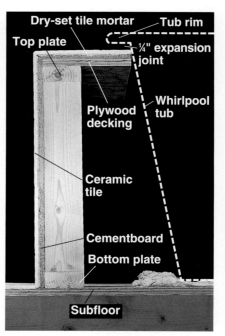

1 Outline the planned location of the deck frame on the subfloor. Use the plumbing stub-outs as starting points for measuring. Before you begin to build the deck, check the actual dimensions of your whirlpool tub to make sure they correspond to the dimensions listed in the manufacturer's directions. NOTE: Plan your deck so it will be at least 4" wide at all points around the whirlpool.

2 Cut top plates, bottom plates, and studs for the deck frame. The height of the frame should allow ¾" for the plywood decking, ¼" for an expansion gap between the deck and the tub rim, and 1" for cementboard, tile, and mortar.

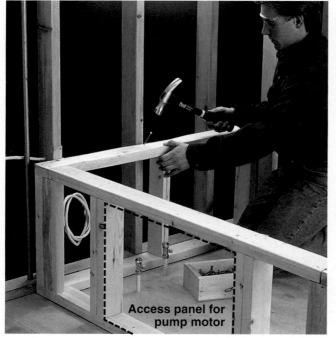

3 Assemble the deck frame. Make sure to leave a framed opening for access panels at the pump location and the drain location. Nail the frame to the floor joists and wall studs or blocking, using 10d nails.

4 Cover the deck frame with ¾" exterior-grade plywood, and attach with deck screws spaced every 12". Using a template of the whirlpool cutout (usually included with the tub), mark the deck for cutting. If no template is included, make one from the shipping carton. (Cutout will be slightly smaller than the outside dimensions of the whirlpool rim.)

5 Drill a starter hole inside the cutout line, then make the cutout hole in the deck, using a jig saw.

6 Measure and mark holes for faucet tailpieces and spout tailpiece according to the faucet manufacturer's suggestions. Drill holes with a spade bit or hole saw.

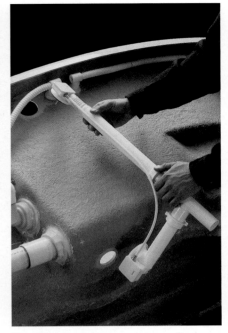

7 Attach drain-waste-overflow assembly (included with most whirlpools) at the drain and over-flow outlets in the tub (page 162). Trim the drain pipe in the floor to the proper height, using a hacksaw.

8 Apply a layer of dry-set mortar to the subfloor where the tub will rest. Make 12" spacer blocks, 1¼" thick (equal to expansion gap, tile mortar, and cementboard; see step 2). Arrange blocks along the edges of the cutout.

9 With a helper, lift the tub by the rim and set it slowly into the cutout hole. Lower the tub, pressing it into the mortar base, until the rim rests on the spacers at the edges of the cutout area. Align the tailpiece of the drain-waste-overflow assembly with the P-trap as you set the tub in place. Avoid moving or shifting the tub once it is in place, and allow the mortar to set for 6 to 8 hours before proceeding with the tub installation.

(continued next page)

10 Adjust the length of the tailpiece for the drain-waste-overflow assembly, if necessary, then attach assembly to the P-trap in the drain opening, using a slip nut.

11 Inspect the seals on the built-in piping and hoses for loose connections. If you find a problem, contact your dealer for advice. Attempting to fix the problem yourself could void the whirlpool warranty.

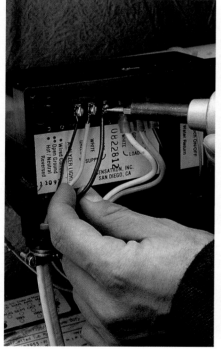

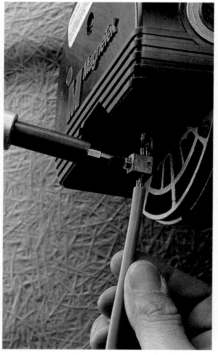

12 With the power off, remove the wiring cover from the pump motor. Feed the circuit wires from the power source or wall timer into the motor. Connect the wires according to the directions printed on the motor.

13 Attach an insulated 8-gauge wire to the ground lug on the pump motor.

14 Attach the other end of the wire to a metal cold water supply pipe in the wall, using a ground clamp. Test the GFCI circuit breaker.

15 Clean out the tub, then fill it so the water level is at least 3" above the highest water jet.

16 Turn on the pump, and allow it to operate for at least 20 minutes while you check for leaks. Contact your whirlpool dealer if leaks are detected.

17 Staple paper-faced fiberglass insulation to the vertical frame supports. The facing should point inward, to keep fibers out of motor. Do not insulate within 6" of pumps, heaters, or lights.

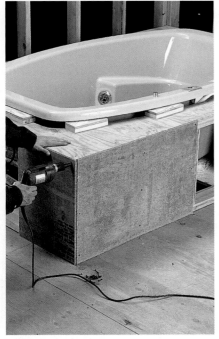 

18 Attach cementboard to the sides and top of the deck frame (pages 182 to 183) if you plan to install ceramic tile on the deck. Use ¾" plywood for access panel coverings.

19 Attach finish surfaces to deck and deck frame, then install grab bar, faucet, and spout (pages 240 to 243). Fill the joints between the floor and deck, and between the tub rim and deck surface, with silicone caulk.

Installing a Sauna

Custom-cut saunas can be tailored to any space or design. This unique hex-shaped sauna includes design elements such as shielded cove lighting, vertical paneling, and mounted backrests.

A Scandanavian tradition for centuries, the sauna has become increasingly popular in North America. The traditional sauna cycle of intense heat followed by a cooling shower helps to soothe, relax, and invigorate the body while providing health benefits such as reduced muscle tension and clean, refreshed skin.

Saunas are typically lined with softwoods, such as cedar, redwood, pine, or spruce, all of which lend a comforting, organic feel to the space. Woods that stay comfortable to the touch at high heat, such as abachi, aspen, and hemlock, are often used for the benches and backrests.

Manufactured saunas generally are sold as either prefabricated or custom-cut kits. Both types include the pre-hung door, benches, electric heater unit, and other accessories. The prefab kits also include finished and insulated wall and ceiling panels, which allow for quick and easy installation.

Custom-cut sauna kits typically are less expensive than prefab kits, but more complicated, requiring you to frame and insulate the space prior to installation. You supply the manufacturer with your project dimensions and they deliver pre-cut and labeled tongue-and-groove boards for the interior paneling. Consult with your manufacturer or dealer about your sauna plans before beginning the framing process.

As you plan the location of your sauna, keep in mind that the flooring should be a water-resistant surface such as concrete, resilient flooring, or ceramic tile. Locating the sauna near a floor drain will ease cleaning.

Check with your manufacturer before attempting to install and connect the electrical wiring for your sauna's systems. Some manufacturers' warranties require that all electrical work be completed by a licensed electrician.

When framing your sauna, use pressure-treated 2 × 4s for the bottom plates for added moisture protection. The rest of the framing can be built with standard 2 × 4s. See pages 80 to 84 for additional tips on framing the walls and doors of your sauna.

Everything You Need:

Tools: tape measure, chalk line, 4-ft. level, circular saw, caulk gun, powder-actuated nailer, hammer, stud finder, plumb bob, stapler, pneumatic nailer and compressor, drill.

Materials: custom-cut sauna kit, treated 2 × 4s (for bottom plates), standard 2 × 4s (for all additional framing), caulk, galvanized common nails (8d, 10d, 16d), 3½" unfaced fiberglass insulation, ⅜" staples, 1½" galvanized pin nails or 4d galvanized finish nails, 3" stainless steel screws, exterior wall material.

How to Install a Custom-cut Sauna

Stud layout for 6 x 6-ft. sauna built in this project

15¼"

16"

Detail area

Door rough opening

Door cripple stud

←15¼"→ ←16"→ ← 26" →

1 Measure and mark the sauna framing dimensions on the floor, then snap chalk lines to mark your framing layout. Cut bottom plates from treated 2 × 4s, then mark the 16" on-center stud layout onto the plates. Include the door rough opening and extra nailer studs in the corners to allow for fastening the tongue-and-groove boards (detail). Cut top plates to length, pair them with bottom plates, and transfer the stud markings to the top plates (inset). Caulk beneath the bottom plates, then fasten them to the floor, using 16d nails (or use masonry screws or a powder-actuated nailer on a concrete floor).

2 The sauna door requires a double plate to provide a proper sill. Transfer the stud layout markings to another 2 × 4 and install it on top of the front wall plate, using 10d nails driven at a slight angle.

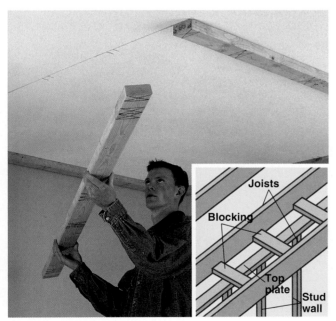

3 Locate and mark the joists in the area, using a stud finder. If a wall falls between parallel joists, remove the ceiling drywall and install 2× blocking between the joists (inset). Use a plumb bob to transfer the plate locations from the floor to the ceiling, then snap chalk lines through the ceiling marks. Attach the top plates to the joists or blocking, using 16d nails.

Joists

Blocking

Top plate

Stud wall

4 Measure and cut the wall studs to length from standard 2 × 4s. Install the studs by toenailing them through the sides of the studs and into the top and bottom plates, using 8d nails. On each end, drive two nails through one side of the stud and one more through the center on the other side (see page 82).

(continued next page)

5 Install the king studs for the door frame. Make sure that these studs are plumb, using a level. Cut and install a 2 × 4 header flat between the king studs, using 16d nails. Cut and install jack studs to fit snugly beneath the header. Cut and install a cripple stud above the header, centered over the rough opening.

6 Measure up 7 ft. from the floor and mark a stud. Use a 4-ft. level to transfer the mark across the studs. Align 2 × 4 nailers on the marks and attach them to the studs with 16d nails. Mark the joist layout onto the nailers, using 16" on-center spacing. Cut 2 × 4 joists to fit and fasten them to the nailers, using 10d nails. NOTE: If the joist span is over 8 ft., use 2 × 6s for the nailers and joists.

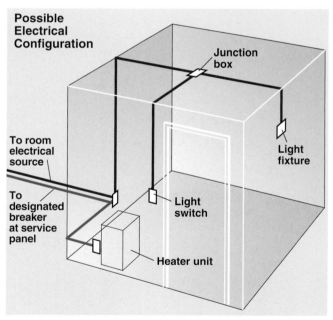

7 Frame openings for the sauna vents according to the manufacturer's directions. Locate the framing for the inlet vent at floor level, near the heater. Frame the outlet vent on another wall, located just below the top bench height (about 30"). If you have a wall-mount heater unit, attach 2 × 4 supports between the studs at the heater location according to the manufacturer's directions.

8 Install electrical boxes and route cable to the lights, switches and heater unit as directed by the manufacturer. See pages 126 to 136 for more information on wiring techniques. NOTE: Some manufacturers may require that all electrical work be completed by a licensed electrician.

9 Install a double layer of 3½" unfaced fiberglass insulation at the ceiling. Lay the first layer on top of the ceiling framing, perpendicular to the joists. Install a second layer between the joists. If necessary, drive nails partially into the joists to hold the second layer in place.

10 Install insulation between the studs along the finished walls. For easier access while paneling the sauna, leave the outer walls open until you are ready to panel them. (See step 15.) Install the included vapor barrier over the insulation on the walls and ceiling, attaching it to the framing with ⅜" staples. Begin at the bottom of the walls and overlap the foil pieces as you go up. Repair tears and seal joints with foil tape.

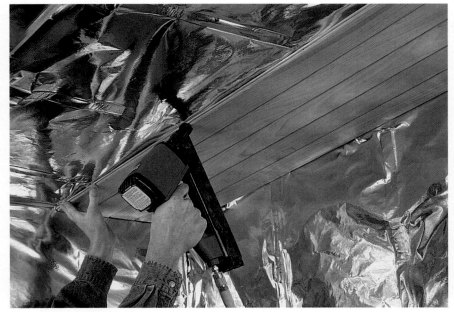

11 Install the pre-cut ceiling boards, starting at the back of the sauna. If the boards are slightly shorter than the framing, split the difference and allow equal space on each side. Nail the first board to the joists through its face, then "blind-nail" the board by driving 1½" galvanized pin nails (or 4d galvanized finish nails) at an angle through the inside of the tongue. If you are not using a pneumatic nailer, drive the nail heads below the wood surface with a nail set. For the remaining boards, fit the groove over the tongue of the preceding board and drive nails through the inside of the tongue only.

12 Measure periodically to make sure the boards are straight and parallel to the far wall, adjusting the following few boards, if necessary. When you get to the final board, measure the space remaining, rip the board to fit, and face-nail it into place.

(continued next page)

13 Check to see if the floor is level by moving a level across the floor. If it is uneven, mark the high point. Measure down from the sauna ceiling to this point and subtract ½". Use this measurement to mark the starting point for the tongue-and-groove wall boards at all four corners. This will allow for a minimum ½" gap between the boards and the floor.

14 Align the first board with the starting marks along the back wall and attach it to the studs, using the blind-nailing techniques shown in step 11. Trim the boards, as necessary, to fit around the vent openings. Check the boards for level every few rows, and adjust the next few rows slightly if the boards fall out of level.

VARIATION: If you are installing the paneling vertically, install 1 × 2 furring strips over the studs, spaced 24" on-center, using 8d nails. Install the boards, starting in the corner farthest from the heater. Finish the two walls going toward the heater, then complete the other two walls.

15 On the open stud walls, finish the exterior with the desired paneling or drywall. Then, install the insulation and vapor barrier, as shown in step 10. Finish installing the tongue and groove paneling on the interior side of the walls.

16 Measure from the floor and mark the side walls at 12" and 30" for the bench supports. Align the top edge of each support with the marks and fasten them to the wall studs with 3" screws. Install the prebuilt benches, attaching them to the supports with 3" screws.

17 Position the door in the framed opening with the jamb flush with the exterior wall surface. Check that the door is level, plumb, and centered, shimming, if necessary. Fasten the hinge side to the 2 × 4 frame with the included screws. Check the door again for level, then continue to fasten around the frame.

18 If necessary, install the door jamb extensions flush with the interior wall surface, fastening them to the framed opening, using 3" screws. Mark a setback to indicate the inside edge of the door casings on each of the jambs. Install the casings around the interior and exterior of the door, using 4d galvanized finish nails.

19 Install trim molding to cover the joints at the wall and ceiling corners, cutting the pieces as needed. Fasten the trim with 4d galvanized finish nails. Install the inlet and outlet grills over the vent openings, using the included screws.

20 Install the heater unit, control panel, and light fixtures according to the manufacturer's directions. Assemble and install the heater guard around the heater unit, positioning the top edge of the guard just below the exposed rocks. Follow the manufacturer's directions for operating the heater unit.

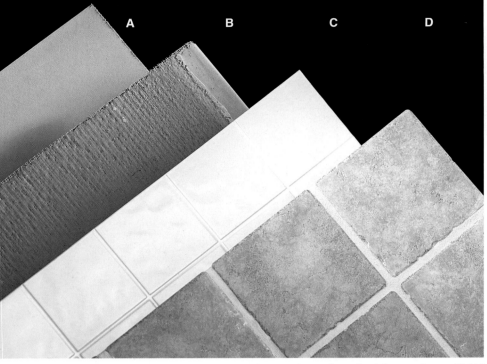

Common wall surfaces: Water-resistant drywall, called "greenboard" (A), is used in moderately damp or dry areas. It can be painted, covered with vinyl wallcovering, or used as a backing for tub surrounds. Cementboard (B) is used as a backing material for ceramic wall tile (pages 184 to 191). Tileboard (C) is made of solid PVC or vinyl and resembles ceramic tile, but is installed in panels or sheets. Ceramic tile (D) is water-resistant and durable. It is sold in a wide range of colors, sizes, and styles.

Common floor surfaces: Resilient vinyl tile (A) is usually sold in 12" × 12" squares. Because it has many seams, vinyl tile flooring should be used only in half baths and dry areas. Ceramic floor tile (B) is sold in sizes ranging from 1" × 1" to 12" × 12". A long-lasting product, it is unglazed and thicker than ceramic wall tile. Sheet vinyl (C) creates a seamless floor surface that is virtually waterproof. Some plastic laminated wood flooring (D) is also available for use in wet areas.

Installing Wall & Floor Surfaces

You can create dramatic changes in your bathroom by replacing old wall and floor surfaces. Even though many products can be installed on top of existing walls and floors, it is best to remove the old surfaces (pages 72 to 75). Because of the high moisture levels in bathrooms, it is possible that old wall and floor surfaces are hiding damaged areas. Removing the old surfaces, including the underlayment, will give you the opportunity to inspect and repair damaged structural members (pages 72 to 75), as well as provide ready access for upgrading wiring and plumbing.

Choose materials and finishes that will stand up to high moisture levels. Bathroom walls will be "greenboard" a moisture-resistant wallboard, or cementboard, the backing for ceramic tile. Select products that are designed for bathroom use.

Install new wall surfaces first so you will not damage new floors while finishing the walls. Follow the manufacturer's recommendations for adhesive products and installation techniques.

This section shows:

- Installing & Finishing Drywall (pages 180 to 181)
- Installing Cementboard (pages 182 to 183)
- Installing Ceramic Wall Tile (pages 184 to 191)
- Installing Vinyl Flooring (pages 192 to 197)
- Installing a Floor-Warming System (pages 198 to 201)
- Installing Ceramic Floor Tile (pages 202 to 209)

Tips for Finishing Walls & Floors

Fill dips and knotholes in floors with latex underlayment before installing vinyl flooring. Locate low spots with a long straightedge, then apply underlayment with a large drywall knife. Let underlayment dry, sand it smooth, then clean the surface thoroughly.

Apply silicone caulk to flanges on bathtubs and shower bases before installing cementboard or water-resistant drywall. The caulk creates a solid bond and keeps water from seeping into the wall.

Staple a vapor barrier over insulation in exterior bathroom walls or walls that adjoin unheated spaces. The plastic vapor barrier prevents moisture from condensing in the walls.

Patch holes in walls, those made when installing pipes or wires, using pieces of drywall cut to fit the openings. Attach small patches to the framing members with hot glue or construction adhesive; attach large patches with drywall screws. Cover seams with fiberglass drywall tape and drywall compound (page 180).

Make access openings in wall surfaces so bathtub and shower fittings and shutoff valves can be reached easily. A whirlpool may require two access panels—one for the drain plumbing and one for the pump motor. Trim the opening with mitered wood moldings, and cover it with a removable plywood panel finished to match the surrounding wall or whirlpool deck.

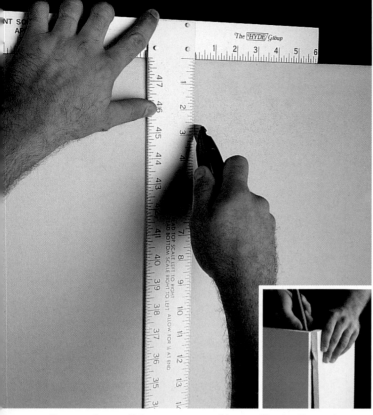

Installing & Finishing Drywall

Use drywall panels both to finish new walls and to patch existing wall areas exposed during the installation of a window or door.

Openings in smooth plaster walls usually can be patched with drywall, but if you need to match a textured plaster surface, it is best to hire a plasterer to do the work.

Drywall panels are available in 4 x 8-ft. or 4 x 10-ft. sheets, and in ⅜", ½", and ⅝" thicknesses. For new walls, ½" thick is standard. Moisture-resistant greenboard is recommended for use in bathrooms.

Use all-purpose drywall compound and paper joint tape. Lay out drywall panels so that seams fall over the center of openings, not at sides, or use solid pieces at openings. Insulate all framing cavities around each opening.

Score drywall face paper with a utility knife, using a drywall T-square as a guide. Bend the panel away from the scored line until the core breaks, then cut through the back paper (inset) with a utility knife, and separate the pieces.

Everything You Need

Tools: tape measure, utility knife, drywall T-square, 6" and 12" wallboard knives, 150-grit sanding sponge.

Materials: drywall, drywall tape, 1¼" coarse-thread drywall screws, drywall compound, metal inside corner bead.

How to Install & Finish Drywall

1 Install panels with their tapered edges butted together. Fasten with 1¼" screws, driven every 8" along the edges, and every 12" in the field. Drive screws deep enough to dimple surface without ripping face paper (inset).

2 Finish the seams by applying an even bed layer of compound over the seam, about ⅛" thick, using a 6" taping knife.

3 Center the tape over the seam and lightly embed it into the compound, making sure it's smooth and straight.

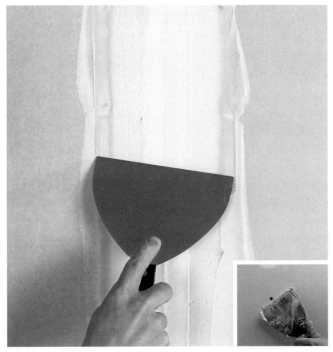

4 Smooth the tape with the taping knife. Apply enough pressure to force compound from underneath the tape, leaving the tape flat and with a thin layer underneath. Cover all exposed screw heads with the first of three coats of compound (inset). Let compound dry overnight.

5 Second-coat the seams with a thin, even layer of compound, using a 12" knife. Feather the sides of the compound first, holding the blade almost flat and applying pressure to the outside of the blade so that the blade just skims over the center of the seam.

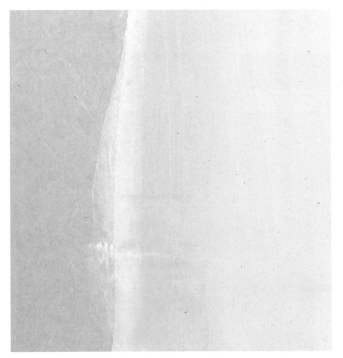

6 After feathering both sides, make a pass down the center of the seam, leaving the seam smooth and even, the edges feathered out to nothing. Completely cover the joint tape. Let second coat dry, then apply a third coat, using the 12" knife. After the third coat dries completely, sand the compound lightly with a drywall sander or a 150-grit sanding sponge.

TIP: Finish any inside corners using paper-faced metal inside corner bead to produce straight, durable corners with little fuss. Embed the bead into a thin layer of compound, then smooth the paper with a taping knife. Apply two finish coats to the corner, then sand the compound smooth.

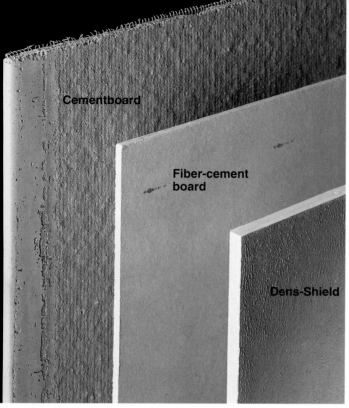

Cementboard

Fiber-cement board

Dens-Shield

Common tile backers are cementboard, fiber-cement board, and Dens-Shield. Cementboard is made from portland cement and sand reinforced by an outer layer of fiberglass mesh. Fiber-cement board is made similarly, but with a fiber reinforcement integrated throughout the panel. Dens-Shield is a water-resistant gypsum board with a waterproof acrylic facing.

Installing Cementboard

Use tile backer board as the substrate for tile walls in wet areas. Unlike drywall, tile backer won't break down and cause damage if water gets behind the tile. The three basic types of tile backer are cementboard, fiber-cement board, and Dens-Shield®.

Though water cannot damage either cementboard or fiber-cement board, it can pass through them. To protect the framing members, install a water barrier of 4-mil plastic or 15# building paper behind the backer.

Dens-Shield has a waterproof acrylic facing that provides the water barrier. It cuts and installs much like drywall but requires galvanized screws to prevent corrosion, and must be sealed with caulk at all untaped joints and penetrations.

Everything You Need

Tools: T-square, utility knife, drill with a small masonry bit, hammer, jig saw with a bimetal blade, drywall knife.

Materials: 4-mil plastic sheeting, cementboard, 1¼" cementboard screws, cementboard joint tape, latex-portland cement mortar.

How to Install Cementboard

1 Staple a water barrier of 4-mil plastic sheeting or 15# building paper over the framing. Overlap seams by several inches, and leave the sheets long at the perimeter. NOTE: Framing for cementboard must be 16" on-center; steel studs must be 20-gauge.

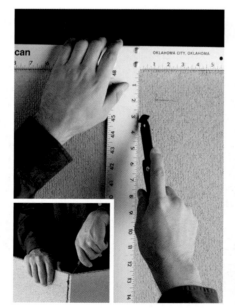

2 Cut cementboard by scoring through the mesh just below the surface, using a utility knife or carbide-tipped cutter. Snap the panel back, then cut through the back-side mesh (inset). NOTE: For tile applications, the rough face of the board is the front.

3 Make cutouts for pipes and other penetrations by drilling a series of holes through the board, using a small masonry bit. Tap the hole out with a hammer or a scrap of pipe. Cut holes along edges with a jig saw and bimetal blade.

4 Install the sheets horizontally. Where possible, use full pieces to avoid cut-and-butted seams, which are difficult to fasten. If there are vertical seams, stagger them between rows. Leave a ⅛" gap between sheets at vertical seams and corners. Use spacers to set the bottom row of panels ¼" above the tub or shower base. Fasten the sheets with 1¼" cementboard screws, driven every 8" for walls and every 6" for ceilings. Drive the screws ½" from the edges to prevent crumbling. If the studs are steel, don't fasten within 1" of the top track.

5 Cover the joints and corners with cementboard joint tape (alkali-resistant fiberglass mesh) and latex-portland cement mortar (thin-set). Apply a layer of mortar with a drywall knife, embed the tape into the mortar, then smooth and level the mortar.

Variation: How to Finish Cementboard

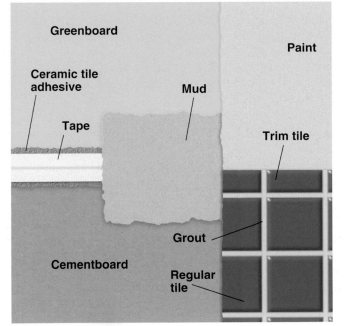

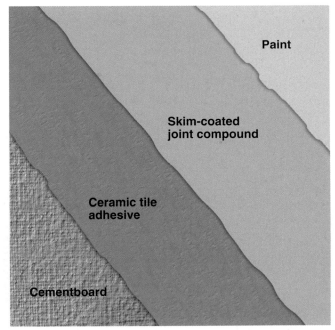

To finish a joint between cementboard and greenboard, seal the joint and exposed cementboard with ceramic tile adhesive, a mixture of four parts adhesive to one part water. Embed paper joint tape into the adhesive, smoothing the tape with a tape knife. Allow the adhesive to dry, then finish the joint with at least two coats of all-purpose drywall joint compound.

To finish small areas of cementboard that will not be tiled, seal the cementboard with ceramic tile adhesive, a mixture of four parts adhesive to one part water, then apply a skim-coat of all-purpose drywall joint compound, using a 12" drywall knife. Then, paint the wall.

Installing Ceramic Wall Tile

Ceramic wall tile is one of the most durable surface materials for bathroom walls and ceilings because it's virtually impervious to water and easy to clean. However, a tiled surface surround for a bathtub or shower must be prepared using the proper materials to ensure that the wall system will be protected if water does get through the surface.

Install tile over cementboard (pages 182 to 183). Made from cement and fiberglass, cementboard cannot be damaged by water, though moisture can pass through it. To protect the framing, install a waterproof membrane, such as roofing felt or polyethylene sheeting, between the framing members and the cementboard. Be sure to tape and finish the seams between cementboard panels before laying the tile.

When shopping for tile, keep in mind that tiles that are at least 6" × 6" are easier to install than small tile, because they require less cutting and cover more surface area. Larger tiles also have fewer grout lines that must be cleaned and maintained. Check out the selection of trim and specialty tiles and ceramic accessories that are available to help you customize your project.

Most wall tile is designed to have narrow grout lines (less than ⅛" wide) filled with unsanded grout. Grout lines wider than ⅛" should be filled with sanded floor-tile grout. Either type will last longer if it contains, or is mixed with, a latex additive. To prevent staining, it's a good idea to seal your grout after it fully cures, then once a year thereafter.

If you are planning to tile all the walls in your bathroom, you can use standard drywall or water-resistant drywall (called "greenboard") as a backer for walls in dry areas. See page 191 for information on laying out full rooms.

Everything You Need

Tools: tile-cutting tools (pages 204 to 205), marker, tape measure, 4-ft. level, notched trowel, mallet, grout float, sponge, small paintbrush, caulk gun.

Materials: straight 1 × 2, dry-set tile mortar with latex additive, ceramic wall tile, ceramic trim tile (as needed), 2 × 4, carpet scrap, tile grout with latex additive, tub & tile caulk, alkaline grout sealer, cardboard.

Materials for Wall Tiling Projects

Use planning brochures and design catalogs to help you create decorative patterns and borders for your ceramic tile projects. Brochures and catalogs are available free of charge from many tile manufacturers.

Choose moisture-resistant backing materials. Water-resistant drywall (A), or greenboard, is made from gypsum and has a water-resistant facing. Use it only in moderately damp or dry areas. Cementboard (B) is a rigid material with a fiberglass facing and a cement core. Because water does not damage cementboard, use it as a tile backer in bathtub and shower surrounds.

Ceramic wall tile is available in a wide range of shapes, styles, and colors. The most basic types of tile are: 4 × 4 glazed wall tiles (A), self-spacing mosaic sheet tiles (B), and trim tiles for borders (C) and accents (D).

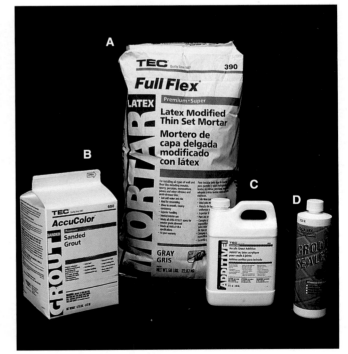

Bonding materials for ceramic tile include: dry-set mortar (A), grout mix (B), and latex grout additive (C). Latex additive makes grout lines stronger and more crack-resistant. Grout sealer (D) is used to protect grout lines from staining.

How to Lay Out Tile Walls in a Bathtub Alcove

1 Make a story pole to mark the tile layout on walls. For square tiles, set a row of tiles (and plastic spacers, if they will be used) in the selected pattern on a flat surface. Mark a straight 1 × 2 to match the tile spacing. Include any narrow trim tiles or accent tiles. For rectangular and odd-shaped tiles, make separate sticks for the horizontal and vertical layouts.

2 Beginning with the back wall, measure up and mark a point at a distance equal to the height of one ceramic tile (if the tub edge is not level, measure up from the lowest spot). Draw a level line through this point, along the entire back wall. This line represents a tile grout line and will be used as a reference line for making the entire tile layout.

Tile height

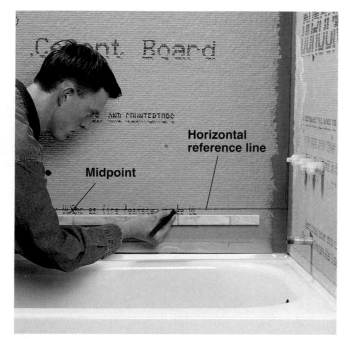

Horizontal reference line

Midpoint

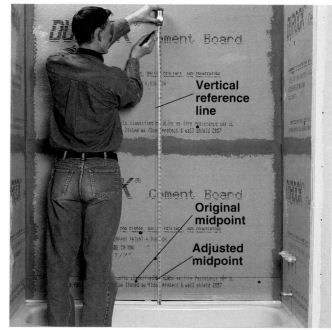

Vertical reference line

Original midpoint

Adjusted midpoint

3 Measure and mark the midpoint on the horizontal reference line. Using the story pole, mark along the reference line where the vertical grout joints will be located. If the story pole shows that the corner tiles will be less than half of a full tile width, move the midpoint half the width of a tile in either direction and mark (shown in next step).

4 Use a level to draw a vertical reference line through the adjusted midpoint from the tub edge to the ceiling. Measure up from the tub edge along the vertical reference line and mark the rough height of the top row of tiles.

5 Use the story pole to mark the horizontal grout joints along the vertical reference line, beginning at the mark for the top row of tiles. If the cut tiles at the tub edge will be less than half the height of a full tile, move the top row up half the height of a tile. NOTE: If tiling to a ceiling, evenly divide the tiles to be cut at the ceiling and tub edge, as for the corner tiles in steps 3 and 4.

6 Use a level to draw an adjusted horizontal reference line through the vertical reference line at a grout joint mark close to the center of the layout. This splits the tile area into four workable quadrants.

7 Use a level to transfer the adjusted horizontal reference line from the back wall to both side walls, then follow step 3 through step 6 to lay out both side walls. Adjust the layout as needed so the final column of tiles ends at the outside edge of the tub. Use only the adjusted horizontal and vertical reference lines for ceramic tile installation (pages 188 to 190).

Tile shown installed for clarity

VARIATION: To wrap the final column of tile around the outside edge of the bathtub, begin your layout on a side wall. Make adjustments based on the tile to be notch-cut for the edge of the bathtub—the tile should be at least half a tile width and height. Transfer the adjusted horizontal reference line to the other walls and finish the layout.

How to Install Ceramic Wall Tile in a Bathtub Alcove

1 Mark the tile layout (pages 186 to 187). Mix a small batch of thin-set mortar containing a latex additive. (Some mortar has additive mixed in by the manufacturer and some must have additive mixed separately.) Spread adhesive on a small section of the wall, along both legs of one quadrant, using a ¼" notched trowel.

2 Use the edge of the trowel to create furrows in the mortar. Set the first tile in the corner of the quadrant where the lines intersect, using a slight twisting motion. Align the tile exactly with both reference lines. When placing cut tiles, position the cut edges where they will be least visible.

3 Continue installing tiles, working from the center out into the field of the quadrant. Keep the tiles aligned with the reference lines and tile in one quadrant at a time. If the tiles are not self-spacing, use plastic spacers inserted in the corner joints to maintain even grout lines (inset). The base row against the tub edge should be the last row of tiles installed. To cut tiles at inside corners, see step 5 on the opposite page.

VARIATION: In some instances it is more practical to apply mortar to the tile rather than the wall. Cover the back of the tile with mortar, then press the tile in position with a slight twisting motion.

4 As small sections are completed, set the tile by laying a scrap of 2 × 4 wrapped with carpet onto the tile and rapping it lightly with a mallet. This embeds the tile solidly in the adhesive and creates a flat, even surface.

5 To mark tiles for straight cuts, begin by taping ⅛"-thick spacers against the surfaces below and to the side of the tile. Position a tile directly over the last full tile installed (A), then place a third tile so the edge butts against the spacers (B). Trace the edge of the top tile onto the middle tile to mark it for cutting.

6 Install trim tiles, such as the bullnose tiles shown above, at border areas. Wipe away excess mortar along the top edges of the edge tiles.

7 Mark and cut tiles to fit around all plumbing accessories or plumbing fixtures. Refer to pages 204 to 205 for tile cutting techniques.

(continued next page)

8 Install any ceramic accessories, such as soap dishes, by applying thin-set mortar to the back side, then pressing the accessory into place. Use masking tape to support the weight until the mortar dries (INSET).

9 Let mortar dry completely (12 to 24 hours), then mix a batch of grout containing latex additive. Apply the grout with a rubber grout float, using a sweeping motion, and hold at a 30° angle to force it deep into the joints (page 208). Do not grout the joints adjoining the bathtub, floor, and corners. These will serve as expansion joints and will be caulked later.

10 Wipe a damp grout sponge diagonally over the tiles, rinsing the sponge between wipes. Wipe each area only once; repeated wiping can pull grout from the joints. Allow the grout to dry for about 4 hours, then buff the tile surface with a soft cloth to remove any remaining grout film.

11 When the grout has cured completely, use a small foam brush to apply grout sealer to the joints, following the manufacturer's directions. Avoid brushing sealer on the tile surfaces, and wipe up excess sealer immediately.

12 Fill the tub with water, then seal expansion joints around the bathtub, floor, and corners with silicone caulk. After the caulk dries, buff the tile with a dry, soft cloth.

Variation: How to Tile Bathroom Walls

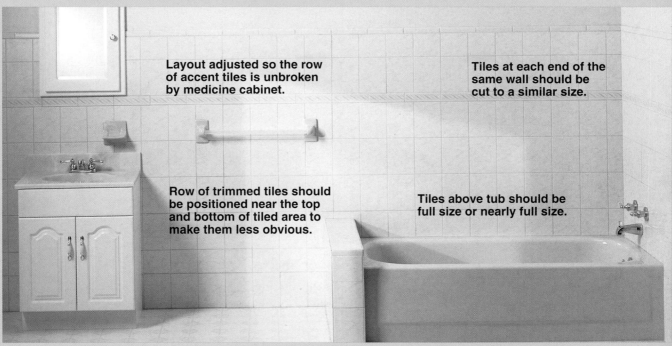

Layout adjusted so the row of accent tiles is unbroken by medicine cabinet.

Tiles at each end of the same wall should be cut to a similar size.

Row of trimmed tiles should be positioned near the top and bottom of tiled area to make them less obvious.

Tiles above tub should be full size or nearly full size.

Tiling an entire bathroom requires careful planning. The bathroom shown here was designed so that the tiles directly above the bathtub (the most visible surface) are nearly full height. To accomplish this, cut tiles were used in the second row up from the floor.

The short second row also allows the row of accent tiles to run uninterrupted below the medicine cabinet. Cut tiles in both corners should be of similar width to maintain a symmetrical look in the room.

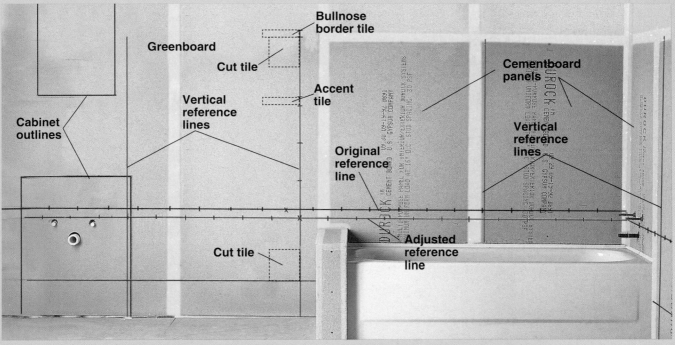

Bullnose border tile

Greenboard

Cut tile

Accent tile

Cabinet outlines

Vertical reference lines

Cementboard panels

Vertical reference lines

Original reference line

Adjusted reference line

Cut tile

The key to a successful wall-tile project is the layout. Mark the wall to show the planned location of all wall cabinets, fixtures, and wall accessories, then locate the most visible horizontal line in the bathroom, which is usually the top edge of the bathtub. Follow steps on pages 186 to 187 to establish the layout, using a story pole to see how the tile pattern will run in relation to the

other features in the room. After establishing the working reference lines, mark additional vertical reference lines on the walls every 5 to 6 tile spaces along the adjusted horizontal reference line to split large walls into smaller, workable quadrants, then install the tile (pages 188 to 190). NOTE: Premixed, latex mastic adhesives generally are acceptable for wall tile in dry areas.

Installing Vinyl Flooring

Vinyl flooring is available both in sheets and tiles. Sheet vinyl is a good choice for bathrooms since it has few seams for water to seep through; in most bathrooms, you can install sheet vinyl with no seams at all. Vinyl tiles perform best in drier locations, such as a half bath, where a floor with many seams is not a liability.

The quality of resilient flooring varies significantly and is based primarily on the amount of vinyl in the material. The thickness of the flooring is a good clue to its quality; thicker materials have more vinyl and are therefore more durable. Solid vinyl is the best and most expensive flooring.

Sheet vinyl comes in 6- and 12-ft.-wide rolls. The most important aspect of installing sheet vinyl is to create a near-perfect underlayment surface. It's also important to cut the material so it fits perfectly along the contours of the room. Making a cutting template is the best way to ensure that your cuts will be correct (page 193). When handling sheet vinyl (especially felt-backed), remember that it can crease and tear easily if not handled carefully.

Make sure to use the recommended adhesive for the sheet vinyl you are installing. Many manufacturers require the use of their glue to install their flooring products, and will void their warranties if their directions are not followed exactly. Apply adhesive sparingly, using a ⅛" or ¼" notched trowel.

Most vinyl tiles are 12" squares, though 9" square tiles and narrow, 2-ft. long border strips are also available. If installing vinyl tile in your bathroom, be sure to carefully position the layout lines. Once those are established, the actual installation of the tile is relatively easy, especially if you are using self-adhesive tile. Before committing to any layout, however, be sure to dry-fit the tiles to identify potential problems.

Sheet vinyl comes in full-spread and perimeter-bond types. Full-spread flooring has a felt-paper backing, and is secured with adhesive that is spread over the floor before installation. It bonds tightly to the floor and is unlikely to come loose, but is more difficult to install, requiring a flawlessly smooth and clean underlayment. Perimeter-bond flooring has a white PVC backing, and is secured to the floor using a special adhesive along only the edges and seams. It is easy to install and will tolerate some minor underlayment flaws.

Resilient tile comes in dry-back tile and self-adhesive styles. Dry-back tile is secured with adhesive spread onto the underlayment before installation. Self-adhesive tile has a preapplied adhesive protected by a wax paper backing that is peeled off as the tiles are installed. Though self-adhesive tile is easier to install than dry-back tile, the bond is less reliable. Do not use additional adhesives with self-adhesive tile.

Everything You Need

Tools: utility knife, framing square, compass, scissors, non-permanent felt-tipped pen, linoleum knife, straightedge, ¼" V-notched trowel, J-roller, stapler, flooring roller, chalk line, heat gun.

Materials: vinyl flooring, masking tape, heavy butcher or brown wrapping paper, duct tape, flooring adhesive, ⅜" staples, metal threshold bars, nails.

How to Make a Cutting Template

1 Place sheets of heavy butcher or brown wrapping paper along the walls, leaving a ⅛" gap. Cut triangular holes in the paper with a utility knife. Fasten the template to the floor by placing masking tape over the holes.

2 Follow the outline of the room, working with one sheet of paper at a time. Overlap the edges of adjoining sheets by about 2" and tape the sheets together.

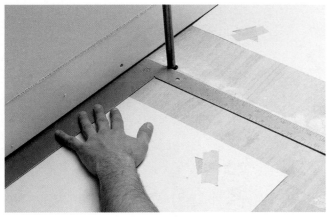

3 To fit the template around pipes, tape sheets of paper on either side. Measure the distance from the wall to the center of the pipe, and subtract ⅛".

4 Transfer the measurement to a separate piece of paper. Use a compass to draw the pipe diameter onto the paper, then cut out the hole with scissors or a utility knife. Cut a slit from the edge of the paper to the hole.

5 Fit the hole cutout around the pipe. Tape the hole template to the adjoining sheets.

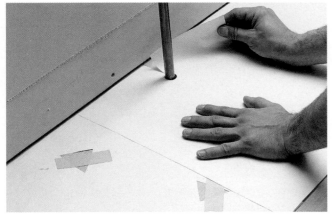

6 When completed, roll or loosely fold the paper template for carrying.

How to Install Perimeter-bond Sheet Vinyl

1 Unroll the flooring on any large, flat, clean surface. To prevent wrinkles, sheet vinyl comes from the manufacturer rolled with the pattern side out. Unroll the sheet and turn it pattern-side up for marking.

2 For two-piece installations, overlap the edges of sheets by at least 2". Plan to have the seams fall along the pattern lines or simulated grout joints. Align the sheets so that the pattern matches, then tape the sheets together with duct tape.

3 Position the paper template over the sheet vinyl, and tape it in place. Trace the outline of the template onto the flooring with a non-permanent felt-tipped pen.

4 Remove the template. Cut the sheet vinyl with a sharp linoleum knife or a utility knife with a new blade. Use a straightedge as a guide for making longer cuts.

5 Cut holes for pipes and other permanent obstructions, then cut a slit from each hole to the nearest edge of the flooring. Whenever possible, make slits along pattern lines.

6 Roll up flooring loosely and transfer it to the installation area. Do not fold the flooring. Unroll and position the sheet vinyl carefully. Slide the edges beneath undercut door casings.

7 Cut the seams for two-piece installations, using a straightedge as a guide. Hold the straightedge tightly against the flooring, and cut along the pattern lines through both pieces of vinyl flooring.

8 Remove both pieces of scrap flooring. The pattern should now run continuously across the adjoining sheets of flooring.

(continued next page)

9 Fold back the edges of both sheets and apply a 3" band of flooring adhesive to the underlayment or old flooring, using a ¼" V-notched trowel or wallboard knife.

10 Lay the seam edges one at a time into the adhesive. Make sure the seam is tight, pressing the gaps together with your fingers, if needed. Roll the seam edges with a J-roller or wallpaper seam roller.

11 Apply flooring adhesive underneath the flooring cuts at pipes or posts and around the entire perimeter of the room. Roll the flooring with the roller to ensure good contact with the adhesive.

12 If you are applying flooring over a wood underlayment, fasten the outer edges of the sheet with ⅜" staples driven every 3". Make sure the staples will be covered by the base molding.

How to Install Full-spread Sheet Vinyl

1 Cut the sheet vinyl using the techniques described on pages 194 to 195 (steps 1 through 5), then lay the sheet vinyl into position, sliding the edges underneath the door casings.

2 Pull back half of the flooring, then apply a layer of flooring adhesive over the underlayment or old flooring, using a ¼" V-notched trowel. Lay the flooring back onto the adhesive.

3 Roll the floor with a heavy flooring roller (available at rental centers), moving toward the edges of the sheet. The roller creates a stronger bond and eliminates air bubbles. Pull back the unbonded section of flooring, apply adhesive, then replace and roll the flooring. Wipe up any adhesive that oozes up around the edges of the vinyl, using a damp rag.

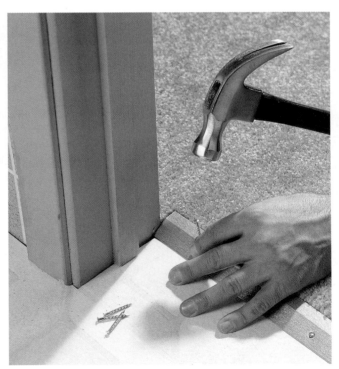

4 Measure and cut metal threshold bars to fit across doorways, then position each bar over the edge of the vinyl flooring and nail it in place.

Installing a Floor-Warming System

Floor-warming systems require very little energy to run and are designed to heat ceramic tile floors only; they generally are not used as sole heat sources for rooms.

A typical floor-warming system consists of one or more thin mats containing electric resistance wires that heat up when energized, like an electric blanket. The mats are installed beneath the tile and are hardwired to a 120-volt GFCI circuit. A thermostat controls the temperature, and a timer turns the system on or off automatically.

The system shown in this project includes two plastic mesh mats, each with its own power lead that is wired directly to the thermostat. The mats are laid over a concrete floor and then covered with thin-set adhesive and ceramic tile. If you have a wood subfloor, install cementboard before laying the mats.

A crucial part of installing this system is to perform several resistance checks to make sure the heating wires have not been damaged during shipping or during the installation.

Electrical service required for a floor-warming system is based on size. A smaller system may connect to an existing GFCI circuit, but a larger one will need a dedicated circuit (pages 127 to 128); follow the manufacturer's requirements.

To order a floor-warming system, contact the manufacturer or dealer. In most cases, you can send them plans and they'll custom-fit a system for your project area.

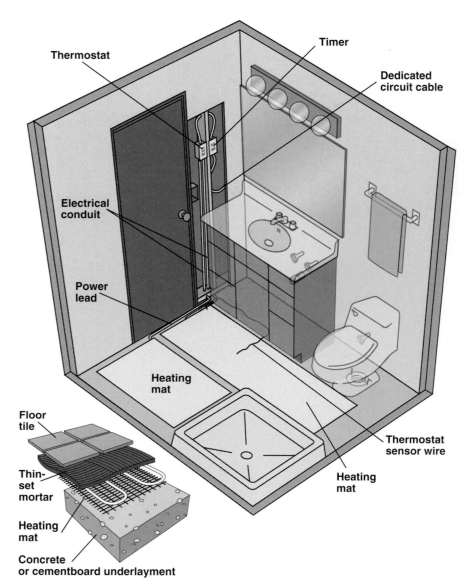

Thermostat · Timer · Dedicated circuit cable · Electrical conduit · Power lead · Floor tile · Thin-set mortar · Heating mat · Concrete or cementboard underlayment · Heating mat · Thermostat sensor wire · Heating mat

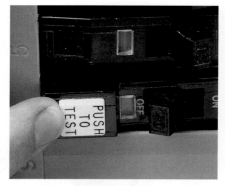

Floor-warming systems must be installed on a circuit with adequate amperage and a GFCI breaker (some systems have built-in GFCIs). Smaller systems may tie into an existing circuit but larger ones need a dedicated circuit. Follow local building and electrical codes that apply to your project.

How to Install a Floor-Warming System

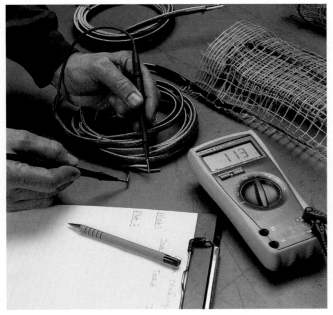

1 Check the resistance value (ohms) of each heating mat, using a digital multi-tester. Record the reading. Compare your reading to the factory-tested reading noted by the manufacturer—your reading must fall within the acceptable range determined by the manufacturer. If it does not, the mat has been damaged and should not be installed; contact the manufacturer for assistance.

2 Install electrical boxes for the thermostat and timer at an accessible location. Remove the wall surface to expose the framing, then locate the boxes approximately 60" from the floor, making sure the power leads of the heating mats will reach the double-gang electrical box. Mount a 2½"-deep × 4"-wide double-gang electrical box (for the thermostat) to the stud closest to the determined location, and a single-gang electrical box (for the timer) on the other side of the stud.

3 Use a plumb bob to mark points on the bottom plate directly below the two knockouts on the thermostat box. At each mark, drill a ½" hole through the top of the plate, then drill two more holes as close as possible to the floor through the side of the plate, intersecting the top holes. (The holes will be used to route the power leads and thermostat sensor wire.) Clean up the holes with a chisel to ensure smooth routing.

4 Cut two lengths of ½" thin-wall electrical conduit to fit between the thermostat box and the bottom plate, using a tube cutter. Place the bottom end of each length of conduit about ¼" into the holes in the bottom plate, and fasten the top end to the thermostat box, using a setscrew fitting. NOTE: If you are installing three or more mats, use ¾" conduit instead of ½".

(continued next page)

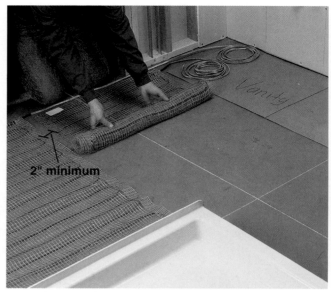

Branch cable

Cable from power source

5 Run 12-gauge NM electrical cable from the service panel (power source) to the timer box (pages 130 to 131). Attach the cable to the box with a cable clamp, leaving 8" of extra cable extending from the box. Drill a ⅝" hole through the center of the stud, about 12" above the boxes. Run a short branch cable from the timer box to the thermostat box, securing both ends with clamps. The branch cable should make a smooth curve where it passes through the stud.

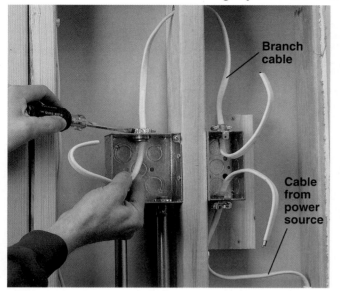

2" minimum

6 Vacuum the floor thoroughly. Plan the ceramic tile layout and snap reference lines for the tile installation (pages 202 to 209). Spread the heating mats onto the floor with the power leads closest to the electrical boxes. Position the mats 3" to 6" away from walls, showers, bathtubs, and toilet flanges. You can lay the mats into the kick space of a vanity but not under the vanity cabinet or over expansion joints in the concrete slab. Set the edges of the mats close together, but do not overlap them: The heating wires in one mat must be at least 2" from the wires in the neighboring mat.

7 Confirm that the power leads still reach the thermostat box. Then, secure the mats to the floor using strips of double-sided tape spaced every 24". Make sure the mats are lying flat with no wrinkles or ripples. Press down firmly to secure the mats to the tape.

8 Create recesses in the floor for the connections between the power leads and the heating-mat wires, using a grinder or a cold chisel and hammer. These insulated connections are too thick to lay under the tile and must be recessed to within ⅛" of the floor. Clean away any debris, and secure the connections in the recesses with a bead of hot glue.

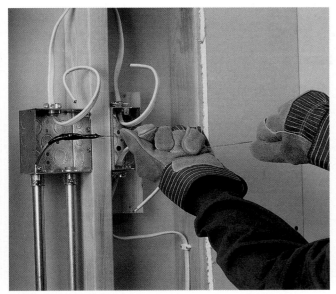

9 Thread a steel fish tape down one of the conduits, and attach the ends of the power leads to the fish tape, using electrical tape. Pull the fish tape and leads up through the conduit. Disconnect the fish tape, and secure the leads to the box with insulated cable clamps. Cut off the excess from the leads, leaving 8" extending from the clamps.

10 Feed the heat sensor wire down through the remaining conduit and weave it into the mesh of the nearest mat. Use dabs of hot glue to secure the sensor wire directly between two blue resistance wires, extending it 6" to 12" into the mat. Test the resistance of the heating mats with a multi-tester (step 1, page 199) to make sure the resistance wires have not been damaged. Record the reading.

11 Install the ceramic floor tile (pages 202 to 208). Use thin-set mortar as an adhesive, and spread it carefully over the floor and mats with a ⅜" × ¼" square-notched trowel. Check the resistance of the mats periodically during the tile installation. If a mat becomes damaged, clean up any exposed mortar and contact the manufacturer. When the installation is complete, check the resistance of the mats once again and record the reading.

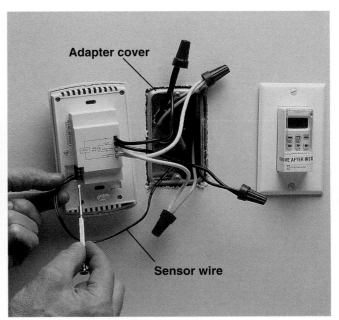

Adapter cover

Sensor wire

12 Install an adapter cover (mud ring) to the thermostat box, then patch the wall opening with drywall (pages 180 to 181). Complete the wiring connections for the thermostat and timer, following the manufacturer's instructions. Attach the sensor wire to the thermostat setscrew connection. Apply the manufacturer's wiring labels to the thermostat box and service panel. Mount the thermostat and timer. Complete the circuit connection at the service panel or branch connection. After the flooring materials have fully cured, test the system.

Installing Ceramic Floor Tile

Tile flooring should be durable and slip-resistant. Look for floor tile that is textured or soft-glazed—for slip resistance—and has a Class or Group rating of 3, 4, or 5—for strength. Floor tile also should be glazed for protection from staining. If you use unglazed tile, be sure to seal it properly after installation. Standard grouts also need stain-protection. Mix your grout with a latex additive, and apply a grout sealer after the new grout sets, then reapply the sealer once a year thereafter.

Successful tile installation involves careful preparation of the floor and the proper combination of materials. For an underlayment, cementboard is the best for use over wood subfloors in bathrooms, since it is stable and undamaged by moisture (page 203). Thin-set is the most common adhesive for floor tile. It comes as a dry powder that is mixed with water. Premixed organic adhesives generally are not recommended for floors.

Ceramic tile installations start with snapping perpendicular layout lines and dry-laying tiles for best placement (page 203). If you want to install trim tiles, consider their placement as you plan the layout. Some base-trim tile is set on the floor, with its finished edge flush with the field tile; other types are installed on top of the field tile (page 209).

See pages 204 to 205 for tips on cutting tile.

Everything You Need

Tools: chalk line, ¼" square-notched trowel, rubber mallet, tile-cutting tools (pages 204 to 205), needlenose pliers, utility knife, grout float, grout sponge, buff rag, foam brush.

Materials: tile, thin-set mortar, tile spacers, 2 × 4, threshold material, grout, latex additive (mortar and grout), grout sealer, silicone caulk.

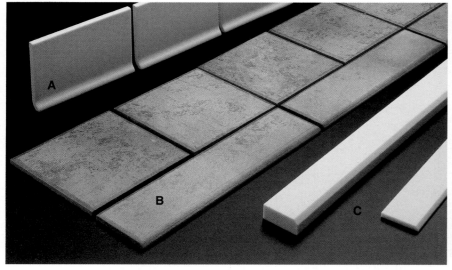

Trim and finishing materials for tile installations include base-trim tiles (A), which fit around the room perimeter, and bullnose tiles (B), used at doorways and other transition areas. Doorway thresholds (C) are made from synthetic materials as well as natural materials, such as marble, and come in thicknesses ranging from ¼" to ¾" to match different floor levels.

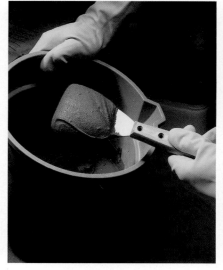

To prepare thin-set mortar, add liquid, a little at a time, to the dry powder and stir the mixture until it has a creamy consistency. If the mortar does not already have a latex additive in the dry mix, you'll need to add liquid latex additive to the mixture.

How to Install Cementboard Underlayment

1 Mix thin-set mortar (page 202) according to the manufacturer's directions. Starting at the longest wall, spread mortar on the subfloor in a figure-eight pattern, using a ¼" notched trowel. Spread only enough mortar for one sheet at a time. Set the cementboard on the mortar with the rough side up, making sure the edges are offset from the subfloor seams.

2 Fasten cementboard to the subfloor, using 1½" cementboard screws driven every 6" along the edges and 8" throughout the sheet. Drive the screw heads flush with the surface. Continue spreading mortar and installing sheets along the wall, leaving a ⅛" gap at all joints and a ¼" gap along the room perimeter. See pages 182 to 184 for cutting cementboard, and taping and mudding the joints.

How to Establish Perpendicular Lines for Floor Tile Installation

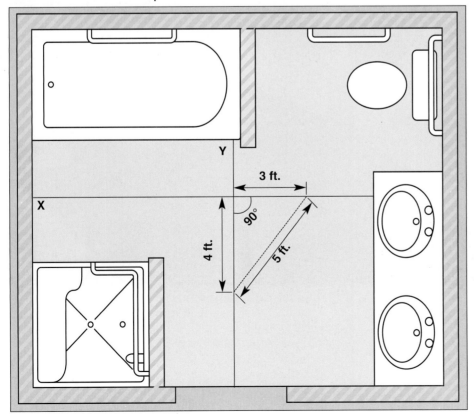

To establish perpendicular reference lines, position a reference line (X) by measuring between opposite sides of the room and marking the center of each side. Snap a chalk line between these marks.

Next, measure and mark the centerpoint of the chalk line. From this point, use a framing square to establish a second line perpendicular to the first. Snap a second reference line (Y) across the room.

Check for squareness using the "3-4-5 triangle" method. Measure and mark one reference line 3 ft. from the centerpoint on line X, then mark another reference line 4 ft. from the centerpoint on line Y.

Finally, measure the distance between the marks. If the reference lines are perpendicular, the distance will measure exactly 5 ft. If not, adjust the reference lines until they are exactly perpendicular to each other.

How to Cut Tile Using a Tile Cutter

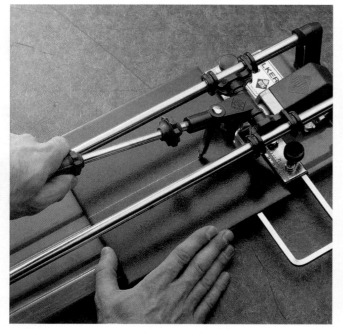

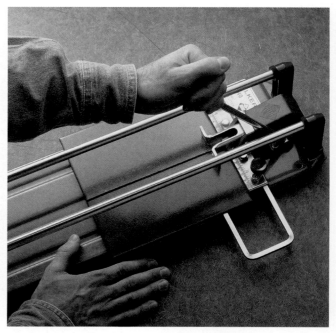

1 Mark a cutting line on the tile with a pencil, then place the tile in the cutter so the cutting wheel is directly over the line. While pressing down firmly on the wheel handle, run the wheel across the tile to score the surface. For a clean cut, score the tile only once.

2 Snap the tile along the scored line, as directed by the tool manufacturer. Usually, snapping the tile is accomplished by depressing a lever on the tile cutter.

How to Cut Tile Using Power Saws

Tile saws (also called *wet saws* because they use water to cool blades and tiles) are used primarily for cutting natural-stone tiles. They are also useful for quickly cutting notches in all kinds of hard tile. Wet saws are available for rent at tile dealers and rental shops.

To make square notches, clamp the tile down on a worktable, then use a jig saw with a tungsten-carbide blade to make the cuts. If you need to cut many notches, a wet saw is more efficient.

How to Cut Tile Using Curved Cuts

1 Mark a cutting line on the tile face, then use the scoring wheel of a handheld tile cutter to score the cut line. Make several parallel scores, no more than ¼" apart, in the waste portion of the tile.

2 Use tile nippers to nibble away the scored portion of the tile. TIP: To cut circular holes in the middle of a tile (step 7, page 207), first score and cut the tile so it divides the hole in two, using the straight-cut method, then use the curved-cut method to remove waste material from each half of the circle. To cut a hole through a whole tile, see below.

How to Cut Tile Using Specialty Cuts

To cut mosaic tiles, use a tile cutter to score tiles in the row where the cut will occur. Cut away excess strips of mosaics from the sheet, using a utility knife, then use a handheld tile cutter to snap tiles one at a time. NOTE: Use tile nippers to cut narrow portions of tiles after scoring.

Cut holes for plumbing stub-outs and other obstructions by marking the outline on the tile, then drilling around the edges, using a ceramic tile bit (inset). Gently knock out the waste material with a hammer. The rough edges of the hole will be covered by protective plates on fixtures (called *escutcheons*).

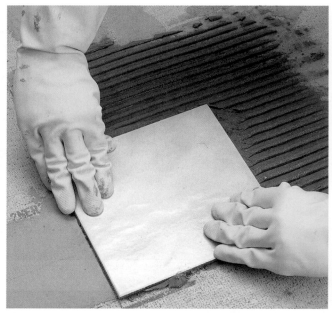

1 Draw reference lines (page 203) and establish the tile layout by dry-fitting full tiles along both lines, adjusting the layout as necessary. Mix a batch of thin-set mortar, and spread it evenly against both reference lines of one quadrant, using a ¼" square-notched trowel. Use the notched edge of the trowel to create furrows in the mortar bed. NOTE: For large or uneven tiles, you may need a trowel with ⅜" or larger notches.

2 Set the first tile in the corner of the quadrant where the reference lines intersect. TIP: When setting tiles that are 8" square or larger, twist each tile slightly as you set it into position.

3 Using a soft rubber mallet, gently rap the central area of each tile a few times to set it evenly into the mortar.

VARIATION: For mosaic sheets, use a ³⁄₁₆" V-notched trowel to spread the mortar, and use a grout float to press the sheets into the mortar. Apply pressure gently to avoid creating an uneven surface.

4 To ensure consistent spacing between tiles, place plastic tile spacers at corners of the set tile. NOTE: With mosaic sheets, use spacers equal to the gaps between tiles.

5 Position and set adjacent tiles into the mortar along the reference lines. Make sure the tiles fit neatly against the spacers. To make sure the tiles are level with one another, lay a straight piece of 2 × 4 across several tiles, and rap the board with a mallet. Lay tile in the remaining area covered with mortar. Repeat steps 1 through 5, continuing to work in small sections, until you reach walls or fixtures.

6 Measure and mark tiles for cutting to fit against walls and into corners, then cut the tiles to fit, following the tips on pages 204 to 205. Apply thin-set mortar directly to the back of the cut tiles, instead of the floor, using the notched edge of the trowel to furrow the mortar. Set the tiles.

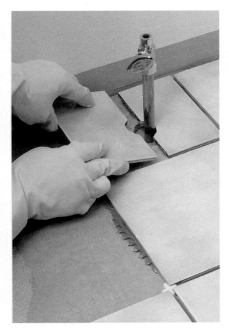

7 Measure, cut, and install tiles requiring notches or curves to fit around obstacles, such as exposed pipes or toilet drains.

8 Remove the spacers with needlenose pliers before the mortar hardens. TIP: Inspect the tile joints and remove high spots of mortar that could show through the grout, using a utility knife or small screwdriver. Install tile in the remaining quadrants, completing one quadrant at a time.

9 Install threshold material in doorways. Set the threshold in thin-set mortar so the top is even with the tile. Keep the same space between the threshold as between tiles. Let the mortar cure for at least 24 hours.

(continued next page)

10 Mix a small batch of grout, following the manufacturer's directions. TIP: For unglazed or stone tile, add a release agent to prevent the grout from bonding to the tile surfaces. Starting in a corner, pour the grout over the tile. Use a rubber grout float to spread the grout outward from the corner, pressing firmly on the float to completely fill the joints. For best results, tilt the float at a 60° angle to the floor and use a figure-eight motion.

11 Use the grout float to remove excess grout from the surface of the tile. Wipe diagonally across the joints, holding the float in a near-vertical position. Continue applying grout and wiping off excess until about 25 sq. ft. of the floor has been grouted.

12 Remove excess grout by wiping a damp grout sponge diagonally over about 2 sq. ft. of the tile at a time. Rinse the sponge in cool water between wipes. Wipe each area only once; repeated wiping can pull grout from the joints. Repeat steps 10 through 12 to apply grout to the rest of the floor. Allow the grout to dry for about 4 hours, then use a soft cloth to buff the tile surface and remove any remaining grout film.

13 After the grout has cured completely (check the manufacturer's instructions), apply grout sealer to the grout lines, using a small sponge brush or sash brush. Avoid brushing sealer on the tile surfaces. Wipe up any excess sealer immediately.

How to Install Base & Trim Tile

1 Dry-fit the trim tiles to determine the best spacing (grout lines in base tile do not always align with grout lines in the floor tile). Use rounded bullnose tiles at outside corners, and mark tiles for cutting as needed.

2 Leaving a ⅛" expansion gap between tiles at corners, mark any contour cuts necessary to allow the coved edges to fit together. Use a jig saw with a tungsten-carbide blade to make curved cuts.

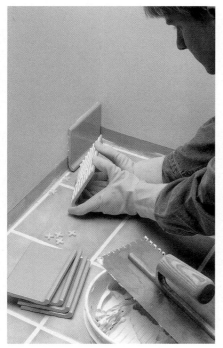

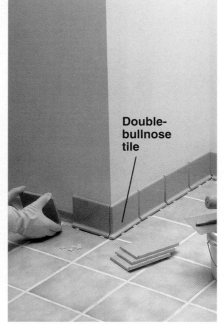

Double-bullnose tile

3 Begin installing base-trim tiles at an inside corner. Use a notched trowel to apply wall-tile adhesive to the back of each tile. Slip ⅛" spacers under the tiles to create an expansion joint. Set the tiles by pressing them firmly onto the wall.

4 At outside corners, use a double-bullnose tile on one side, to cover the edge of the adjoining tile.

5 After the adhesive dries, grout the vertical joints between tiles, and apply grout along the tops of the tiles to make a continuous grout line. After the grout cures, fill the expansion joint at the bottom of the tiles with silicone caulk.

Photo courtesy of Andersen Windows, Inc.

Bow windows include side windows set at an angle with a middle window or windows parallel to the wall. Bow and bay windows expand a space and bring more light into a room, making them attractive options for whirlpool alcoves.

Installing Windows & Doors

When selecting bathroom windows, look for windows that will resist moisture, give you a good combination of light, ventilation, and privacy, and last for many years. Quality and price can vary dramatically from window to window, as can installation requirements. Some models are geared toward the do-it-yourself homeowner, while others should be installed only by experienced professionals. Make sure to read the manufacturer's literature carefully before placing an order.

Make the most of the space that you have for windows. You may decide to combine two types of windows or even design a nontraditional window solution in order to get the results you want. Most window manufacturers offer each of their styles in a limited range of stock sizes, but for an additional fee, you can order windows in unusual sizes and shapes.

Doors are available in many styles and standard sizes and are sold in 2" increments ranging from 24" to 36". Bathroom doors should provide plenty of privacy for the user and be equipped with a locking door handle.

When designing for accessibility, doorways must be at least 32" wide; 36" is preferred. Pocket doors are available for small bathrooms that cannot accommodate the swing radius of a standard hinged door.

This section shows:

- Installing a Glass Block Window
  (pages 212 to 215)
- Installing a Tubular Skylight
  (pages 216 to 217)
- Installing a Prehung Interior Door
  (pages 218 to 219)
- Installing a Pocket Door
  (pages 220 to 223)

Windows & Doors for Bathrooms

Replace a large window in a tub alcove with a smaller window, especially when adding a shower and surround. An awning window (above) provides as much ventilation as the larger, double-hung window that it replaced. Be sure to check wall studs and window framing for water damage. NOTE: All glass in shower surrounds, including windows, must be safety glass.

Glass block windows are ideal for bathrooms as they provide security and privacy while allowing in plenty of natural light. Louvered vents (inset) are available for installation to provide ventilation.

Skylights let in more natural light per square foot than do wall windows. They are a great lighting solution for a small interior bathroom, or can be a luxurious addition in a master suite.

Pocket doors take up no floor space in a room, making them a great option to traditional swinging doors in a bathroom. Pocket doors are available in kits and can be installed in a standard 2 × 4 stud wall.

Installing a Glass Block Window

Glass block is a durable material that transmits light while reducing visibility, making it a perfect material for creating unique windows. Glass block windows are energy-efficient and work particularly well as accent windows, or in rooms where privacy is desired, such as bathrooms.

Glass block is available in a wide variety of sizes, shapes, and patterns. It can be found, along with other necessary installation products, at specialty distributors or home centers.

Building with glass block is much like building with mortared brick, with two important differences. First, glass block must be supported by another structure and cannot function in a loadbearing capacity. Second, glass block cannot be cut, so take extra time to make sure the layout is accurate.

When installing a glass block window, the size of the rough opening is based on the size and number of blocks you are using. It is much easier to make an existing opening smaller to accommodate the glass block rather than make it larger, which requires reframing the rough opening. To determine the rough opening width, multiply the nominal width of the glass block by the number of blocks horizontally, and add ¼". For the height, multiply the nominal height by the number of blocks vertically and add ¼".

Because of its weight, a glass block window requires a solid base. The framing members of the rough opening will need to

Photo courtesy of Pittsburgh Corning Corporation

be reinforced. Contact your local building department for requirements in your area.

Use ¼" plastic T-spacers between blocks to ensure consistent mortar joints and to support the weight of the block to prevent mortar from squeezing out before it sets. (T-spacers can be modified into L or flat shapes for use at corners and along the channel.) For best results, use premixed glass block mortar. This high-strength mortar is a little drier than regular brick mortar, because glass doesn't wick water out of the mortar as brick does.

Because there are many applications for glass block, and installation techniques may vary,

ask a glass block retailer or manufacturer about the best products and methods for your specific project.

Everything You Need

Tools: tape measure, circular saw, hammer, utility knife, tin snips, drill, mixing box, trowel, 4-ft. level, rubber mallet, jointing tool, sponge, scrub brush, caulk gun.

Materials: 2 × 4 lumber, 16d common nails, glass block perimeter channels, 1" galvanized flat-head screws, glass block mortar, glass blocks, ¼" T-spacers, expansion strips, silicone caulk, construction adhesive, mortar sealant.

How to Install a Glass Block Window

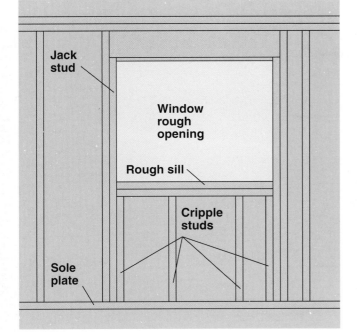

1 Measure the size of the rough opening and determine the size of the glass block window you will install (opposite page). Reinforce the rough opening framing by doubling the rough sill and installing additional cripple studs. Cut all pieces to size and fasten with 16d common nails.

2 Cut perimeter channel to length for the sill and side jambs, mitering the ends at 45°. Align front edge of channel flush with front edge of exterior wall sheathing. Drill pilot holes every 12" through the channels (if not provided), and fasten the channels in place with 1" galvanized flat-head screws. NOTE: Paint screw heads white to help conceal them.

3 For the header, cut a channel to length, mitering the ends at 45°, then cut it in half lengthwise, using a utility knife. Align one half of the channel flush with the exterior face of the sheathing, and fasten in place with 1" galvanized flat-head screws.

4 Set two blocks into the sill channel, one against each jamb—do not place mortar between blocks and channels. Place a ¼" flat spacer against the first block. Mix glass block mortar and liberally butter the leading edge of another block, then push it tight against the first block. Make sure the joint is filled with mortar.

(continued next page)

5 Lay the remainder of the first course, building from both jambs toward the center. Use flat spacers between blocks to maintain proper spacing. Plumb and level each block as you work, then check the entire course for level. Tap blocks into place using the rubber handle of the trowel—do not use metal tools with glass block. Butter both sides of the final block in the course to install it.

6 At the top of the course, fill any depression at the top of each mortar joint with mortar and insert a ¼" T-spacer, then lay a ⅜" bed of mortar for the next course. Lay the blocks for each course, using T-spacers to maintain proper spacing. Check each block for level and plumb as you work.

7 Test the mortar as you work. When it can resist light finger pressure, remove the T-spacers (inset) and pack mortar into the voids, then tool the joints with a jointing tool. Remove excess mortar with a damp sponge, or a nylon or natural-bristle brush.

8 To ease block placement in the final course, trim the outer tabs off one side of the T-spacers, using tin snips. Install the blocks of the final course. After the final block is installed, work in any mortar that has been forced out of the joints.

9 Cut an expansion strip for the header 1½" wide and to length. Slide it between the top course of block and the header of the rough opening. Apply a bead of construction adhesive to the top edge of the remaining half of the header channel, and slide it between the expansion strip and header.

10 Clean glass block thoroughly with wet sponge, rinsing often. Allow surface to dry, then remove cloudy residue with clean, dry cloth. Caulk between glass block and channels, and between channels and framing members before installing exterior trim. After molding is installed, allow mortar to cure for two weeks, then apply silicone caulk.

Variation: Glass Block Window Kits

Some glass block window kits do not require mortar. Instead, the blocks are set into the perimeter channels and the joints are created using plastic spacer strips. Silicone caulk is then used to seal the joints.

Preassembled glass block windows are simple to install. These vinyl-clad units have a nailing flange around the frame, which allows them to be hung using the same installation techniques as for standard windows with a nailing flange.

Installing a Tubular Skylight

Any bathroom can be brightened with a tubular skylight. Unlike traditional skylights, tubular skylights are quite energy-efficient and are relatively easy to install, with no complicated framing involved.

Tubular skylights vary among manufacturers, with some using solid plastic reflecting tubes and others using flexible tubing. Various diameters are also available. Measure the distance between the framing members in your attic before purchasing your skylight.

This project shows the installation of a tubular skylight on a sloped, asphalt-shingled roof. Consult the dealer or manufacturer for installation procedures on other roof types.

Photos courtesy of Sun Tunnel Systems, Inc.

Everything You Need

Tools: pencil, ladder, drill, tape measure, wallboard saw, reciprocating saw or jig saw, pry bar, screwdriver, hammer, wire cutters, utility knife, chalk.

Materials: tubular skylight kit, stiff wire, 2" roofing nails or flashing screws, roofing cement.

How to Install a Tubular Skylight

1 Drill a pilot hole through the ceiling at the approximate location for your skylight. Fish a stiff wire into the attic to help locate the hole. In the attic, make sure the space around the hole is clear and pull back any insulation. Drill a second hole through the ceiling at the centerpoint between two joists.

2 Center the ceiling ring frame over the hole and trace around it with a pencil. Carefully cut out along the pencil line with a wallboard saw or reciprocating saw. Save the wallboard ceiling cutout to use as your roof-hole pattern. Attach the ceiling frame ring around the hole with the included screws.

3 In the attic, choose the most direct route for the tubing to reach the roof. Find the center between the appropriate rafters and drive a nail up through the roof sheathing and shingles.

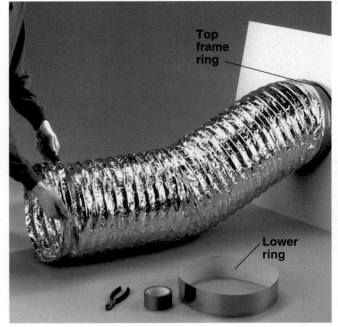

4 Use the wallboard ceiling cutout, centered over the nail hole, as a template for the roof opening. Trace the cutout onto the roof with chalk. Drill a starter hole to insert the reciprocating saw blade, then cut out the hole in the roof. Pry up the lower portion of the shingles above the hole. Remove any staples or nails around the hole edge.

5 Pull the tubing over the top frame ring. Bend the frame tabs out through the tubing, keeping two or three rings of the tubing wire above the tabs. Wrap the junction three times around with included PVC tape. Then, in the attic, measure from the roof to the ceiling. Stretch out the tubing and cut it to length with a utility knife and wire cutters. Pull the loose end of tubing over the lower ring and wrap it three times around with PVC tape.

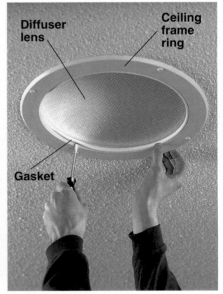

6 Lower the tubing through the roof hole and slide the flashing into place with the upper portion of the flashing underneath the existing shingles. This is easier with two people, one on the roof and one in the attic.

7 Secure the flashing to the roof with 2" roofing nails or flashing screws. Seal under the shingles and over all nail heads with roofing cement. Attach the skylight dome and venting to the frame with the included screws.

8 Pull the lower end of the tubing down through the ceiling hole. Attach the lower tubing ring to the ceiling frame ring and fasten it with screws. Attach the gasket to the diffuser lens and work the gasket around the perimeter of the ceiling frame. Repack any insulation around the tubing in the attic.

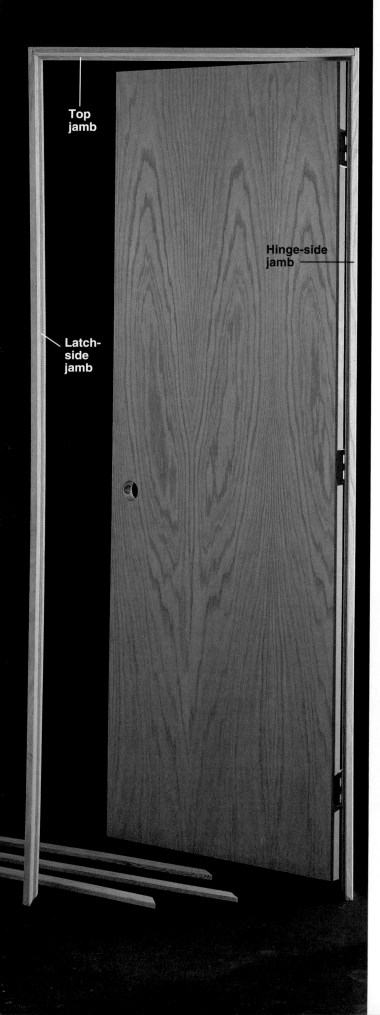

Top jamb

Hinge-side jamb

Latch-side jamb

Installing a Prehung Interior Door

Prehung doors come as single units with the door already hung on hinges attached to a factory-built frame. To secure the unit during shipping, most prehung doors are fastened shut. These fasteners must be removed before you install the door.

The key to installing doors is to plumb and fasten the hinge-side jamb first. After that's in place, you can position the top and latch-side jambs by checking the reveal—the gap between the closed door and the jamb.

Standard prehung doors have 4½"-wide jambs and are sized to fit walls with 2 × 4 construction and ½" drywall. If you have thicker walls, you can special-order doors to match, or you can add jamb extensions to standard-size doors. You will need to note which direction the door will open in relation to which side has the hinges before purchasing your door.

Everything You Need

Tools: 4-ft. level, nail set, hammer, handsaw.

Materials: prehung door unit, wood shims, 8d casing nails.

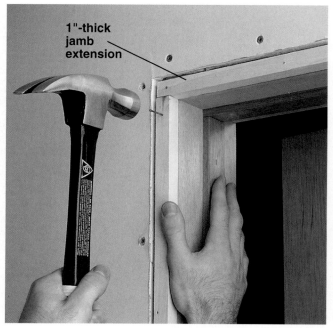

1"-thick jamb extension

Tip: If your walls are built with 2 × 6 studs, extend the jambs by attaching 1"-thick wood strips to the jamb edges on both sides. Use glue and 4d casing nails to attach these extensions to the jambs.

How to Install a Prehung Interior Door

1 Set the door unit into the framed opening so the jamb edges are flush with the wall surfaces and the unit is centered from side to side. Using a level, adjust the unit so the hinge-side jamb is plumb.

2 Starting near the top hinge, insert pairs of shims driven from opposite directions into the gap between the framing and the jamb, sliding the shims in until they are snug. Check the jamb to make sure it remains plumb and does not bow inward. Install shims near each hinge.

3 Anchor the hinge-side jamb with 8d casing nails driven through the jamb and shims and into the framing. Drive nails only at the shim locations.

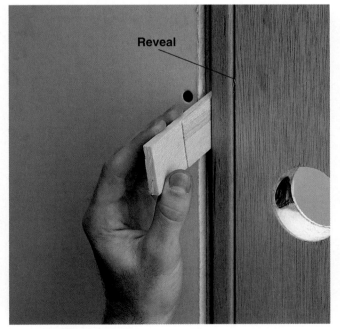

Reveal

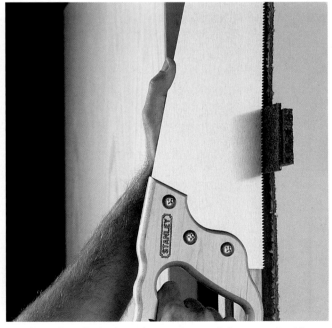

4 Insert pairs of shims into the gap between the framing members and the top jamb and latch-side jamb, aligning them roughly with the hinge-side shims. With the door closed, adjust the shims so the reveal is $\frac{1}{16}$" to $\frac{1}{8}$" wide. Drive casing nails through the jambs and shims and into the framing members.

5 Set all nails below the surface of the wood with a nail set, then cut off the shims flush with the wall surface, using a handsaw or utility knife. Hold the saw vertically to prevent damage to the door jamb or wall. Install the door casing.

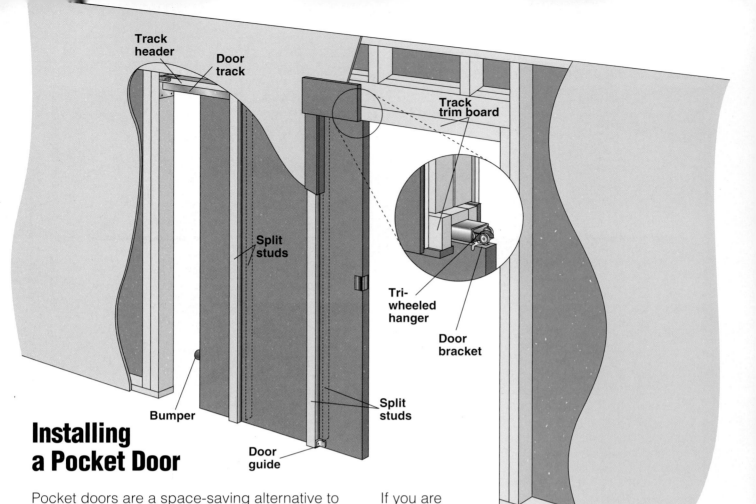

Track
header

Door
track

Track
trim board

Split
studs

Tri-
wheeled
hanger

Door
bracket

Bumper

Split
studs

Door
guide

Installing
a Pocket Door

Pocket doors are a space-saving alternative to traditional hinged interior doors. Swinging doors can monopolize up to 16 sq. ft. of floor space in a room, which is why pocket doors are a perfect choice for tight spaces, like small bathrooms. Installed in pairs, pocket doors can divide large rooms into more intimate spaces and can still be opened to use the entire area.

Pocket door hardware kits generally are universal and can be adapted for almost any interior door. In this project, the frame kit includes an adjustable track, steel-clad split studs, and all the required hanging hardware. The latch hardware, jambs, and the door itself are all sold separately. Pocket door frames can also be purchased as preassembled units that can be easily installed into a rough opening.

Framing and installing a pocket door is not difficult in new construction or a major remodel. But retrofitting a pocket door in place of a standard door, or installing one in a wall without an existing door, is a major project that involves removing the wall material, framing the new opening, installing and hanging the door, and refinishing the wall. Hidden utilities, such as wiring, plumbing, and heating ducts, must be rerouted if encountered.

The rough opening for a pocket door is at least twice the width of a standard door opening.

If you are installing the pocket door in a non-loadbearing wall, see pages 84 to 86 to learn how to frame the opening. If the wall is loadbearing, you will need to install an appropriately sized header (page 84).

Because pocket doors are easy to open and close and require no threshold, they offer increased accessibility for wheelchair or walker users, provided the handles are easy to use. If you are installing a pocket door for this purpose, be aware that standard latch hardware may be difficult to use for some individuals. Page 223 includes some handle variations for easier accessibility.

Everything You Need

Tools: tape measure, circular saw, hammer, nail set, screwdriver, level, drill, handsaw, hacksaw, wallboard tools.

Materials: 2 × 4 lumber, 16d, 8d & 6d common nails, pocket door frame kit, door, 1¼" wallboard screws, wallboard materials, manufactured pocket door jambs (or build jambs from 1× material), 8d & 6d finish nails, 1½" wood screws, door casing.

How to Install a Pocket Door

1 Prepare the project area and frame the rough opening to the manufacturer's recommended dimensions (pages 84 to 86). Measuring from the floor, mark each jack stud at the height of the door plus ¾" to 1½" (depending on the door clearance above the floor) for the overhead door track. Drive a nail into each jack stud, centered on the mark. Leave about ⅛" of the nail protruding.

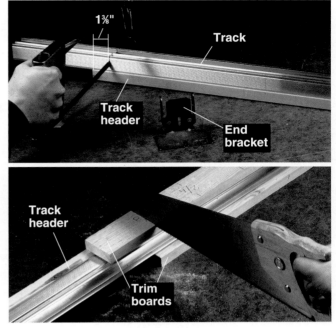

2 Remove the adjustable end bracket from the overhead door track. Cut the wooden track header at the mark that matches your door size. Turn the track over and cut the metal track 1⅜" shorter than the wooden track header, using a hacksaw (top). Replace the end bracket. Cut the side trim boards along the marks corresponding to your door size, being careful not to cut the metal track (bottom).

3 Set the end brackets of the track on the nails in the jack studs. Adjust the track to level and set the nails. Then drive 8d common nails through the remaining holes in the end brackets.

4 Snap chalk lines on the floor across the opening, even with the sides of the rough opening. Tap floor plate spacers into the bottom ends of the pairs of steel-clad split studs. Butt one split stud pair against the door track trim board, check it for plumb, and fasten it to the track header using 6d common nails (left). Center the other split stud pair in the "pocket" and fasten it to the track header. Plumb the split studs again and attach them to floor with 8d common nails or 2" screws driven through spacer plates (right).

(continued next page)

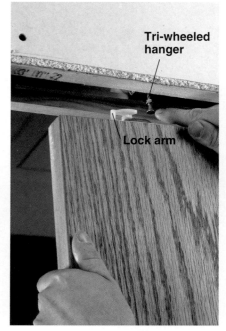

5 Install drywall over the pocket to the edge of the opening. You may want to leave the drywall off one side of the wall to allow for door adjustment. Do not finish drywall until the door has been completely installed and adjusted. Use 1¼" drywall screws, which will not protrude into the pocket.

6 Paint or stain the door as desired. When the door has dried, attach two door brackets to the top of the door, using included screws driven through pilot holes. Install the rubber bumper to the rear edge of the door with its included screw.

7 Slide two tri-wheeled hangers into the overhead door track. Set the door in the frame, aligning the hangers with the door brackets. Then raise the door and press each hanger into the door bracket until it snaps into place. Close the lock arm over the hanger.

8 Cut the strike-side jamb to length and width. Fasten it to the jack stud, using 8d finish nails, shimming jamb to plumb as necessary. Close door and adjust the hanger nuts to fine-tune the door height so the door is parallel with the jamb from top to bottom.

9 Measure and cut the split jambs to size. Fasten each split jamb to front edge of split stud, using 8d finish nails. Maintain ³⁄₁₆" clearance on both sides of door. If necessary, shim between the bumper and door until the door is flush with the jambs when open.

10 Measure and cut the split head jambs to size. Use 1½" wood screws driven through countersunk pilot holes to attach the head jamb on the side that has access to the lock arm of the hangers, to allow for easy removal of the door. Attach the other head jamb using 6d finish nails. Maintain ³⁄₁₆" clearance on each side of the door.

11 Install the included door guides on both sides of the door near the floor at the mouth of the pocket. Install the latch hardware according to the manufacturer's directions. Finish the drywall and install casing around the door. Fill all nail holes, then paint or stain the jambs and casing as desired.

Improving Pocket Door Accessibility

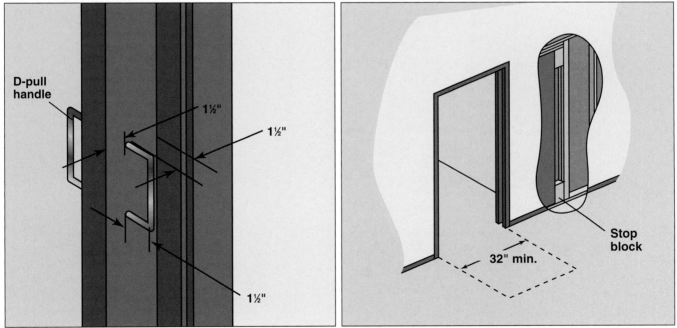

D-pull handle

1½"

1½"

1½"

1½"

Stop block

32" min.

D-pull handles are easier to use than standard recessed hardware. Choose pulls that project at least 1½" from the door. Mount the pulls 1½" from the edge of the door to provide room for fingers when the door is closed (left). Install a stop block at the back of the frame (right), so the door stops 1½" short of the D-pull to provide room for fingers when the door is open. Because this design reduces the width of the door opening by 3", you must use a 36"-wide door to maintain the recommended doorway width of 32".

Installing Cabinets, Countertops & Sinks

When selecting cabinets, countertops and sinks, you will find there are many materials, styles, and colors to choose from. As you begin combining the units and fixtures, you will find you have an almost infinite number of options.

One of the first decisions to make is between prebuilt or custom-built units and fixtures. Prebuilt cabinets and countertops are available in familiar styles at home centers, and are perfect for renovating half baths, guest baths, and small family bathrooms. For more unique styles in large family bathrooms, master bathrooms, or home spas, you may want to have your cabinets and countertops custom-built by a professional cabinetmaker. Refer to pages 32 to 35 for more information on different styles of cabinets and countertops.

Sinks are available in a variety of sizes and styles. They can serve as a decorative focal point, or remain purely functional. Many sink manufacturers provide catalogs on the Internet to help make the search for the perfect sink less daunting. See pages 26 to 27 for more information on different types of sinks.

If you are remodeling a bathroom for universal design, there are a number of manufacturers that offer cabinets, countertops and sinks specifically designed to provide accessibility. Examples are provided on the opposite page, as well as more information on universal design on pages 42 to 47.

©Jessie Walker

This section shows:

- Installing Cabinets & Vanities (pages 226 to 229)
- Installing Countertops & Sinks (pages 230 to 233)
- Building a Ceramic Tile Countertop (pages 234 to 239)

Custom cabinets are often professionally installed and can be expensive. Another option is prebuilt cabinets. Manufacturers sell several cabinet types in the same style and finish. When pricing prebuilt cabinets, note that faucets and vanity tops are sold separately.

Cabinet, Countertop & Sink Options for a Universal Bathroom

Height-adjustable countertops and movable base cabinets make this vanity area a versatile workspace. Grab-railings provide support and convenient places for hand towels.

Clear space under sinks and lowered sections of countertop allow seated users to comfortably reach the vanity. A hinged mirror easily adjusts in angle for users of all heights.

Accessible sinks are wider and are installed closer to the front edge of the countertop than standard sinks. Some designs jut out past the counter's edge, providing easy access from a seated position.

Installing Cabinets & Vanities

Common bathroom cabinets include vanities, medicine cabinets, linen cabinets, and "tank topper" cabinets that mount over the toilet area. See pages 32 to 33 for more information on cabinets.

When installing cabinets in damp locations, like a bathroom, choose the best cabinets you can afford. Look for quality indicators, like doweled construction, hardwood doors and drawers, and high-gloss, moisture-resistant finishes. Avoid cabinets with sides or doors that are painted on one side and finished with laminate or veneer on the other, because these cabinets are more likely to warp.

Remove the door and drawers on heavy cabinets before installing them. This makes the cabinets easier to move and provides better access for making the plumbing hookups (pages 240 to 242). Reattach the doors and install drawers after the plumbing hookups are completed.

Everything You Need

Tools: electronic studfinder, level, pry bar, hammer, screwdriver, drill, circular saw, reciprocating saw, bar clamp, framing square.

Materials: duplex nails, 10d common nails, finish nails, 1 × 4 lumber, 2½" wood screws, wood shims.

How to Install a Surface-mounted Cabinet

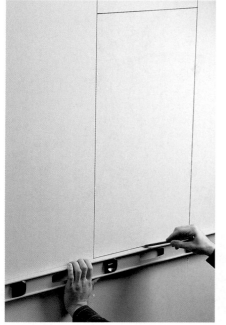

1 Locate the wall studs and mark them clearly on the wall surface. Draw a level line at the desired top height of the cabinet body, then measure and mark a second line to indicate the bottom of the cabinet.

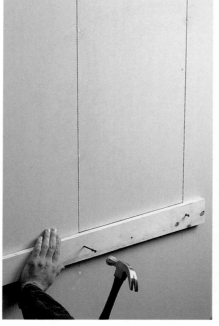

2 Attach a temporary ledger board (usually 1 × 4) just below the lower level line, using duplex nails. Rest the base of the cabinet on the ledger, and hold it in place, or brace it with 2 × 4s.

3 Attach the cabinet to the wall at the stud locations by drilling pilot holes and driving wood screws. Remove ledger when finished, and patch the nail holes with drywall compound.

How to Install a Recessed Cabinet

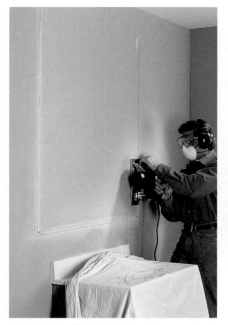

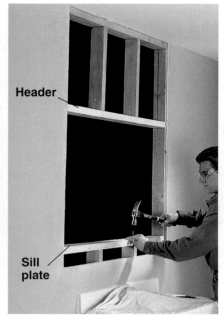

1 Locate the first stud beyond either side of the planned cabinet location, then remove the wall surface between the studs. (Removing the wall surface all the way to the ceiling simplifies patch work.) Cut along the center of the studs, using a circular saw with the blade depth set to the thickness of the wall surface.

2 Mark a rough opening ½" taller than the cabinet frame onto the exposed wall studs. Add 1½" for each header and sill plate, then cut out the studs in the rough opening area.

3 Frame out the top and bottom of the rough opening by installing a header and a sill plate between the cut wall studs. Make sure the header and sill plate are level, then nail them in place with 10d common nails.

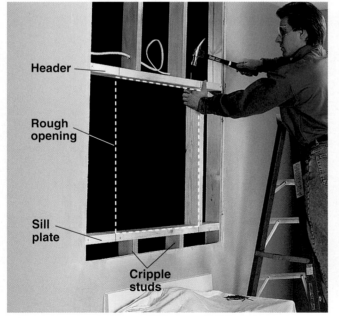

4 Mark the rough opening width on the header and sill plates, centering the opening over the sink. Cut and nail jack studs between the header and the sill plate, just outside the rough opening marks. Install any wiring for new light fixtures and receptacles (pages 126 to 137), then patch the wall where necessary with drywall (pages 180 to 181).

5 Position the cabinet in the opening. Check it for level with a carpenter's level, then attach the cabinet by drilling pilot holes and driving wood screws through the top and bottom of the cabinet sides and into the wall studs, header, and sill plate. Attach the doors, shelves, and hardware.

How to Install a Vanity

1 Measure and mark the top edge of the vanity cabinet on the wall, then use a 4-ft. level to mark a level line at the cabinet height mark. Use an electronic stud finder to locate the framing members, then mark the stud locations along the line.

2 Slide the vanity into position, so that the back rail of the cabinet can later be fastened to studs at both corners and in the center. The back of the cabinet should also be flush against the wall. (If the wall surface is uneven, position the vanity so it contacts the wall in at least one spot, and the back cabinet rail is parallel with the wall.)

3 Using a 4-ft. level as a guide, shim below the vanity until the unit is level.

VARIATION: To install two or more cabinets, set the cabinets in position against the wall, and align the cabinet fronts. If one cabinet is higher than the other, shim under the lower cabinet until the two are even. Clamp the cabinet faces together, then drill countersunk pilot holes through the face frames, spaced 12" apart, at least halfway into the face frame of the second cabinet. Drive wood screws through the pilot holes to join the cabinets together.

4 At the stud locations marked on the wall, drive 3" drywall screws through the rail on the cabinet back and into the framing members. The screws should be driven at both corners and in the center of the back rail.

5 Run a bead of caulk along small gaps between the vanity and the wall, and between the vanity and floor. For larger gaps, use quarter-round molding between the vanity and wall. Between the vanity and the floor, install the same baseboard material used to cover the gap between the wall and floor.

Variation: Installing a Vanity with a Back

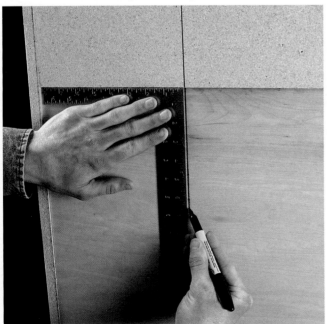

1 Mark a line on the wall where the top of the vanity will fit, then draw a line down the wall from the midpoint of this line. Draw a corresponding centerline down the back of the vanity.

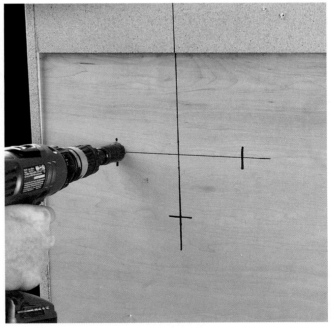

2 Measure the distance from the supply and drain pipes to the centerline on the wall. Transfer distances to the back of the vanity, measuring from the centerline. Mark pipe cutouts, drill a hole at the center, then cut out with a hole saw or jig saw.

Installing Countertops & Sinks

Most bathroom countertops installed today are integral (one-piece) sink-countertop units made from cultured marble or other solid materials, like Corian® or Swanstone®. Integral sink-countertops are convenient, and many are inexpensive, but style and color options are limited.

Some remodelers and designers still prefer the distinctive look of a custom-built countertop with a self-rimming sink basin, which gives you a much greater selection of styles and colors. Installing a self-rimming sink is very simple.

For more information regarding countertops and sinks, refer to pages 34 to 35 for countertops and pages 26 to 27 for sinks.

Everything You Need

Tools: pencil, scissors, carpenter's level, screwdriver, channel-type pliers, ratchet wrench, basin wrench.

Materials: cardboard, masking tape, plumber's putty, lag screws, tub & tile caulk.

Integral sink-countertops are made in standard sizes to fit common vanity widths. Because the sink and countertop are cast from the same material, integral sink-countertops do not leak, and do not require extensive caulking and sealing.

Tips for Countertops

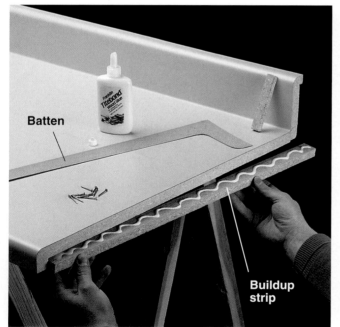

Postform countertops are made from inexpensive, factory-laminated particleboard, usually with a built-in backsplash and front flange. Buildup strips and battens are used to finish the edges of the countertops, and holes for the sink basins are cut to size using a jig saw. Countertops are held in place with corner braces (page opposite) and caulk.

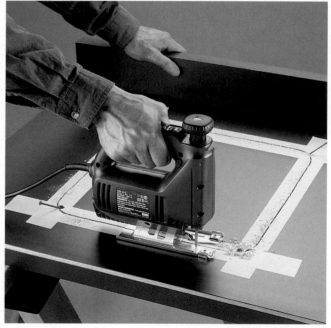

To make the sink cutout in a countertop or the backer material for a tile countertop (pages 234 to 239), trace the sink cutout onto strips of masking tape on the countertop, using a sink template. Drill a starter hole just inside the outline, then carefully complete the cutout using a jig saw. NOTE: Apply tape to the foot of the jig saw to prevent scratching.

How to Install an Integral Sink-Countertop

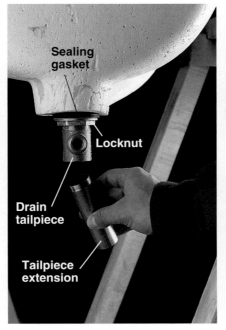

1 Set the sink-countertop unit onto sawhorses. Attach the faucet (page 241), and slip the drain lever through the faucet body. Place a ring of plumber's putty around the drain flange, then insert the flange in the drain opening.

2 Thread the locknut and sealing gasket onto the drain tailpiece, then insert the tailpiece into the drain opening and screw it onto the drain flange. Tighten the lock-nut securely. Attach the tailpiece extension. Insert the pop-up stopper linkage (page 62).

3 Apply a layer of tub & tile caulk (or adhesive, if specified by the countertop manufacturer) to the top edges of the vanity, and to any corner braces.

4 Center the sink-countertop unit over the vanity, so the overhang is equal on both sides and the backsplash of the countertop is flush with the wall. Press the countertop evenly into the caulk.

Cabinets with corner braces: Secure the counter-top to the cabinet by driving a mounting screw through each corner brace and up into the counter-top. NOTE: Cultured marble and other hard counter-tops require predrilling and a plastic screw sleeve.

(continued next page)

How to Install an Integral Sink-Countertop (continued)

5 Attach the drain arm to the drain stub-out in the wall, using a slip nut. Attach one end of the P-trap to the drain arm, and the other to the tailpiece of the sink drain, using slip nuts. Connect supply tubes to the faucet tailpieces (page 242).

6 Seal the gap between the backsplash and the wall with tub & tile caulk.

How to Install a Surface-mounted Sink

1 Use a template that is ½" narrower than the sink rim to mark the countertop cutout. Drill a ⅜" starter hole, then use a jig saw to make the cutout (page 230). For countertop-mounted faucets, drill holes for the tailpieces, according to the faucet manufacturer's directions.

2 Apply a ring of plumber's putty around the sink cutout. Before setting the sink in place, attach the faucet body to the sink or countertop (page 241), and the drain flange and pop-up drain assembly (page 231, step 1).

3 Set the sink into the cutout area, and gently press the rim of the sink into the plumber's putty. Hook up the drain and supply fittings (step 5, above), then caulk around the sink rim.

How to Install a Pedestal Sink

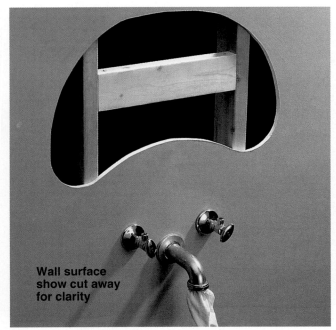

Wall surface show cut away for clarity

1 Install 2 × 4 blocking between the wall studs, behind the planned sink location. Cover the wall with water-resistant drywall (pages 180 to 181).

2 Set the basin and pedestal in position, bracing the basin with 2 × 4s. Outline the top of the basin on the wall, and mark the base of the pedestal on the floor. Mark reference points on the wall and floor through the mounting holes found on the back of the sink and the bottom of the pedestal.

3 Set aside the basin and pedestal. Drill pilot holes in the wall and floor at the reference points, then reposition the pedestal. Anchor the pedestal to the floor with lag screws.

4 Attach the faucet (page 241), then set the sink on the pedestal. Align the holes in the back of the sink with the pilot holes drilled in the wall, then drive lag screws and washers into the wall brace, using a ratchet wrench. Do not overtighten the screws.

5 Hook up the drain and supply fittings (page 232, step 5). Caulk between the back of the sink and the wall when installation is finished.

Building a Ceramic Tile Countertop

Ceramic tile is a popular choice for countertops and backsplashes for a number of reasons. It's available in a vast range of sizes, styles, and colors; it's durable and can be repaired; and some tile—not all—is reasonably priced. With careful planning, tile is also easy to install, and building a custom countertop with tile is a good do-it-yourself project.

The best tile for most countertops is glazed ceramic floor tile. Glazed tile is better than unglazed because of its stain resistance, and floor tile is better than wall tile because it's harder and more durable. Most residential floor tile is rated for light commercial or commercial use, with a hardness rating of Class 3 or better. Porcelain tile also is suitable for countertops; it's very hard and durable, but typically much more expensive than ceramic tile.

While glazing protects tile from stains, the grout between tiles is still vulnerable because it's so porous. To minimize staining, use a grout that contains a latex additive, or mix the grout powder with a liquid latex additive instead of water. After the grout cures fully, apply a quality grout sealer, and reapply the sealer once a year thereafter.

The countertop in this project has a core of ¾" exterior-grade plywood that's cut to fit and fastened to the cabinets. (Treated plywood, particleboard, and oriented-strand board are not acceptable backers for this project.) The plywood is covered with a layer of plastic (for a moisture barrier) and a layer of ½"-thick cementboard. Cementboard is an effective backer for tile because it won't break down if water gets through the tile layer. The tile is adhered to the cementboard with thin-set adhesive, which also can survive prolonged water contact. The over-all thickness of the finished countertop is about 1½". If you want a thicker countertop, you can fasten an additional layer of plywood (of any thickness) to the core.

When laying out the tile for your countertop, account for the placement of the sink and any other fixtures. The tile should break evenly where it meets the sink and along the counter's perimeter. If you'll be installing a tile-in sink, make sure the tile thickness matches the rim of the sink to create a smooth transition.

Everything You Need

Tools: tape measure, circular saw, drill, utility knife, straightedge, stapler, drywall knife, framing square, notched trowel, tile cutter, carpeted 2 × 4, mallet, rubber grout float, sponge, foam brush, caulk gun.

Materials: ceramic tile, tile spacers, ¾" exterior-grade (CDX) plywood, 4-mil polyethylene sheeting, packing tape, ½" cementboard, 1¼" galvanized deck screws, fiberglass mesh tape, thin-set mortar, grout with latex additive, silicone caulk, silicone grout sealer.

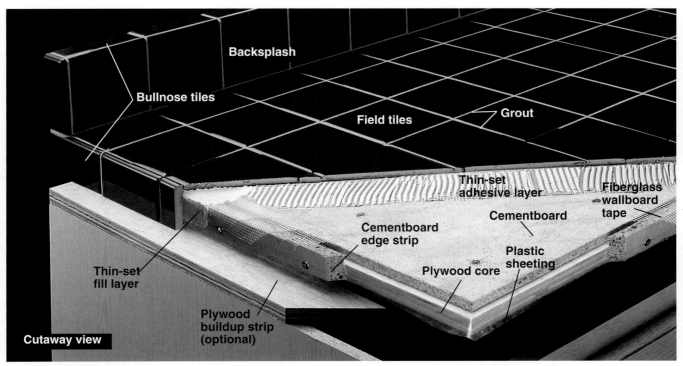

A ceramic tile countertop starts with a core of ¾" exterior-grade plywood that's covered with a moisture barrier of 4-mil polyethylene sheeting. Half-inch cementboard is screwed to the plywood, and the edges are capped with cementboard and finished with fiberglass mesh tape and thin-set mortar. Tiles for edging and backsplashes may be bullnose or another type of specialty tile (see below).

Options for Backsplashes & Countertop Edges

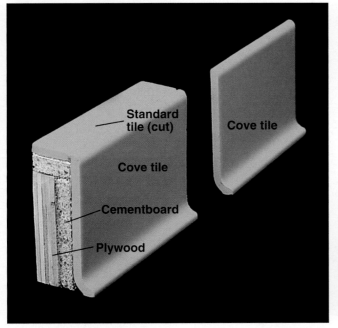

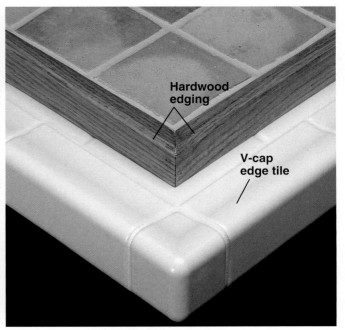

Backsplashes can be made from cove tile (right) attached to the wall at the back of the countertop. You can use the tile alone or build a shelf-type backsplash (left), using the same construction used for the countertop. Attach the plywood backsplash to the plywood core of the countertop. Wrap the front face and all edges of the plywood backsplash with cementboard before laying tile.

Edge options include V-cap edge tile and hardwood strip edging. V-cap tiles have raised and rounded corners that create a ridge around the countertop perimeter—good for containing spills and water. V-cap tiles must be cut with a tile saw. Hardwood strips should be prefinished with at least three coats of polyurethane finish. Attach the strips to the plywood core so the top of the wood will be flush with the faces of the tiles.

How to Build a Ceramic Tile Countertop

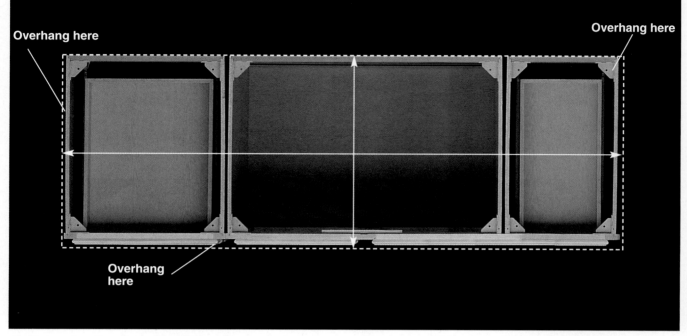

Overhang here

Overhang here

Overhang here

1 Determine the size of the plywood core by measuring across the top of the cabinets. The finished top should overhang the drawer fronts by at least ¼". Be sure to account for the thickness of the cementboard, adhesive, and tile when deciding how large to make the overhang. Cut the core to size from ¾" plywood, using a circular saw. Also make any cutouts for sinks and other fixtures (page 230).

Corner bracket

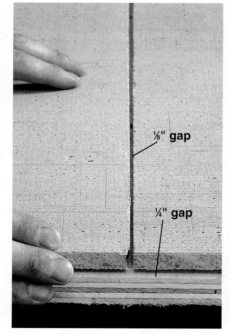

⅛" gap

¼" gap

2 Set the plywood core on top of the cabinets, and attach it with screws driven through the cabinet corner brackets. The screws should not be long enough to go through the top of the plywood core.

3 Cut pieces of cementboard to size, then mark and make the cutout for the sink. Dry-fit them on the plywood core with the rough sides of the panels facing up. Leave a ⅛" gap between the cementboard sheets and a ¼" gap along the perimeter.

TIP: Cut cementboard using a straightedge and utility knife or a cementboard cutter with a carbide tip. Hold the straightedge along the cutting line, and score the board several times with the knife. Bend the piece backwards to break it along the scored line. Back-cut to finish.

236

4 Lay the plastic moisture barrier over the plywood core, draping it over the edges. Tack it in place with a few staples. Overlap the seams in plastic by 6", and seal them with packing tape.

5 Lay the cementboard pieces rough-side up on the plywood and attach them with 1¼" galvanized deck screws driven every 6". If needed, predrill holes through the cementboard using a masonry bit. Make sure all screw heads are flush with the surface. Wrap the countertop edges with 1¼"-wide cementboard strips, and attach them to the core with deck screws.

6 Tape all cementboard joints with fiberglass mesh tape. Apply three layers of tape along the front edge where the horizontal cementboard sheets meet the cementboard edging.

7 Fill all gaps and cover all of the tape with a layer of thin-set mortar. Feather out the mortar with a drywall knife to create a smooth, flat surface. NOTE: Do not use joint compound.

(continued next page)

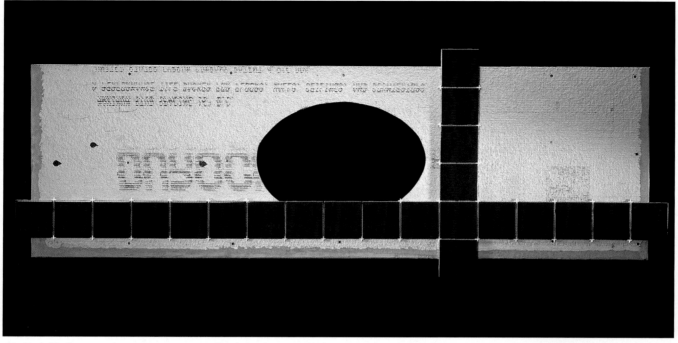

8 Dry-fit tiles on the countertop to find the layout that works best. If the tiles do not have spacing lugs on their edges, use plastic spacers to set the grout-joint gaps between tiles. Once the layout is established, make marks along the vertical and horizontal rows. Draw reference lines through the marks and use a framing square to make sure the lines are perpendicular.

Bullnose edges

9 Install the edge tiles by applying a layer of thin-set mortar to the back of the tile and the edges of the countertop, using a notched trowel. Place the tiles with a slight twisting motion. Add plastic spacers, if needed. Use a dry tile set on top of the countertop to determine the height of the edge tiles.

10 Use bullnose corner tile (with adjacent bullnose edges) to finish the corner edges of the countertop. Place dry tile glazed-side down on the edge face. Mark and cut the tile so the bullnose edge will sit directly on the corner. Install the piece with thin-set mortar. See pages 204 to 205 for help with cutting tile.

11 Install the field tile after the edge tiles have set. Spread a layer of thin-set on the cement-board along the layout lines, and install perpendicular rows of tile. Make sure the spacing is correct, and use a framing square to check your work as you go.

12 To mark border tiles for cutting, allow space for backsplash tiles, grout, and mortar by placing a tile against the back wall. Set another tile (A) on top of the last full tile in the field, then place a third tile (B) over tile A and hold it against the upright tile. Mark tile A where the cut will be. Cut tile A on the marked line and install it with the cut edge toward the wall.

13 As you install small sections of tile, lay a carpeted 2 × 4 block over the tile and tap the block lightly with a mallet or hammer. Run your hand over the tiles to make sure they are flush with one another. Remove any plastic spacers with a toothpick, and carefully scrape any excess mortar from the grout joints. Let the mortar dry completely.

14 Mix a batch of grout with a latex additive and apply it with a rubber float, forcing the grout into the joints with a sweeping motion (page 208). Wipe away excess grout with a damp sponge. Wait one hour and wipe away the powdery haze. Let the grout cure fully.

15 Caulk along the backsplash and around penetrations with a fine bead of silicone caulk. Smooth the bead with a wet finger. After the grout cures completely, apply silicone sealer to the grout with a foam brush. Let the sealer dry, and apply a second coat.

Bathroom sink faucets come in many styles, allowing you to match the decorating theme of your bathroom. A basin wrench (inset) enables you to reach faucet locknuts from inside cabinets.

Making Plumbing & Wiring Connections

Careful, accurate finishing work helps ensure that all the parts of your bathroom remodeling project function properly and look good.

Shop carefully when purchasing faucets and electrical fixtures. With these products, spending a few dollars more for better quality is always a good investment.

Be extra careful when working with wiring in a bathroom, where the closeness of water poses a constant threat. Always turn off electrical power at the main service panel before you begin an electrical project.

Take special precautions to avoid damaging faucets and accessories that have a polished finish. Wrap the jaws of pliers with masking tape

before tightening visible nuts, and use care when driving screws so the screwdriver does not slip and cause damage. Block drain openings to avoid losing small pieces of hardware in sinks and bathtubs.

This section shows:

- Installing Faucets & Spouts (pages 241 to 243)
- Installing a Slide-bar Showerhead (pages 244 to 245)
- Installing Toilets (pages 246 to 247)
- Installing Light Fixtures (pages 248 to 249)
- Installing Recessed Light Fixtures (pages 250 to 251)
- Installing a Bathroom Vent Fan (pages 252 to 255)

Installing Faucets & Spouts

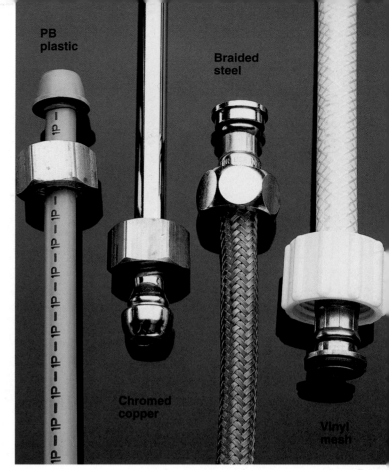

Bathroom sink faucets come in a variety of designs, materials, and prices. Better faucets are made of solid brass, while less expensive models may be made of other metals surface-coated with chrome.

The handle is one of the most distinguishing features of the faucet. Variations include single handles, double handles, or electronic sensors in place of handles. Most types are available in a range of designs, from modern to antique.

Whenever possible, install a faucet before installing the sink. This will allow you the greatest freedom of movement for making connections.

Everything You Need

Tools: drill with spade bit, basin wrench, adjustable wrench, screwdriver.

Materials: plumber's putty, Teflon tape, joint compound.

Supply tubes are used to connect water pipes to faucets, toilets, and other fixtures. They come in 12", 20", and 30" lengths. Plastic and chromed copper tubes are inexpensive. Braided steel and vinyl mesh supply tubes are easy to install.

Installing a One-piece Faucet

1 Apply a ring of plumber's putty around the base of the faucet body. (Some faucets use a gasket that does not require plumber's putty—read the manufacturer's directions carefully.)

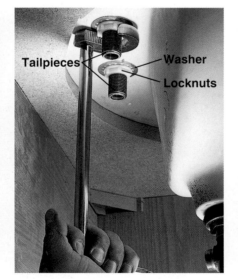

2 Insert the faucet tailpieces through holes in the countertop or sink. From below, thread washers and locknuts over the tailpieces, then tighten the locknuts with channel-type pliers or a basin wrench until snug.

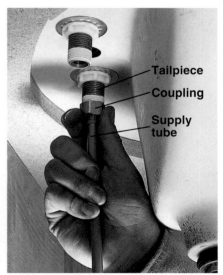

3 Wrap Teflon tape around the tailpiece threads, then cut supply tubes to fit (page 242). Attach the supply tube couplings and tighten them with a basin wrench until snug. Connect the drain linkage (page 232), then attach the faucet handles and trim caps.

How to Install Shutoff Valves & Flexible Copper Supply Tubes

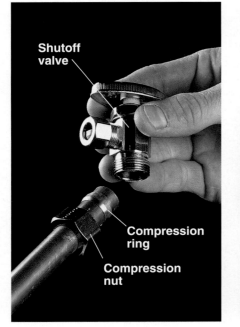

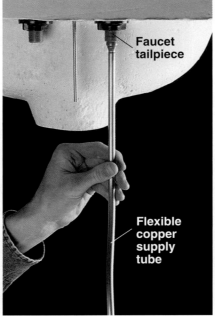

1 Slide a compression nut and ring over the copper water pipe, with the nut threads facing the end of the pipe. Apply pipe joint compound to the compression ring. Screw the nut onto the shutoff valve and tighten it with an adjustable wrench.

2 Bend a flexible copper supply tube to reach between the faucet tailpiece and the shutoff valve (page 96). Fit the bell-shaped end of the tube into the end of the tailpiece, and mark the other end to length. Include a ½" portion that will fit inside the valve. Cut the tube (page 99).

3 Wrap the threads of the tailpiece with Teflon tape, then connect the bell-shaped end of the supply tube to the faucet tailpiece, using a coupling nut. Tighten the nut with a basin wrench or channel-type pliers.

4 To connect the supply tube to the valve, slide a compression nut over the end of the pipe, with the threads facing the valve, then slide on the compression ring.

5 Insert the pipe into the valve until the end rests at the bottom of the fitting socket. Apply a layer of joint compound over the compression ring and hand-tighten the nut onto the valve.

6 Gently tighten the compression nut with an adjustable wrench. Do not overtighten. Turn on the water and check for leaks. If the fitting leaks, carefully tighten the nut.

How to Install Tub & Shower Faucets

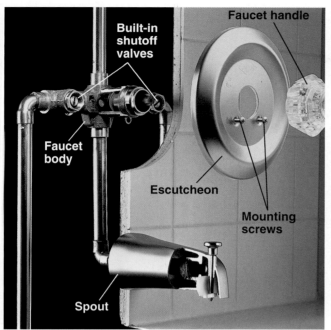

Single-handled faucet: Open the built-in shutoff valves, using a screwdriver, then attach the escutcheon to the faucet body with mounting screws. Attach the faucet handle, then attach the spout (below) and trim cap. NOTE: Attach the faucet body before installing the wall surface.

Anti-scald valves are safety devices that protect against sudden changes in water temperature. They are required by most building codes for faucets in showers and combination tub-showers. Once installed, faucets with anti-scald valves look like standard faucets (inset).

How to Connect Tub Spouts

1 Apply joint compound or Teflon tape to the threaded end of the spout nipple that extends from the wall.

2 Screw the spout onto the nipple, using a long screwdriver as a lever. Use tub & tile caulk to caulk around spout.

TIP: Some spouts have a setscrew on the underside that must be tightened. Find the small access slot, then tighten the setscrew inside, using an Allen wrench.

Installing a Slide-Bar Showerhead

The slide-bar showerhead is an attractive and practical shower addition for any bathroom. It combines the flexibility of a handheld sprayer with a sliding mounted showerhead. This convenient height adjustability makes it perfect for all family members, including children or disabled users who must sit to shower. The model shown uses a slide-lock mechanism that allows you to easily set the sprayer height anywhere along the 2-ft. span of the bar.

Slide-bar showerheads are generally sold as a kit that includes the bar, sprayer, hose, and mounting hardware. Many basic kits contain only a simple coupling that attaches the hose to the end of the shower arm. For a cleaner look, purchase a matching supply elbow that attaches to the pipe stub at the wall via a galvanized nipple connector, as shown in this project.

Everything You Need:

Tools: pipe wrench or strap wrench, ³⁄₁₆" masonry drill bit, ½" masonry drill bit, screwdriver, level, nailset, hammer, drill, caulk gun.

Materials: slide-bar showerhead kit, ½"-diameter × 1½"-long galvanized nipple, Teflon tape, chrome supply elbow, wall anchors or toggle bolts, ¼"-20 stainless steel machine bolt, silicone caulk.

How to Install a Slide-Bar Showerhead

1 Remove the existing shower-head and arm (page 66). Wrap the threads of a galvanized nipple with Teflon tape and thread it into the stub-out, leaving about ⁹⁄₁₆" of the nipple protruding from the wall. Thread the supply elbow onto the nipple. Cover the elbow with a soft cloth and tighten it with a pipe wrench or strap wrench.

2 Attach a mounting bracket to each end of the slide-bar. Place the bar 4" to 6" to the side of the wall supply elbow to avoid the water pipes. Locate the lower end of the bar about 48" from the bottom of the tub or shower. Use a level to make sure the bar is plumb, then mark the location of the mounting holes.

3 Drill holes in the tile using a masonry bit. If you hit a stud, attach the slide-bar to the wall, using the screws and wall anchors provided with the kit.

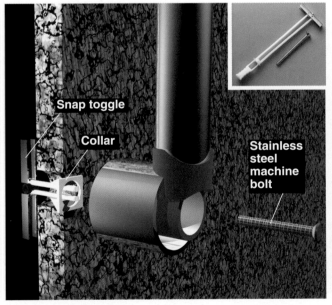

VARIATION: If you don't hit a stud, enlarge the hole, using a ½" masonry bit, then insert a toggle anchor (inset) into the hole. Slide the collar forward to hold the toggle against the back of the wall, then snap off the plastic straps. Attach the slide-bar to the wall with ¼"-20 stainless steel machine bolts.

4 Slide the decorative end caps onto the mounting brackets. Thread the shower hose onto the wall supply elbow. Clip the showerhead into the slide-lock mechanism. Apply silicone caulk around the supply elbow and mounting brackets.

245

Installing Toilets

Building codes now require the installation of water-conserving, low-flow toilets in all new construction and bathroom remodeling projects. Low-flow toilets, which use only 1.6 gallons of water per flush, are available in gravity-flush and pressure-assisted models.

Gravity-flush toilets work much like old models, but with a more efficient water flow. Pressure-assisted toilets use pressurized air and water to flush wastes. There is great variety in price, style, and function, so inspect several models before choosing a toilet. Also measure from your bathroom wall to the floor bolts on the toilet flange to determine whether you will need a 12" or 14" offset model.

Like standard toilets, low-flow models are available in both one- and two-piece units. Two-piece, vitreous china toilets are the least expensive, and gravity-flush models cost less than pressure-assisted varieties.

Everything You Need

Tools: adjustable wrench, ratchet wrench or basin wrench, tubing cutter, screwdriver.

Materials: toilet wax ring and sleeve, plumber's putty, tank bolts with rubber washers, supply tube, coupling nuts, seat bolts and mounting nuts.

Install a toilet by anchoring the bowl to the floor first, then mounting the tank onto the bowl. China fixtures crack easily, so use care when handling them.

How to Install a Toilet

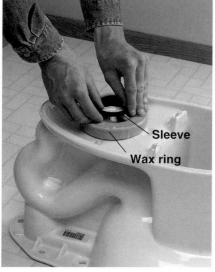

Sleeve

Wax ring

1 Turn the bowl upside down and place a new wax ring and sleeve onto the toilet horn.

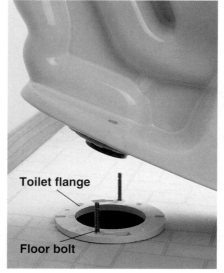

Toilet flange

Floor bolt

2 Position the toilet over the toilet flange so the floor bolts fit through the holes in the base of the toilet. The flange should be clean, and the floor bolts should point straight up.

3 Press down on the toilet bowl to compress the wax ring. Attach washers and nuts to the floor bolts and tighten with an adjustable wrench until they are snug—do not overtighten. Attach the trim caps.

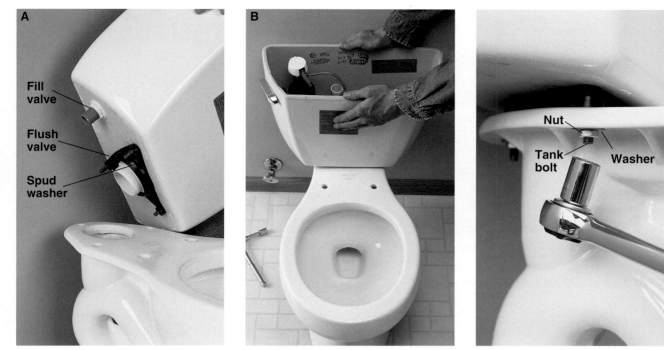

4 Center the spud washer on the bottom of the tank over the water inlet opening near the back edge of the bowl, aligning the tank bolts with the bolt holes in the bowl flange (photo A). On some toilets, the spud washer and tank bolts are installed separately. Set the tank onto the bowl (photo B). NOTE: with some toilets, you will have to purchase a flush handle, fill valve, and flush valve separately.

5 From beneath the bowl flange, attach washers and nuts to the tank bolts, and tighten them with a ratchet wrench or basin wrench until they are snug—do not over-tighten.

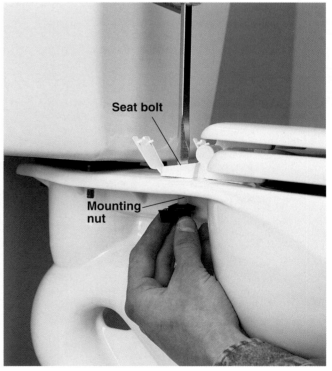

6 Cut a piece of supply tube to fit between the shutoff valve and the toilet tank. Attach a supply tube to the shutoff valve, then to the fill valve tailpiece. Use an adjustable wrench to tighten coupling nuts until they are snug.

7 Mount the toilet seat onto the bowl by tightening the mounting nuts onto the seat bolts from below the seat flange. Fill the toilet bowl and tank with water and test-flush to make sure there are no leaks, then seal around the toilet base at the floor with silicone caulk.

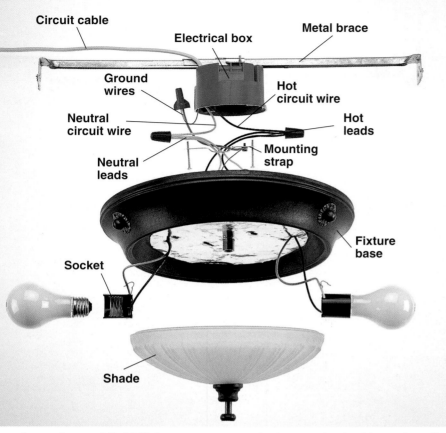

Circuit cable

Electrical box

Metal brace

Ground wires

Hot circuit wire

Neutral circuit wire

Hot leads

Neutral leads

Mounting strap

Fixture base

Socket

Shade

Incandescent light fixtures connect to the house circuit with pre-installed wire leads. Fixtures are secured directly to electrical boxes or to mounting straps attached to the boxes.

Installing Light Fixtures

Running cables for new electrical fixtures is easiest if wall surfaces have been removed (pages 72 to 74). Make the final wiring hookups at the fixtures after the wall surfaces are finished (pages 178 to 191). If it's not practical to remove wall surfaces, install fixtures designed for "retrofit" installations.

Always follow your local code requirements for wiring bathrooms. Reduce shock hazard by protecting all bathroom circuits with GFCI receptacles, and install only electrical fixtures that are UL approved.

Most wiring connections for bathroom fixtures are easy to make, but wiring configurations in electrical boxes vary widely depending on the fixture and the circuit layout. If you are not confident in your skills, have an electrician install and connect fixtures and circuits.

Refer to pages 126 to 137 for more information on wiring bathrooms.

> **CAUTION:** Always shut off electrical power at the main service panel and test for power before working with wiring.

Everything You Need

Tools: neon circuit tester, screwdriver.

Materials: light fixtures, twist-on wire connectors.

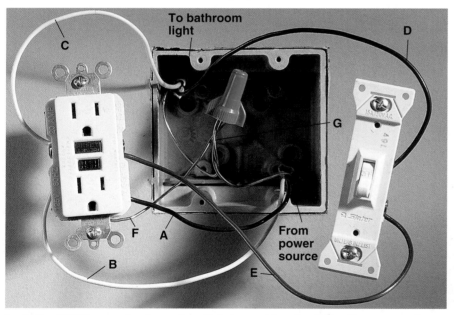

To bathroom light

From power source

Install a GFCI receptacle and switch by making the following connections: black wire from power source (A) to screw marked HOT LINE on GFCI; white wire from power source (B) to screw marked WHITE LINE; white wire to light (C) to GFCI screw marked WHITE LOAD; black wire to light (D) to a screw terminal on switch. Cut a short length of black wire (E), and attach one end to GFCI screw marked HOT LOAD, and other end to a screw terminal on switch. Connect a bare grounding pigtail wire to GFCI grounding screw (F), and join all bare grounding wires (G) with a wire connector. Tuck wires into box, then attach switch, receptacle, and coverplate. Use the circuit maps on pages 127 to 128 as a guide for making connections.

How to Install Bathroom Vanity Fixtures

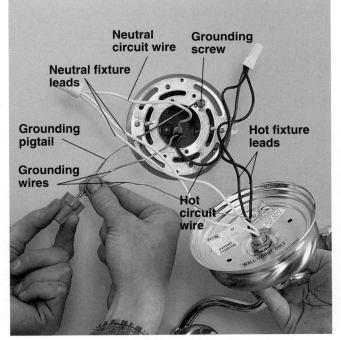

1 Turn the power off. Test for power with a circuit tester. Prepare the fixture mounting plate as directed by the manufacturer. Feed the cable from the wall box through the holes in the mounting plate. Fasten the plate to the electrical box, using included mounting screws.

Neutral circuit wire

Grounding screw

Neutral fixture leads

Grounding pigtail

Grounding wires

Hot fixture leads

Hot circuit wire

2 Using twist-on wire connectors, connect the white wire from the cable to the white fixture wires, and the black wire from the cable to the black fixture wires. Pigtail the copper grounding wires from the cable and the fixture to the grounding screw on the mounting plate. (On some fixtures, connect the grounding wire from the cable directly to the grounding wire from the fixture, using a wire connector.)

3 Tuck the wires into the fixture, then attach the fixture or coverplate with included fasteners. Install light bulbs and globes only after the rest of the remodeling project is completed.

VARIATION: Combine side-mounted vanity lights located at eye level with a light fixture mounted over the mirror to eliminate shadows and provide the most flattering lighting configuration.

249

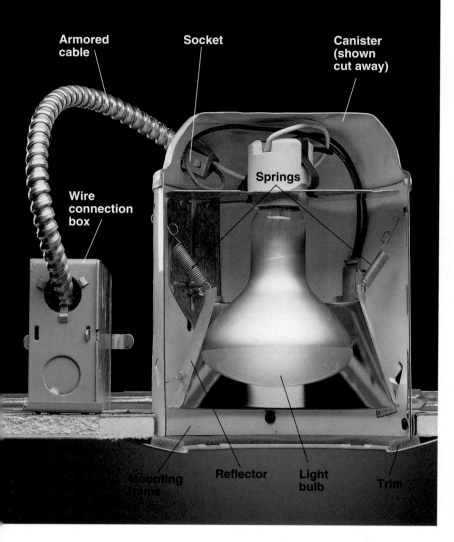

Armored cable   **Socket**   **Canister (shown cut away)**

Springs

Wire connection box

Mounting frame   **Reflector**   **Light bulb**   **Trim**

Installing Recessed Light Fixtures

Recessed light fixtures are mounted so that the light is flush with the surface of the ceiling or wall. They are unobtrusive choices for overall lighting, casting light without drawing attention to themselves.

Locate recessed light fixtures where they will best illuminate activity areas. Run bathroom light fixtures on a GFCI protected circuit. If you are uncomfortable working with electricity, hire an electrician to complete the installation.

See pages 130 to 133 for installing cables, and pages 134 to 135 for connecting switches and creating GFCI circuits.

Everything You Need

Tools: hammer, screwdriver, drill, utility knife, cable stripper.

Materials: recessed light fixture, nails, cable clamps, NM cable, wire connectors.

How to Install Recessed Light Fixtures

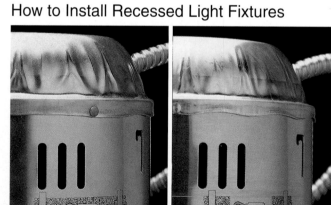

Rating symbol   **Rating symbol**

TIP: Choose the proper type of recessed light fixture for your project. There are two types of fixtures: those rated for installation within insulation (left), and those that must be kept at least 3" from insulation (right). Self-contained thermal switches shut off power if the unit gets too hot for its rating. A recessed light fixture must be installed at least ½" from combustible materials.

1 Extend the mounting bars on the recessed fixture to reach the framing members. Adjust the position of the light unit on the mounting bars to locate it properly. Align the bottom edges of the mounting bars with the bottom face of the framing members, then nail or screw the mounting bars to the framing members.

Open knockout

Cable clamp

Cutaway view

2 Remove the wire connection box cover and open one knockout for each cable entering the box. Install a cable clamp for each open knockout, and tighten the locknut, using a screwdriver to drive the lugs. Mount any remaining fixtures.

3 With the recessed fixtures mounted, install the feeder cable that runs from the service panel to the switch gang box, then install cable to the first fixture in the circuit (pages 130 to 133). Strip the cable sheathing back 6" to 8" from the end, using a cable ripper. Insert the cable through a cable clamp and into the wire connection box with ½" of sheathing extending into the box, then tighten the clamp. Cut and install cable to run to any remaining fixtures to complete the circuit. Arrange for the rough-in inspection before making the final connections.

4 Make the final connections before installing drywall (the work must be inspected first). For each fixture, strip ½" of insulation from the white cable wires, then connect them to the white fixture lead, using a wire connector.

5 Strip ½" of insulation from the black cable wires, then connect them to the black fixture lead, using a wire connector.

6 Attach a grounding pigtail to the grounding screw on the fixture, then connect all grounding wires. Tuck all wires into the junction box, and replace the cover. Make hookups at the service panel (pages 136 to 137), and arrange for the final inspection.

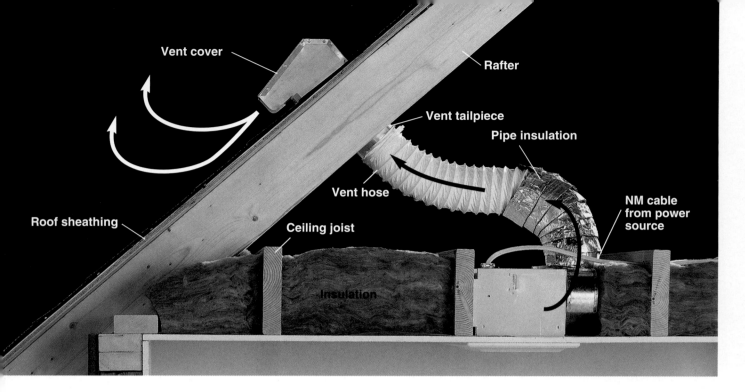

Vent cover · Rafter · Vent tailpiece · Pipe insulation · Vent hose · NM cable from power source · Roof sheathing · Ceiling joist · Insulation

Installing a Bathroom Vent Fan

A bathroom remodeling is a good opportunity to add a new vent fan or replace an existing fan with a quieter, more efficient model. Most building codes require a vent fan in any bathroom without natural ventilation. Fans with only a light fixture usually can be wired into a main bathroom electrical circuit, but units with built-in heat lamps (pages 126 to 127) or blowers require separate circuits.

Most vent fans are installed in the center of the bathroom ceiling or over the toilet area. Do not install a fan over the tub or shower area unless the unit is GFCI-protected and rated for use in wet areas.

If the fan you choose doesn't come with a mounting kit, purchase one separately. A mounting kit should include a vent hose (duct), a vent tailpiece, and an exterior vent cover.

Venting instructions vary among manufacturers, but the most common options are attic venting and soffit venting. Attic venting (shown in this project) routes fan ductwork into the attic and out through the roof. Always insulate ducting in this application to keep condensation from forming and running down into the motor. And carefully install flashing around the outside vent cover to prevent roof leaks.

Soffit venting involves routing the duct to a soffit (roof overhang) instead of through the roof. Check with the vent manufacturer for instructions for soffit venting.

To prevent moisture damage, always terminate the vent outside your home—never into your attic or basement.

You can install a vent fan while the framing is exposed or as a retrofit, as shown in this project. Refer to "Wiring Bathrooms" on pages 126 to 137 for help with running circuit cable, installing an electrical box, and making basic electrical connections.

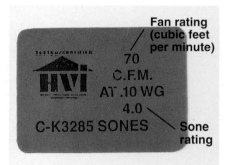

Fan rating (cubic feet per minute)

70 C.F.M. AT .10 WG

4.0

C-K3285 SONES · Sone rating

Check the information label attached to each vent fan unit. Choose a unit with a fan rating at least 5 CFM higher than the square footage of your bathroom. The *sone rating* refers to the relative quietness of the unit, rated on a scale of 1 to 7. (Quieter vent fans have lower sone ratings.)

Everything You Need

Tools: drill, jig saw, combination tool, screwdrivers, caulk gun, reciprocating saw, pry bar.

Materials: drywall screws, double-gang retrofit electrical box, NM cable (14/2, 14/3), cable clamp, hose clamps, pipe insulation, roofing cement, self-sealing roofing nails, shingles, wire connectors, switches.

How to Install a Bathroom Vent Fan

1 Position the vent fan unit against a ceiling joist. Outline the vent fan onto the ceiling surface. Remove the unit, then drill pilot holes at the corners of the outline and cut out the area with a jig saw or drywall saw.

2 Remove the grille from the fan unit, then position the unit against the joist, with the edge recessed ¼" from the finished surface of the ceiling (so the grille can be flush-mounted). Attach the unit to the joist, using drywall screws.

VARIATION: For vent fans with heaters or light fixtures, some manufacturers recommend using 2× lumber to build dams between the ceiling joists to keep the insulation at least 6" away from the fan unit.

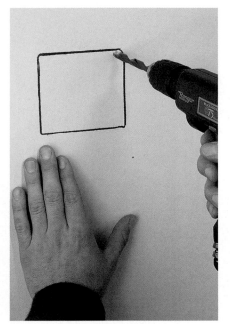

3 Mark and cut an opening for the switch box on the wall next to the latch side of the bathroom door, then run a 14/3 NM cable from the switch cutout to the fan unit. Run a 14/2 NM cable from the power source to the cutout.

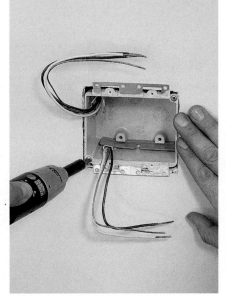

4 Strip 10" of sheathing from the ends of the cables, then feed the cables into a double-gang retrofit switch box so at least ½" of sheathing extends into the box. Clamp the cables in place. Tighten the mounting screws until the box is secure.

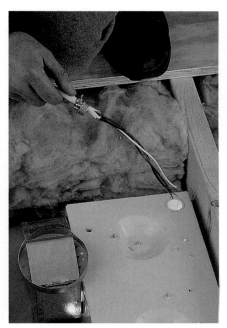

5 Strip 10" of sheathing from the end of the cable at the vent unit, then attach a cable clamp to the cable. Insert the cable into the fan unit. From the inside of the unit, screw a locknut onto the threaded end of the clamp.

(continued next page)

6 Mark the exit location in the roof for the vent hose, next to a rafter. Drill a pilot hole, then saw through the sheathing and roofing material with a reciprocating saw to make the cutout for the vent tailpiece.

Vent cover flange

7 Remove a section of shingles from around the cutout, leaving the roofing paper intact. Remove enough shingles to create an exposed area that is at least the size of the vent cover flange.

8 Attach a hose clamp to the rafter next to the roof cutout, about 1" below the roof sheathing (top). Insert the vent tailpiece into the cutout and through the hose clamp, then tighten the clamp screw (bottom).

9 Slide one end of the vent hose over the tailpiece, and slide the other end over the outlet on the fan unit. Slip hose clamps or straps around each end of the vent hose, and tighten the clamps.

10 Wrap the vent hose with pipe insulation. Insulation prevents moist air inside the hose from condensing and dripping down into the fan motor.

11 Apply roofing cement to the bottom of the vent cover flange, then slide the vent cover over the tailpiece. Nail the vent cover flange in place with self-sealing roofing nails, then patch in shingles around the cover.

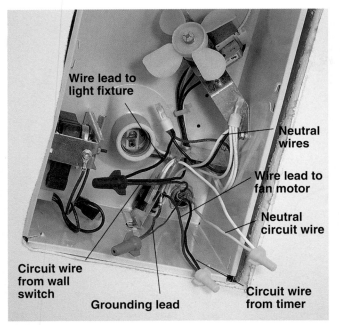

Wire lead to light fixture

Neutral wires

Wire lead to fan motor

Neutral circuit wire

Circuit wire from wall switch

Grounding lead

Circuit wire from timer

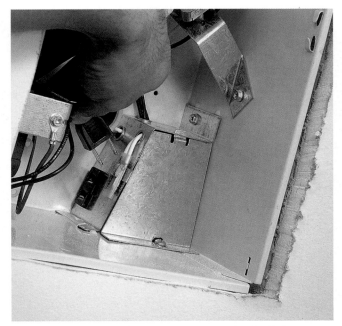

12 Make the following wire connections at the fan unit: the black circuit wire from the timer to the wire lead for the fan motor; the red circuit wire from the single-pole switch (see step 14) to the wire lead for the light fixture in the unit; the white neutral circuit wire to the neutral wire lead; the circuit grounding wire to the grounding lead on the fan unit. Make all connections with wire connectors. Attach the cover plate over the unit when the wiring is completed.

13 Connect the fan motor plug to the built-in receptacle on the wire connection box, and attach the fan grille to the frame, using the mounting clips included with the fan kit. NOTE: If you removed the wall and ceiling surfaces for the installation, install new surfaces before completing this step.

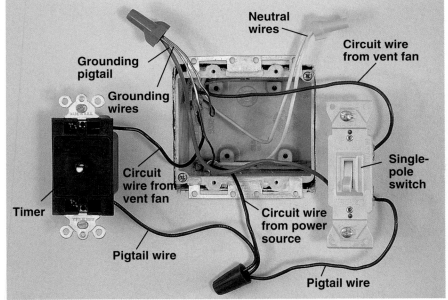

Neutral wires

Circuit wire from vent fan

Grounding pigtail

Grounding wires

Circuit wire from vent fan

Timer

Circuit wire from power source

Single-pole switch

Pigtail wire

Pigtail wire

14 At the switch box, add black pigtail wires to one screw terminal on the timer and to one screw terminal on the single-pole switch; add a green grounding pigtail to the groundling screw on the switch. Make the following wire connections: the black circuit wire from the power source to the black pigtail wires; the black circuit wire from the vent fan to the remaining screw on the timer; the red circuit wire from the vent fan to the remaining screw on the switch. Join the white wires with a wire connector. Join the grounding wires with a green wire connector.

15 Tuck the wires into the switch box, then attach the switch and timer to the box. Attach the coverplate and timer dial. Turn on the power.

Fill bathtubs and whirlpools at least half full of water to approximate the full tub weight before caulking around the edges. Tubs shift position when filled with water; caulking when the tub is full helps ensure that the caulking seal does not stretch and pull apart when the tub is filled.

Options for Attaching Bathroom Accessories

Attach accessories and hardware between wall studs by using screw sleeves or special fasteners that are attached directly to the wall surface. Plastic anchor sleeves (A), often used in ceramic tile, are inserted into pilot holes, where they expand when screws are driven. Grip-it® fasteners (B), molly bolts (C), and toggle bolts (D) provide more holding power than sleeves.

Making Finishing Touches

Hanging towel rods, mirrors, and other accessories, caulking seams, and sealing tile and grout are a few of the small projects that bring your bathroom remodeling project to completion.

Whenever possible, anchor accessories to wall studs or blocking for maximum holding power. If no studs or blocking are located in the area where accessories will be installed, use special fasteners, like toggle bolts or molly bolts, to anchor the accessories to drywall or plaster walls.

Use tub & tile caulk for most bathroom sealing projects. Most tub & tile caulk is a blend of silicone and latex that offers the best features of both. Pure silicone expands and contracts with fixtures, like bathtubs, that can shift position. It is a long-lasting, effective sealant, but it is relatively expensive and cannot be painted.

Latex caulk is inexpensive and it holds paint well. It also is easy to apply in smooth, neat beads, but it breaks down more quickly than silicone, and it can trap odors and mildew. Some tub & tile caulk contains acrylic which yields a hard surface. Caulk of all types should be inspected yearly, and reapplied as needed.

Everything You Need

Tools: tape measure, jig saw with metal-cutting blade or hacksaw, drill, caulk gun, grout float.

Materials: caulk, screws, sleeves and anchors, tape.

Tips for Installing Bathroom Accessories

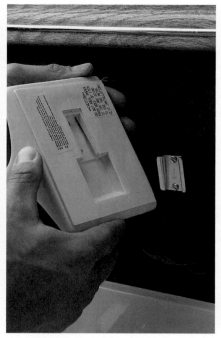

Apply a dab of silicone caulk over pilot holes and screw tips before inserting screws in or near high-moisture areas. Caulk keeps moisture out of walls and enhances the holding power of screws.

Select bathroom accessories that fit onto a metal mounting plate, which can be firmly anchored to the wall. Commonly used with porcelain bathroom accessories, mounting plates are hidden from view once the installation is completed.

Apply a bead of caulk to the back of the mounting flange on recessed wall accessories to keep moisture out and prevent the accessory from shifting. Recessed accessories fit into cutouts in the wall surface and are attached to wall framing members or blocking. If possible, install blocking while wall surfaces are removed.

How to Install a Shower Door

1 Measure the length of the shower curb to make sure the shower door will fit, and to find the required length of the shower door threshold.

2 Cut the shower door threshold to the correct length, using a jig saw with a metal-cutting blade, or a hacksaw.

(continued next page)

How to Install a Shower Door (continued)

3 Apply a heavy bead of silicone caulk to the underside of the threshold, then position it on the curb. Never attach a shower door threshold with screws or other fasteners that can puncture the shower curb.

Jamb shown cut away for clarity

4 Attach the side jambs to the shower stall frame as directed by the shower door manufacturer.

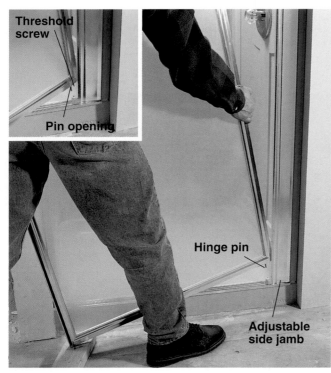

Threshold screw

Pin opening

Hinge pin

Adjustable side jamb

5 Adjust the side jamb so the door opening is the right size for the shower door, then lock the jamb in position (most doors have a threshold screw that secures the adjustable jamb). Slip the hinge pins into the pin openings (inset).

6 Measure the opening and cut the top jamb, then screw it to the side jambs. Attach the door handles and any waterproofing hardware or trim. Caulk all joints thoroughly (page 260).

Options for Installing Shower Curtain Rods

Telescoping shower curtain rod: Spring-loaded and telescoping shower curtain rods are quick and easy to install. They are less sturdy than permanent shower rods, but they will not damage your shower stall or bathtub surround.

Permanent shower curtain rod: Mounting brackets that hold shower curtain rods in place are strong, especially if attached to the framing members. Screws for brackets will puncture walls, so caulk generously around brackets.

How to Install a Bathroom Mirror

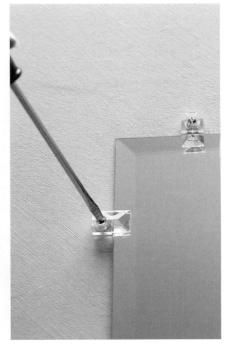

1 Using a pencil, draw a level line at the planned height of the mirror, then hold the mirror top against the level line, and outline each corner of the mirror.

2 Using the corner marks as a reference, mark the location of the screws for mirror clips (two per corner). Drill a pilot hole, then drive a plastic screw anchor at each mark, using a hammer.

3 Screw in the bottom mirror clips, then set the mirror on the bottom clips and attach the remaining clips on the sides and top of the mirror. Have a helper support heavier mirrors while you work.

How to Apply Tub & Tile Caulk

 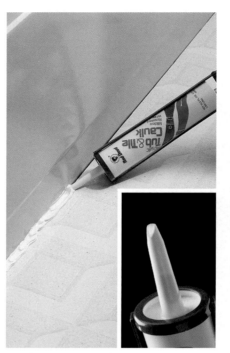 

1 Clean the surface thoroughly, using warm soapy water and a sponge or toothbrush.

2 Cut the top off the caulk tube at a slanted angle, then snip off the point to provide a flat application surface (inset). Apply a smooth bead of caulk to the seam.

3 Moisten one of your fingers and run it along the caulk bead to smooth out any rough or uneven areas.

Tips for Bathroom Tile Maintenance

Apply sealer to grout and unglazed floor tile. Alkaline-based sealer is recommended by most tile manufacturers because it does not scrape off or scuff as quickly as silicone sealer or acrylic floor polish. Sealer should be reapplied every year.

Remove broken tiles carefully. Start by removing the grout from around the tile (opposite page, step 1). Then, use a cold chisel and a hammer to break the tile into small pieces. Always drive the chisel inward to avoid damaging neighboring tiles. After you've removed the tile, scrape the old adhesive from the wall.

How to Regrout Ceramic Tile

1 Scrape out the old grout completely, using an awl, a utility knife, or a grout saw (or all three). Brush out the joints with a grout brush.

2 Clean the grout joints with warm soapy water and a sponge, then rinse and allow the joints to dry. Mix grout according to the manufacturer's directions, but mix only enough for one section, as the grout dries quickly.

3 Spread grout liberally over the tiles, using a rubber grout float. Then, work the grout well into the joints by holding the float face at a 60° angle to the tile and dragging it forcefully over the tiles at a 45° angle to the joints. Let the grout set for 10 to 15 minutes, then wipe away the excess with a damp sponge, rinsing the sponge frequently.

4 Let the grout dry for about 1 hour, then wipe away the powdery residue from the tile faces with a soft, dry cloth. Apply caulk around a bathtub or shower stall. Do not use the tub or shower for 24 hours. Seal the grout after it has fully cured (check the manufacturer's instructions).

Photo courtesy of Ginger®

Installing Grab Bars

Bathrooms are beautiful with their shiny ceramic tubs, showers, and floors, but add water and moisture to the mix and you've created the perfect conditions for a fall. The good news is many falls in the bathroom can be avoided by installing grab bars at key locations.

Grab bars help family members steady themselves on slippery shower, tub, and floor surfaces. Plus, they provide support for people transferring from a wheelchair or walker to the shower, tub, or toilet.

Grab bars come in a variety of colors, shapes, sizes, and textures. Choose a style with a 1¼" to 1½" diameter that fits comfortably between your thumb and fingers. Then properly install it 1½" from the wall with anchors that can support at least 250 pounds.

The easiest way to install grab bars is to screw them into wall studs, or into blocking or backing attached to studs. Blocking is a good option if you are framing a new bathroom or have the wall surface removed during a major remodel (see illustration A). Use 2 × 6 or 2 × 8 lumber to provide room for adjustments, and fasten the blocks to the framing with 16d nails. Note the locations of your blocking for future reference.

As an alternative, cover the entire wall with ¾" plywood backing secured with screws to the wall framing, so you can install grab bars virtually anywhere on the wall (see illustration B).

Grab bars can be installed in areas without studs. For these installations, use specialized, heavy-duty, hollow-wall anchors designed to support at least 250 pounds (page 265).

For grab bar installations near the tub, shower, and toilet, follow the recommendations listed on page 263 and the instructions on page 264.

Grab bars promote independence in the bathroom, where privacy is especially important. Grab bars not only help prevent slips and falls, they also help people steady themselves in showers and lower themselves into tubs.

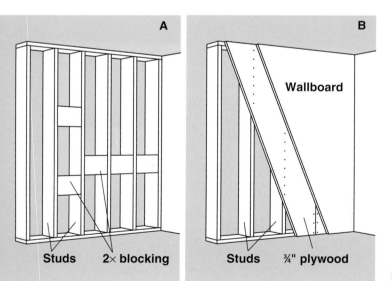

Blocking or backing is required for secure grab bars. If you know where the grab bars will be located, add 2× blocking between studs (photo A). You also can cover the entire wall with ¾" plywood backing, which allows you to install grab bars virtually anywhere on the wall.

Everything You Need

Tools: measuring tape, pencil, studfinder, level, drill, masonry bit.

Materials: grab bar, hollow-wall anchors, #12 stainless steel screws, silicone caulk.

Where to Install Grab Bars

These suggestions for grab bar placement include ADA guidelines and recommendations from universal design specialists.

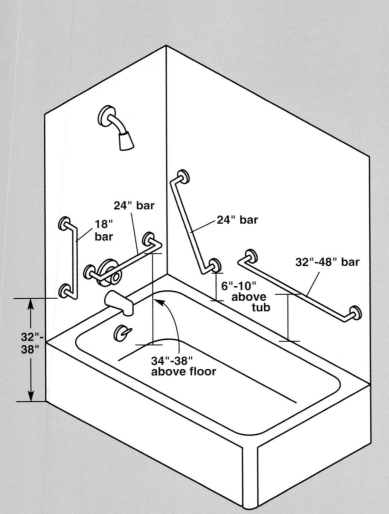

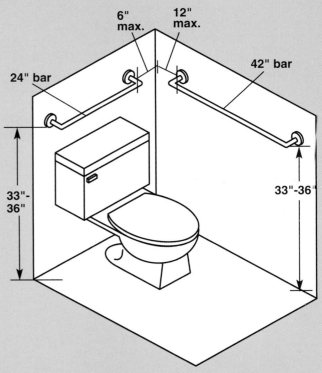

Tub/Shower:

Vertical bar at entrance to tub: 18" long; bottom of bar 32" to 38" above the floor.

Horizontal bar on control wall: 24" long; 34" to 38" above the floor.

Horizontal bar on back wall: 32" to 48" long; 34" to 38" above the floor for shower only; 6" to 10" above top of tub for bath only.

Angled bar: 24" long; bottom end 6" to 10" above top of tub (not necessary in stand-alone showers).

Toilet:

Horizontal bar at side: 42" long (min.); 12" (max.) from the back wall; 33" to 36" above the floor.

Horizontal bar behind: 24" long (min.); 6" (max.) from the side wall; 33" to 36" above the floor.

How to Install Grab Bars into Wood Framing or Backing

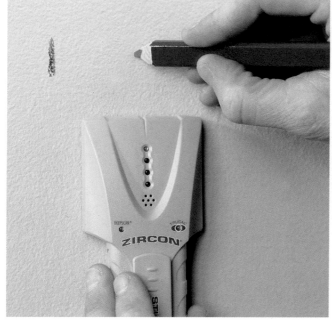

1 Locate the wall studs in the installation area, using a studfinder. If the area is tiled, the studfinder may not detect studs, so try to locate the studs above the tile, if possible, then use a level to transfer the marks lower on the wall. Otherwise, you can drill small, exploratory holes through grout joints in the tile, then fill the holes with silicone caulk to seal them. Be careful not to drill into pipes.

2 Mark the grab bar height at one stud location, then use a level to transfer the height mark to the stud that will receive the other end of the bar. Position the grab bar on the height marks so at least two of the three mounting holes are aligned with the stud centers. Mark the mounting hole locations onto the wall.

3 Drill pilot holes for the mounting screws. If you are drilling through tile, start with a small bit (about ⅛"), then redrill the hole with the larger bit. For screws that won't hit studs, drill holes for wall anchors, following the manufacturer's directions for sizing. Install anchors, if necessary (page 265).

4 Apply a continuous bead of silicone caulk to the back side of each bar end (inset). Secure the bar to the studs using #12 stainless steel screws (the screws should penetrate the stud by at least 1"). Install a stainless steel screw or bolt into the wall anchors. Test the bar to make sure it's secure.

Grab Bar Anchors

Wall anchors are available for a variety of grab bar applications. Make sure the anchors you use can support 250 pounds (contact the grab bar manufacturer for the recommended anchor for your project). Always follow the manufacturer's instructions when installing anchors.

WingIt™ anchors are heavy-duty hollow-wall anchors designed to support grab bars that can't be secured to framing or backing. When installed in walls of ½" wallboard with ceramic tile or in a ¼"-thick fiberglass tub surround, WingIts hold up to 1000 pounds; in ⅝" wallboard alone, 450 pounds; and in ½" wallboard alone, up to 250 pounds. Once installed, the anchor's wing assembly is 3" in diameter, so the bar must be located where no stud interferes.

WingIt anchors are prepared for insertion and temporarily mounted to the grab bar, then are inserted into 1¼" holes. Waterproof adhesive rings hold the anchors in place, and the bar is removed. A tap on the center bolt springs the wing assembly, and the bolt is tightened to draw the wing to the back of the wall. The grab bar is fastened to the anchor mounting plates with stainless steel screws.

Toggler® brand SnapToggle™ anchors help secure grab bars to steel studs. This additional reinforcement is important because bare screws can strip or pull out of light-gauge steel. At each end of the bar, one SnapToggle is used to secure the top screw of the mounting flange to the stud. For the remaining two screws at each end, one is driven into the stud, if possible, and the other is secured to the wall with a hollow wall anchor.

The end of the anchor is inserted into a ½" hole drilled through the center of the stud. A collar is slid along the straps of the anchor to snug it against the back side of the stud. The straps are then broken off, and a ¼"-20 stainless steel bolt is inserted through the grab bar flange and screwed into the anchor.

The Toggler brand Snaptoggle anchor is available in stainless steel and zinc-plated steel. It is important to match the steel of the anchor, bolt, and grab bar—stainless steel is best for damp conditions.

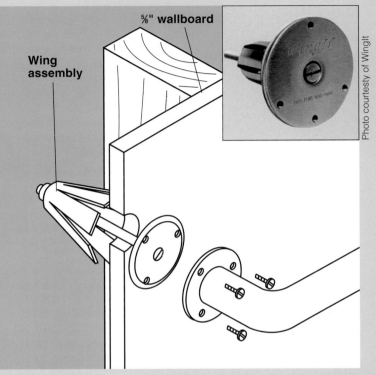

WingIt™ Anchor

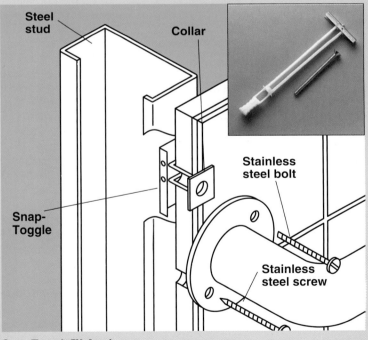

SnapToggle™ Anchor

INDEX

Additional Resources

American Institute of Architects
800-242-3837
www.aia.org

**American Society of
Interior Designers**
202-546-3480
www.asid.org

**Construction Materials
Recycling Association**
630-548-4510
www.cdrecycling.org

**Energy & Environmental
Building Association**
952-881-1098
www.eeba.org

**International Residential
Code** (book) published by
**International Conference of
Building Officials**
800-284-4406
www.icbo.com

**National Association of the
Remodeling Industry (NARI)**
847-298-9200
www.nari.org

**U.S. Environmental Protection
Agency—Indoor Air Quality**
www.epa.gov/iedweb00/pubs
/insidest.html

UNIVERSAL DESIGN RESOURCES

ABLEDATA
800-227-0216
www.abledata.com

Access One, Inc.
800-561-2223
www.beyondbarriers.com

Adaptive Environments Center, Inc.
617-695-1225
www.adaptenv.org

**American Association of
Retired Persons (AARP)**
800-424-3410
www.aarp.org

**Center for Inclusive Design
& Environmental Access
School of Architecture and
Planning—University of Buffalo**
716-829-3485 ext. 329
www.ap.buffalo.edu/~idea

**Center for Universal Design
NC State University**
919-515-3082 (phone)
www.design.ncsu.edu/cud

**National Association of Home
Builders (NAHB)
Research Center**
800-638-8556 (phone)
www.nahbrc.org

Contributors

Andersen Windows
800-426-4261
www.andersenwindows.com

Ariane
c/o Ceramic Tiles of Italy
212-980-1500
www.ariana.it
www.italytiles.com

Armstrong World Industries, Inc.
800-233-3823
www.armstrong.com

Broan-NuTone
800-558-1711
www.broan.com

Craftmaster Manufacturing, Inc.
800-405-2233
www.craftmasterdoordesign.com

Dura Supreme Cabinetry
888-711-3872
www.durasupreme.com

Economic Mobility Inc.
800-342-8801
www.toiletlift.com

Elkay
630-574-8484
www.elkay.com

Ginger
888-469-6511
www.gingerco.com

Kohler Co.
800-4-KOHLER
www.kohlerco.com

Kolbe + Kolbe Millwork Company, Inc.
800-955-8177
www.kolbe-kolbe.com

Marvin Windows and Doors
800-268-7644
www.marvin.com

Pittsburgh Corning Corporation
800-624-2120
www.pittsburghcorning.com

Sun Touch Floor Warming
a divison of Watts Radiant
417-522-6128
www.suntouch.net

Suanatec, Inc.
800-346-6536
www.finnleo.com

Suntunnel Skylights
800-369-7465
www.suntunnel.com

Swanstone
800-325-7008
www.swanstone.com

TOTO USA
800-350-8686
www.totousa.com

VELUX America, Inc.
800-888-3589
www.veluxusa.com

Wellborn Cabinet, Inc.
800-336-8040
www.wellborn.com

Wood-Mode, Inc.
800-635-7500
www.wood-mode.com

Photographers

Henry Cabala
Beateworks, Inc.
Los Angeles, CA
©Henry Cabala/Beateworks.com: p.4

Bill Geddes
Beateworks, Inc.
Los Angeles, CA
©Bill Geddes/Beateworks.com:
    pp.10, 225

Christian Korab
Minneapolis, MN
© Christian Korab p. 16

Karen Melvin
Architectural Stock Images
Minneapolis, MN
©Karen Melvin: pp. 13, 14
    and for the following: p. 7 (bottom)
    Eric Oder AIA, Sara Susanka, AIA-
    mural design, Maureen Lyttle-mural
    painter; p. 9 (top) Lynn Monson
    Interior design; p. 9 (bottom right)

Earl Gutnik Designer; p. 11 (bottom
left) John Sylvestre Construction; p.
11 (bottom right) Pam Enz, ASID
John Sylvestre Construction; p. 15
William Benson Interior Design; pp.
34, 39 (bottom) Proline Audio,
Audio Video Interiors; p. 38 (center) Roddy Turner; pp. 234 Curtis
Hoard, Katherine Shepard Design

Robert Perron
Branford, CT
©Robert Perron: pp. 6, 7, 32, 33, 225

Scott Smith
Beateworks, Inc.
Los Angeles, CA
©Scott Smith/Beateworks.com: p. 211

Tim Street-Porter
Beateworks, Inc.
Los Angeles, CA
©Tim Street Porter/Beateworks.com:
pp. 8, 11

Jessie Walker
Glencoe, Il
©Jessie Walker: pp. 9, 12, 224
    and for the following: p. 6 (bottom)
    Vassa Group LTD; p. 8 (bottom)
    Stephen Knutson-Architect,
    Evanston, IL; p. 12 (bottom right)
    Julie Mcdowell-designer, Chicago,
    IL; p. 25 (bottom left) David Raino-
    Ogden-Architect; p. 32 (top left)
    Marilyn Davis-Designer; p. 211
    George Pappageorge-Architect,
    Chicago, IL

Also from

CREATIVE PUBLISHING INTERNATIONAL

Finishing Basements & Attics

*L*earn how to add new rooms to your home without adding on. This book takes you through the entire remodeling process, from assessing the unfinished space and planning the project to framing new walls and installing trim. You'll find dozens of building projects that show how to convert unused square footage into comfortable living space.

ISBN 0-86573-583-2 . . . .$16.95

Building & Finishing Walls & Ceilings

*W*alls and ceilings define every room in your house, and this book shows you how to make them look their best. You'll find all of the decorating essentials, like wallcoverings, basic painting, and faux-finishing, along with paneling trim, and tin-tile ceilings. For larger remodels, there are projects on framing standard and curved walls, building glass block walls, and sound-proofing walls and ceilings, as well as a comprehensive section on installing, finishing, and texturing drywall.

ISBN 1-58923-042-6 . . . .$16.95

CREATIVE PUBLISHING INTERNATIONAL
18705 LAKE DRIVE EAST
CHANHASSEN, MN 55317

WWW.CREATIVEPUB.COM